THE GREAT BOOK OF
BRAINTEASERS

THE GREAT BOOK OF
BRAINTEASERS

PUZZLES COMPILED BY NORMAN SULLIVAN
with contributions from Ken Russell & Philip Carter

ARCTURUS

Published by
Arcturus Publishing Limited

for Bookmart Limited
Registered Number 2372865
Desford Road
Enderby
Leicester LE9 5AD

This edition published 2001

Printed and bound by Omnia Books Limited

Cover by Dianne Winship
Design and layout by Zeta Fitzpatrick @ Moo Design
Edited by Paua Field

ISBN 1-84193-069-5

Contents

Introduction

Brainteasers is a massive book packed to the brim with word, number and visual puzzles designed to entertain and bewilder.

It is divided into five sections – each of which contains over 150 puzzles. They will challenge you and help you develop your IQ skills, but do remember that they are meant to be fun! The book is not arranged in ascending levels of difficulty but has a good mixture of different puzzle types throughout.

At regular intervals throughout the book you will find puzzles which have a page to themselves and are illustrated with images or diagrams. These are of a slightly different nature to the rest of the puzzles – some are lateral thinking puzzles, some are word puzzles and others are mathematical – they are intended to lighten the load; to give you some breathing space before you dive back into the puzzle-packed pages.

The answers are given at the back of each section, but we recommend that you only check the answers when you absolutely have to!

Section One

The Great Book of Brainteasers

1 Which is the odd one out?

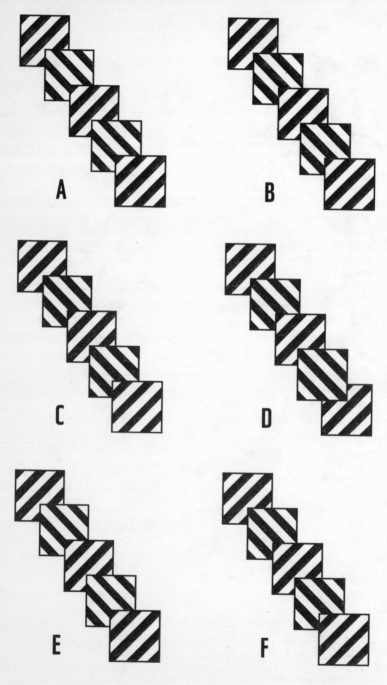

2 Which bowl is nearest to the jack (the white ball) and which is furthest away from it?

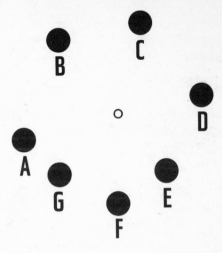

3 The diameter of pulley E is twice that of pulley D. If pinion A rotates eight times clockwise, how many times will pulley E rotate and in which direction?

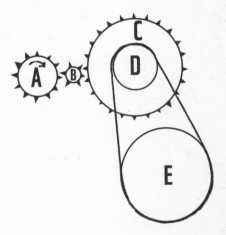

4 **A** What starts the top series?
B What ends the bottom series

–8163264128
1938761523 0–

5 What is the last line?

975949

634536

182018

---

6 Which of these contains the most triangles?

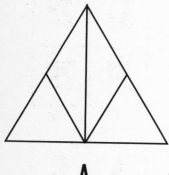

A

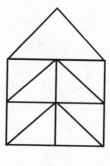

B

C

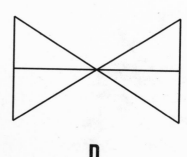

D

7 What are A, B, C and D?

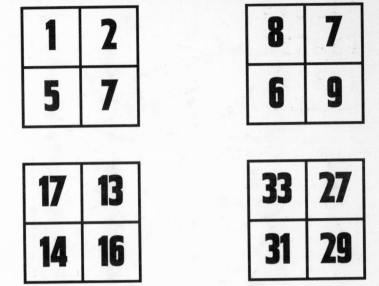

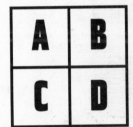

8 In a game of whist, GEORGE partnered MARY, while TED had to select a partner from ANN, EDNA, Joan or ANGELA. Whom did he choose?

9 What comes next?

6 1 3 1 4 −

10 Each letter points to a row of SIX numbers. Which is the odd one out?

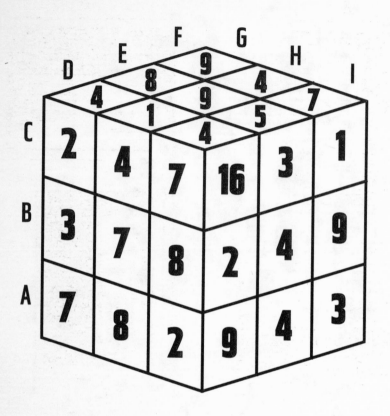

11 How can you make this addition correct?

11
66
88
96

294

12 Which door is wrong?

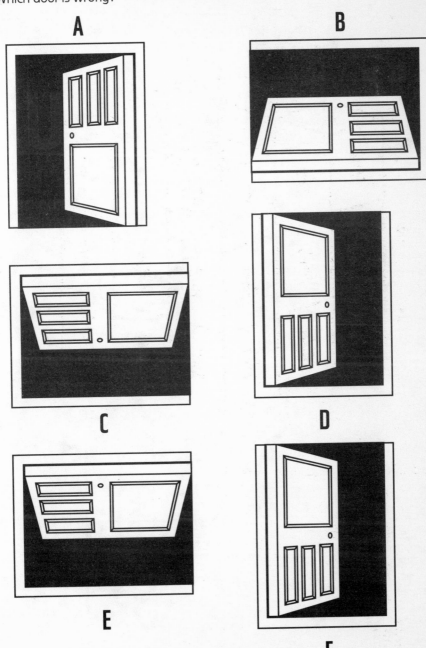

A

B

C

D

E

F

The Great Book of Brainteasers

13 Which clock is the odd one out?

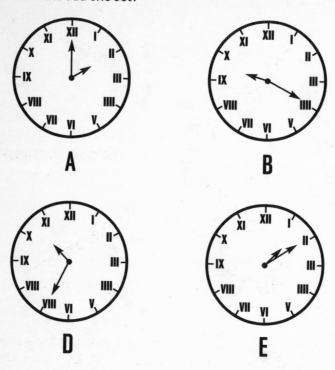

A   B

D   E

14 How many squares are there here?

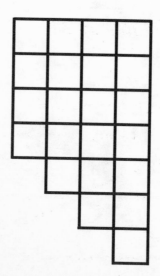

15 Which is the odd one out?

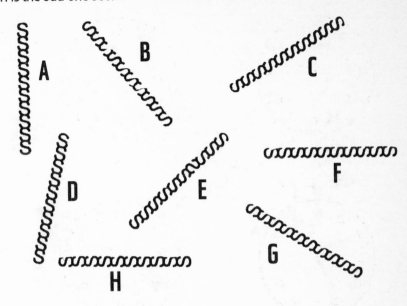

16 Counting down, first by one place, then by two places, then by three and so on (adding one extra place each time), as in this example – 15, 14, 12, 9, 5, 0 – which of these numbers will finish at zero?

102 103 104 105 106

17 How many triangles are there here?

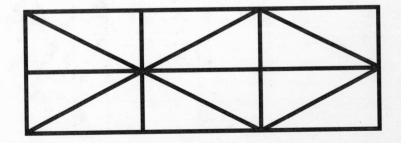

18 In a party of 35 people there are twice as many women as children and twice as many children as men. How many of each are there?

19 Arrange these cubes into four matching pairs

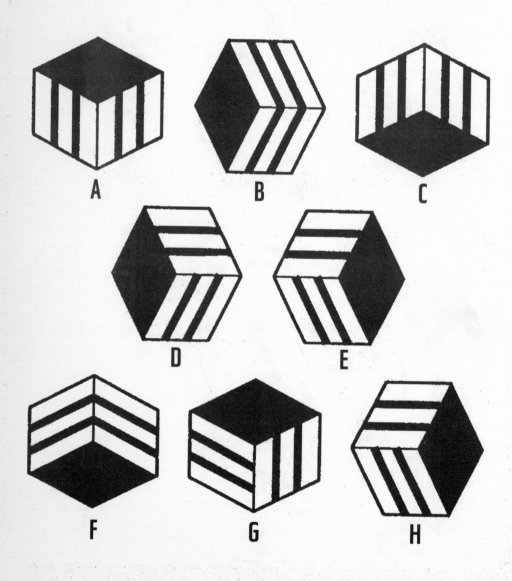

HORSE-RACE

20 There was a 16 horse race in progress at the race-course, but I missed the finish. I asked 6 of my friends to tell me the number of the winner. These were their answers.

A It was even

B It was odd

C It was prime

D It was a square number

E It had 2 digits

F It was between 6 and 12

But only four had told the truth.

Which number was the winner?

The Great Book of Brainteasers

SOCKS

21 A blind man had only black or white socks.
In his drawer he had 4 socks. He went to the drawer and took out 2 socks.

The chances that he had a pair of white socks was $\frac{1}{2}$.

What were the chances that he had drawn out a pair of black socks?

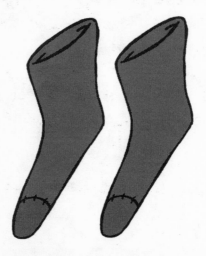

22 Which is the odd one out?

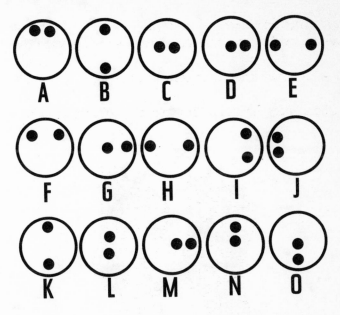

23 Which two of these can be reversed so that the total of each row – across and down – equals 10?

A 5 4 1

B 6 1 3

C 3 5 2

24 What goes into the empty brackets?

1 2 (2 8 4 6) 3 4

4 5 (1 2 2 1 1 5 1 8) 6 7

7 8 (2 8 4 0 3 2 3 6) 9 10

11 12 (   ) 13 14

25 Which is the odd one out?

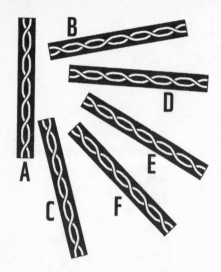

26 Which of the figures at the bottom – A, B, C or D – follows number 4?

27 Choosing from the numbers below, what are A, B, C and D?

A x B + C + D = 5
6 6 9 12

28 Which of the following statements are true and which are false?

A. If this clock is gaining, the pendulum weight should be moved downwards.

B. The majority of these shapes are convex.

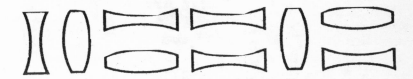

C. A spider has six legs

D. The majority of these are stalagmites.

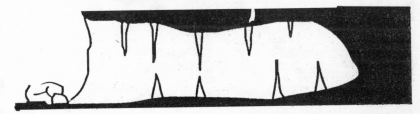

The Great Book of Brainteasers

GROUPS

29 These twelve names of groups of creatures have been mixed up. Can you re-arrange them?

SIEGE	of	HERMITS
TRIP	of	HARPERS
HUSK	of	LARKS
EXALTATION	of	CRANES
MELODY	of	NIGHTINGALES
OBSERVANCE	of	OWLS
WATCH	of	RABBITS
TRIBE	of	SHEEP
KENNEL	of	HARES
PARLIAMENT	of	GOATS
COLONY	of	RACHES
CRY	of	HOUNDS

FLUTES

30 There were 19 flautists in the Orchestra.
One day a consignment of flutes arrived.
The lead flautist took $^1/_{19}$ of the consignment $+ ^1/_{19}$ of a flute
The 2nd flautist took $^1/_{18}$ of the remainder and $^1/_{18}$ of a flute
and so on
until there were only 2 flautists left.

The penultimate flautist took $\frac{1}{2}$ of the remainder and $\frac{1}{2}$ of a flute.

The last flautist felt a little aggrieved.

a Why did he feel aggrieved?

b How many flutes were in the consigment?

31 What is the sum of the numbers in the following list which are consecutive (for example 3, 4, 5)?

15 5 10 28

24 7 18 26

11 21 17 13

22 9 1 20

32 Which one spoils the frieze?

33 Which row is the odd one out?

34 From the example given below, decide what goes into the empty bracket below.

5 1 2 (4 2 3 5 1 6) 6 4 3

7 8 6 (   ) 4 1 2

35 If **13 x 3 = 40**

12 x 3 = 35

15 x 3 = 46

and **16 x 3 = 47**

what does **17 x 3 = ?**

36 How many hexagons (six-sided figures) can you find here?

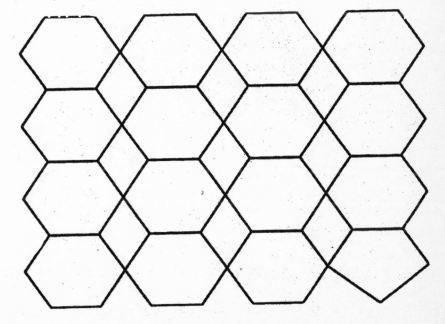

37 Which of the figures at the bottom A, B or C, should take the place of number 3?

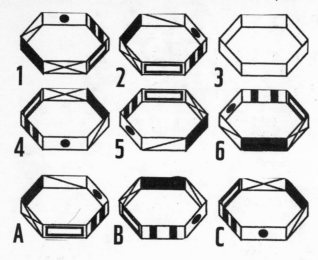

38

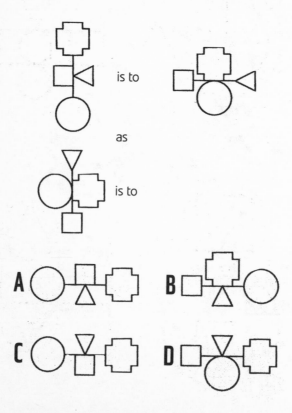

39 Which arithmetical signs should go into the brackets to complete the equations?

A. 5 ( ) 5 ( ) 5 = 2

B. 4 ( ) 4 ( ) 4 = 4

C. 3 ( ) 3 ( ) 3 = 6

D. 2 ( ) 2 ( ) 2 = 8

40 Which is the odd one out?

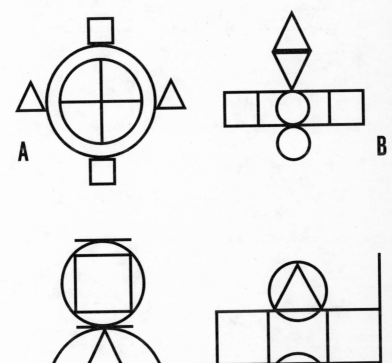

BARBER

41 The barber of Seville shaves all of the men living in Seville.
No man living in Seville is allowed by law to shave himself.
The Barber of Seville lives in Seville.

Who shaves the Barber of Seville?

WATER BUTT

42 Two farm labourers were arguing about a water butt. One said it was less than half full and the other said it was more than half full.
To settle the argument they asked the farmer to adjudicate.

Although there were no other implements or vessels at hand with which to measure the water, the farmer was quickly able to determine who was correct. How did he do it?

43 What number goes into the empty brackets?

16 (4 2 5 6)

9 (3 8 1)

25 (   )

44 Which is the odd one out?

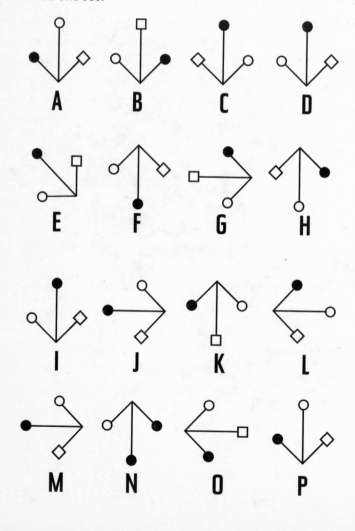

45 If I had one more sister I would have twice as many sisters as brothers. If I had one more brother I would have the same number of each. How many brothers and sisters have I?

46 Using your eyes only and without the aid of a pointer, trace which of the numbered lines will reach any of the goals marked A, B and C. State the number of the line and the goal reached. Right angles must be used only when there is no alternative route.

47 A bag contains 64 balls of eight different colours. There are eight of each colour (including red). What is the least number you would have to pick, without looking, to be sure of selecting 3 red balls?

48 Arrange these shapes into four pairs

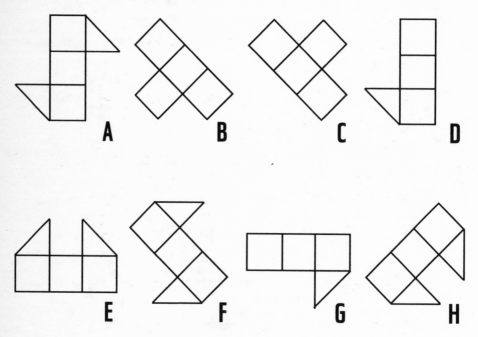

49 Select the number that is midway between the lowest number and the highest number. Which number is midway between that number and the number that is nearest the highest number?

35 5 52 36 67

69 4 51 37 71

55 68 3 53 39

50 If this clock were turned 90 degrees anti-clockwise, which of those below would appear? (Do not turn the page.)

A

B

C

D

51 What goes into the empty brackets?

6 3 (5 9 4 2) 7 1

5 9 (7 1 6 3) 4 2

9 4 (4 2 5 9) 2 8

(– – – –)

The Great Book of Brainteasers

52 If the figure below were held in front of a mirror, which of the figures, A, B, C, D, E or F, would be reflected?

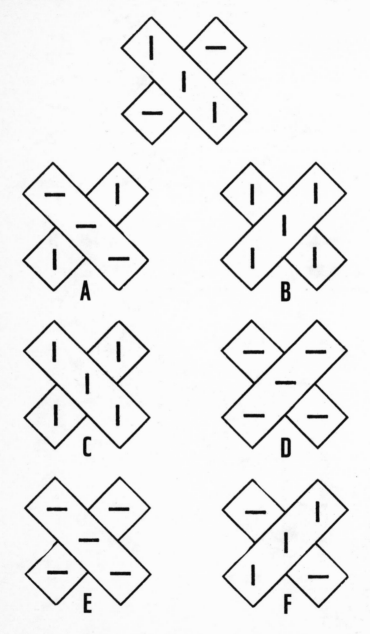

53 Which is the smallest segment and which is the largest segment in thsi circle?

54 Eleven posts have been erected in a straight line and on level ground at regular intervals. Ten are of equal length. Which one is a different length?

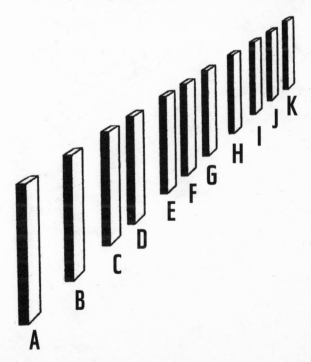

GOLF

55 Two men A and B played a round of golf. A said to B, let us play for a wager on each hole, we will play for half of the money in my wallet at each hole. I have £100 in my wallet, so for the first hole we will play for a stake of £50. If I win you will give me £50, and if I lose you will be given £50. On the second hole I will either have £150 in my wallet or £50, so we will play for £75 or £25.

After the 12th hole it started to rain, so they stopped the game and went back to the club house. As A had won 6 holes and B only 4 holes with 2 holes being tied, A said I will buy the drinks. To his amazement, he had only £71.18 in his wallet. Why was this possible? It makes no difference in the order of winning the holes.

COLLEGE

56 At college, 70% of the students studied Maths, 75% studied English, 85% studied French and 80% studied German.

What percentage at least must have studied all 4?

The Great Book of Brainteasers

57 From the numbers below and using each number only once in each set, select at least five sets of three that add to 29:

18 6 13 9 19 12

11 4 10 5 8 17

58 Which spanner fits the nut?

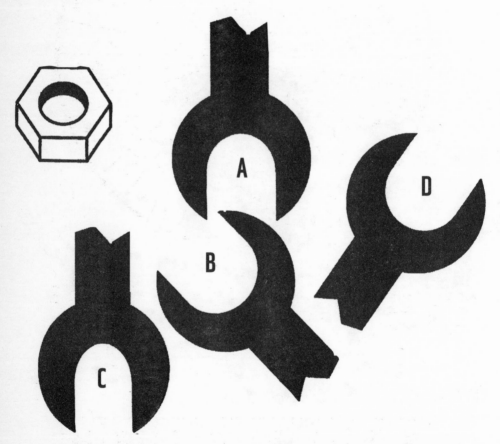

59 Which of the sectors below – A, B, C or D – should fill the empty sector in the circle?

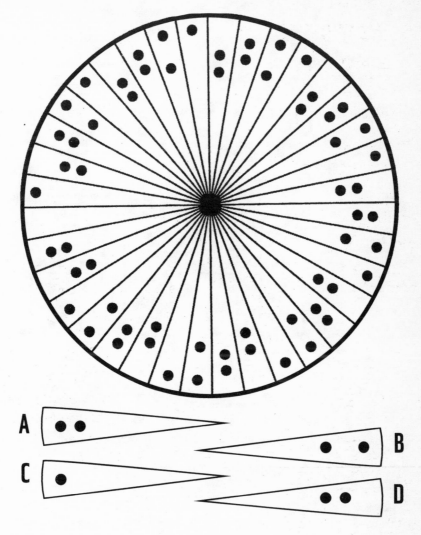

60 What is X?

14	19
8	22

1	50
22	41

22	4
30	8

10	34
28	X

61 What goes into the empty brackets?

2 (38) 3

4 (1524) 5

6 (3548) 7

8 (   ) 9

62 The opposite faces of a die add to seven. The dice below rotate in the directions indicated, one face at a time. After three moves, what will be the total of the front faces?

63 In the game of snooker, a player must pot a red ball each time before potting a 'coloured' ball (that is, a ball other than red). Each red ball scores 1 point; the 'colours' score as follows:

Yellow 2
Green 3
Brown 4
Blue 5
Pink 6
Black 7

If a player potted two blacks, one yellow, one blue and then two brown balls, followed by one red ball, what would the score be?

64 A sheet of paper is folded in half and cuts made into it. The paper is then unfolded to reveal this shape. Which of the figures – A, B, C or D – shows the original cuts?

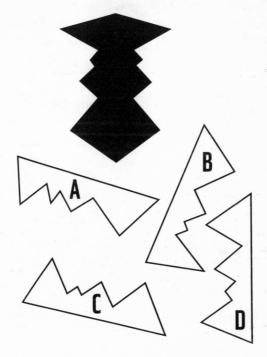

65 How many diamonds are there here?

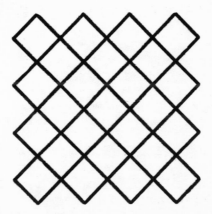

JAPAN

66 This sign was seen in Japan. What does it mean?

P H U S L U L ꟼ

HOUR GLASS

67 With a 7 minute hour glass and an 11 minute hour glass, what is the quickest way to time the boiling of an egg for 15 mins?

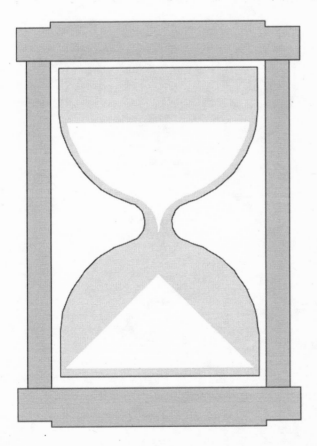

68 If a pack of playing cards measures 1.3cm when viewed sideways, what would be the measurement if all the aces were removed?

69 Match these designs into six pairs.

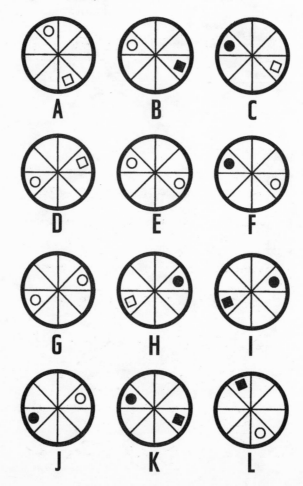

70 Which of the pairs of numbers at the bottom should be placed at X and Y so that each row of four numbers – across, down and diagonally – totals 20?

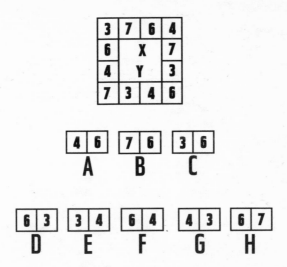

71 Which of these designs is different from the others?

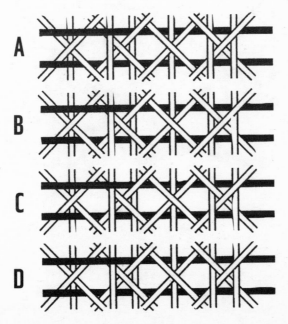

72 All of these except one have one thing in common. Which is the odd one out?

A. 764345896

B. 125612456

C. 367874341

D. 456578325

E. 178652457

F. 279651238

73 A feature of many safe-driving competitions consists of a row of poles set at varying distances from each other, ranging from narrow to wide. Maximum points are scored if the driver chooses the narrowest gap through which he can drive without touching a pole. Thus, the driver must relate the width of his car to the width between the poles. Drivers A and B below are competing here. Which gap should each driver choose?

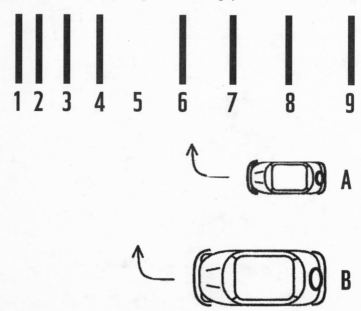

74 Which is the second smallest circle and which is the second largest circle?

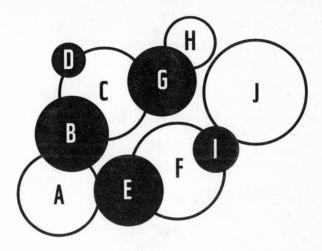

75 Which two dominoes are missing from the set?

PAIR WORDS

76 Here are two lists of words.
List A, each word has two possible pair words in List B.

List B, each word has two possible pair words in List A.

There are two possible solutions.

Pair a word from each list until you have 10 pairs.

List A	List B
SEVERN	TRACTOR
ARROW	RIVER
TURRET	BULLS-EYE
FARM	BOW
YARBOROUGH	TANK
SAND	CARDS
YEW	CASTLE
VEHICLE	BANK
RIPARIAN	WOOD
JACK	BRIDGE

CASINO

77 A croupier in a Casino offered a gambler $100 if he could throw a 6 with one throw of a standard die.
If he failed then he was allowed another throw, if he failed again he was allowed a 3rd throw.

How much should the gambler pay to the croupier for the chance to win $100, stake not returned? Only one $100 to be won.

HINT: One throw chances 1/6
      Two throws chances 2/6
      Three throws chances 3/6 which is even money

So the stake should be $50 or should it?

78 Which string of beads is the odd one out?

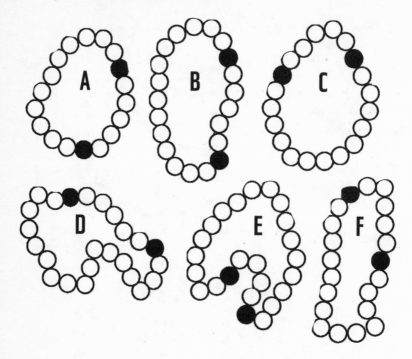

79 What numbers are represented by A, B and C?

A	B	A	B	A	23
B	C	A	A	A	20
B	A	B	C	A	24
B	A	C	C	A	21
B	B	A	A	B	27

31	24	20	21	19

80 Consider these equations and decide which is the odd one out.

$$\text{A. } 6 + 17 - 9 \div 7 + 3$$

$$\text{B. } 3 \times 11 + 6 \div 13 + 2$$

$$\text{C. } 2 \times 6 \times 3 + 4 \div 10$$

$$\text{D. } 1 + 8 - 3 \div 2 + 2$$

$$\text{E. } 7 - 4 + 6 - 1 - 3$$

81 Which of these designs match each other?

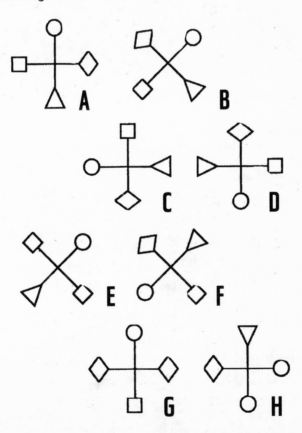

82 What is the total of the four blank squares in the centre when appropriate numbers are filled in?

1	2	9	1	2	3
8	3	3	4	7	5
4	5			5	6
5	9			4	11
7	8	3	13	8	9
2	15	9	10	1	17

83 Which is the odd one out

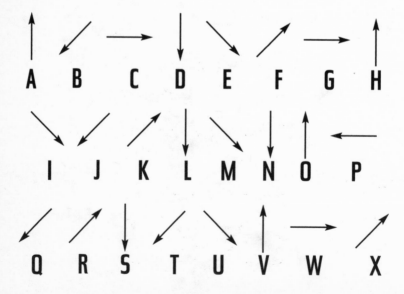

A   B   C   D   E   F   G   H

I   J   K   L   M   N   O   P

Q   R   S   T   U   V   W   X

84 What should go into the last line in the left-hand column?

1812	**9234**
2421	**6437**
1556	**3578**
1436	**2794**
- - - -	**2545**

85 Which of these contains the greatest number of triangles?

   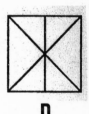

A　　　**B**　　　**C**　　　**D**

86

is to

as

is to

Choose from A, B or C

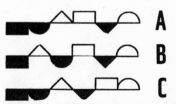

A

B

C

WHAT'S IN A NAME?

87 Arrange the following female names and male names into groups of three:

OLIVE	ISABEL
PRIMROSE	MYRTLE
GARNET	DIAMOND
PEARL	SANDY
MARTIN	MAVIS
ROBIN	POPPY

PUSS IN BOOTS

88 Puss had been called in to MONRAVIA to get rid of the rats. Puss had been told that he could bring as many of his friends as he wished to help him.
After a year every cat had killed an equal number of rats, the total was 1,111,111 rats.

How many cats were there?

89 What is X?

24 81 63 26 412 8 25 X

90 Which triangle is the odd one out

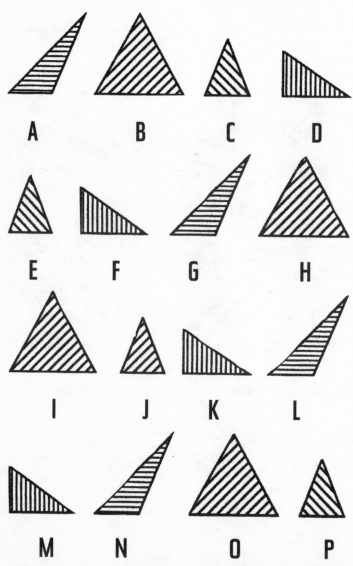

91 If $1 = X$, $2 = C$ and $3 + M$, what is $\frac{3}{2} + \frac{2}{1}$?

92 If the two spirals at the top are correct, which, if any, of those below are wrong?

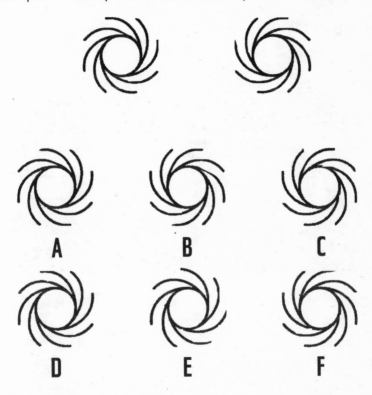

93 What goes into the empty brackets?

3 4 5 6 (7 1)

6 5 9 2 (1 1 7)

7 2 5 1 (9 4)

9 5 9 2 (   )

94 Match these patterns into four groups of three and state which is the odd one out.

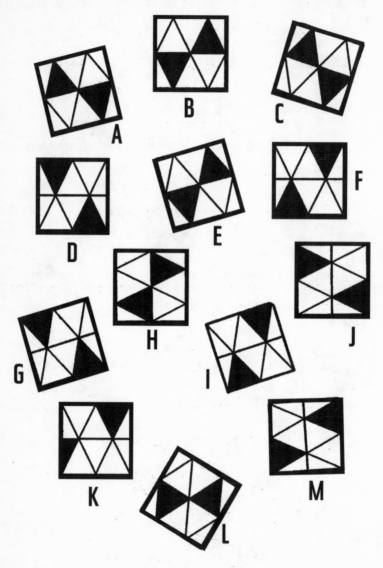

95 What comes next?

1 4 21 13 2 18 1 20 –

96 Which of these matchstick men is the odd man out?

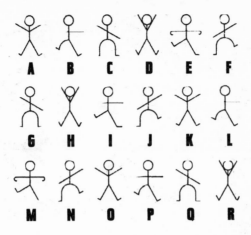

97 The shape of wallpaper at the top has already been hung. Which two of the sheets below will exactly match it when pasted on each side of it?

KEY SEQUENCE

98 The safe can only be opened by using the keys in the correct order that spells out a word. What is that word? Every key must be used just once.

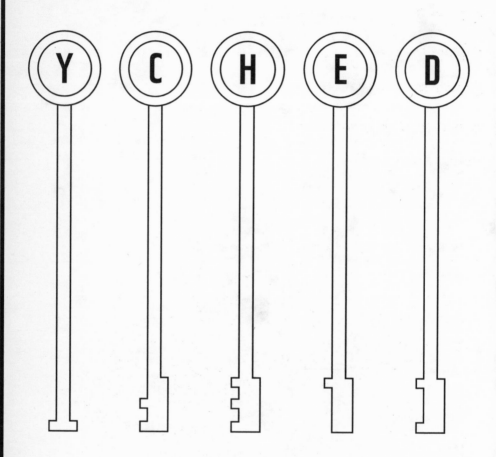

FAIR GROUND DICE

99 3 men are playing dice, each using different numbers, each dice has three numbers repeated. The men can choose their numbers. If

A beat B and

B beat C and

C beat A

What numbers should each dice have?

This is a unique answer

The Great Book of Brainteasers

100 These graphs show the annual profits of four different companies. Which company showed the greatest overall profit in the five years from 1981 to 1985 inclusive?

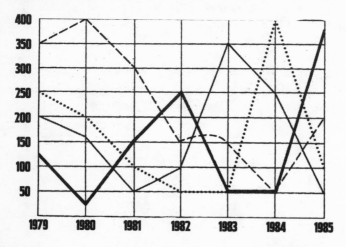

—— company A - - - - - company B —— company C .... company D

101 What are A, B and C?

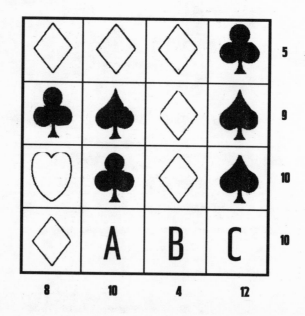

102 If the top clocks are right, which of those below are wrong?

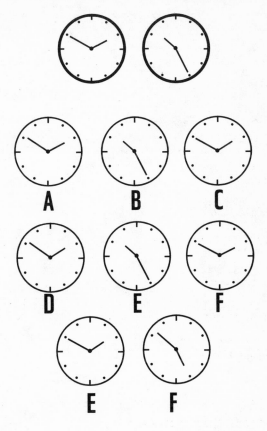

103 Which is the odd one out?

104 Which is th eodd one out?

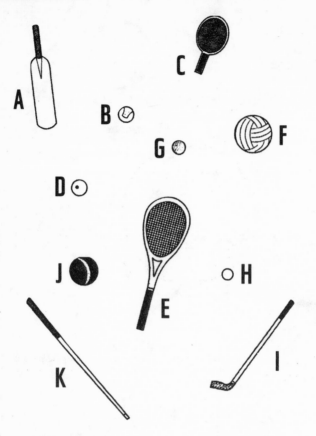

105 Which one spoils the pattern?

106 Tom, Alf, Fred, Bill and Jim sat at a round table.

Alf sat on Fred's left;
Tom sat on Jims's right;
Bill sat on Alf's left.

If Alf sat at A (see below), where were the others seated?

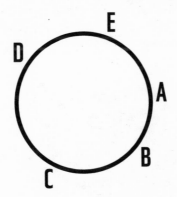

107 Which of these outlines, if any, can be drawn without removing pen from paper, crossing a line, or retracing a line?

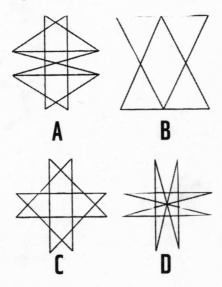

A   B

C   D

The Great Book of Brainteasers

108 Which of those at the bottom takes the place of number 5?

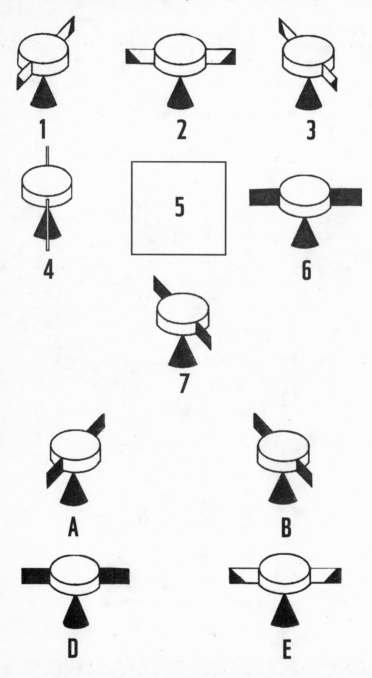

CASINO

109 At the casino I had to pay a £1 entrance fee. I also gave the cloakroom girl £1 tip each evening. Each day for four days I lost half of the money I had left. I went home with £1. How much did I have to start with?

CENSUS

110 A census taker called at a man's house and said, "what are the ages of your 3 daughters?"

The man said "If you multiply their ages together it equals 72 and if you add them it equals your door number". The census taker said "Well if you cannot give me further information I still don't know".

The man said "Well my eldest daughter has a dog with a wooden leg".

The census taker said, "I know now".

What were their ages.

111 Which of the numbered circles belong to A, B, C and D?

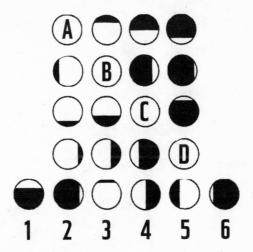

112 Eight of these railway points are set for the up train. Which will let the down-train through?

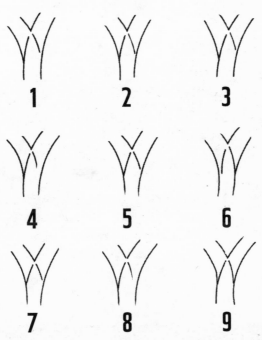

113 What comes next after the top traffic light?

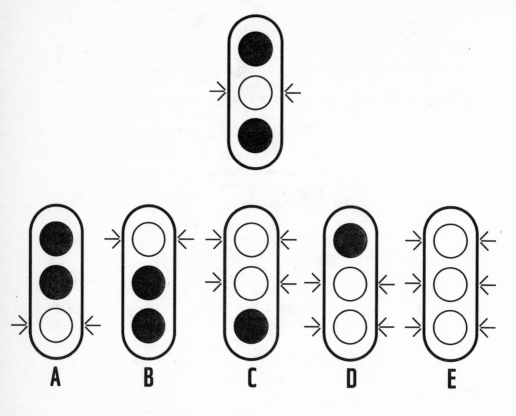

114 Which is the missing keystone?

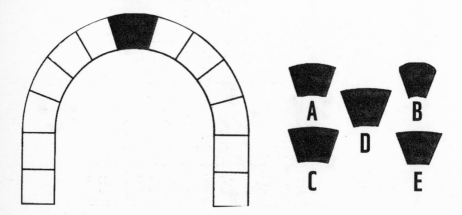

115 What comes next in this series?

1 2 6 24 120 720 –

116 What are X and Y?

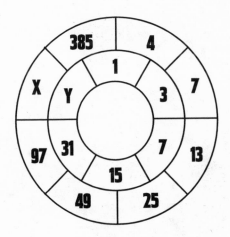

117 What are A, B, C and D?

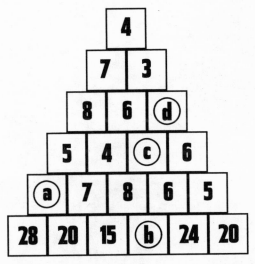

118 Give values for A, B and C?

3	9	A
B	2	2
C	5	6
7	8	2
3	5	10
9	1	9

119 Which globe at the bottom belongs to number 6?

120 Which one is wrong?

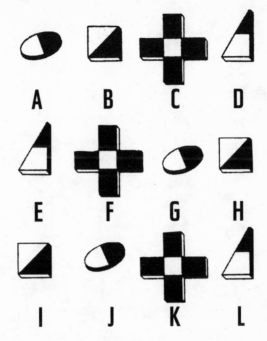

121 Which design is the odd one out?

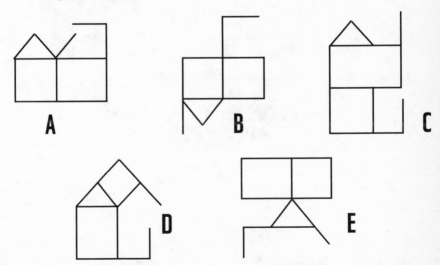

BILLIARD BALL

122 A billiard table is in the form of a rectangle with integral sides and just four pockets, one in each corner. A ball shoots out of one of the pockets at angles of 45° to the sides. Will it bounce around the table or finish up in one of the pockets?

ALIENS

123 100 aliens attended the intergalactic meeting on Earth:

78 had two heads
28 had three eyes
21 had four arms
12 had two heads and three eyes
9 had three eyes and four arms
8 had two heads and four arms
3 had all three unusual features

How many had none of these unusual features?

The Great Book of Brainteasers

124 Add the sum of the odd numbers in square A to that of the even numbers in square B and subtract the sum of the prime numbers in square C.

4	7	9
18	26	2
3	5	15

A

8	10	7
3	1	2
14	13	6

B

6	15	17
3	9	4
21	11	19

C

125 What are X and Y?

```
  3 1 X 4
  6 Y 9 5
  ───────
1 0 0 1 9
```

```
  4 9 1 X
  3 Y 0 1
  ───────
  1 1 1 1
```

126 Whilst driving his two young sons to the seaside, dad hit on an idea to keep the boys occupied. He invited each of them to choose a number between 0 and 9 and to watch for them on the oncoming cars, promising a prize to the first one to reach twenty. Jimmy chose 0 and Freddie chose 1. Why was Freddie more likely to win than Jimmy?

127 Arrange these into five pairs.

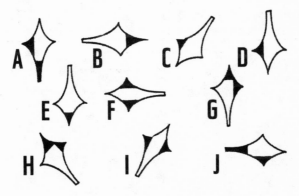

128 Match the five triangles at the bottom with their numbered counterparts in this square?

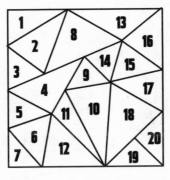

129 Which is the shortest and which is the longest route to X?

A B C

130 Which one does not agree with its counterparts?

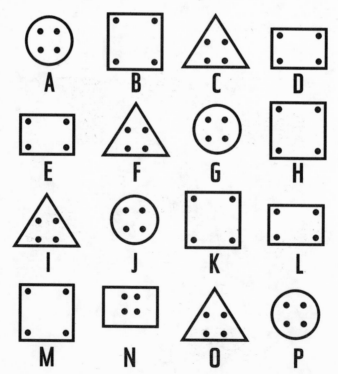

131 Which yacht is the odd one out?

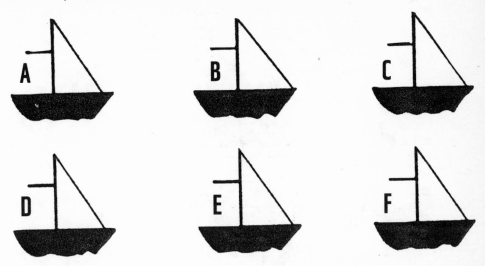

132 Which of these figures is wrong?

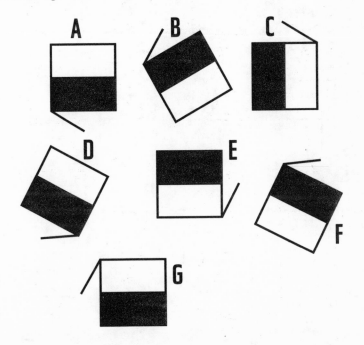

VOWELS

133 All of the vowels have been omitted from this saying. Put them back to produce the saying.

FTFRST   YDNT   SCCD   TRYTRY

GNTHNQTT   HRSNSNS BN

GDMNF   LBTT

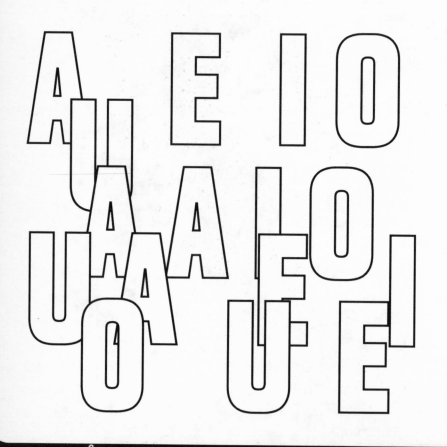

SOCCER

134 An English club had 17 players in their squad. There were 9 English players and 8 foreign players.

How many different teams can they select if each team had 5 English players and 6 foreign players?

135 Add the two highest numbers and take away the sum of the three lowest numbers.

16 13 9 11 23 19
5 14 12 15 18 17

136 If 6 3 5 4 2 equals 5 2 6 3 4, what is B C D E F?

137 Arrange these into four pairs:

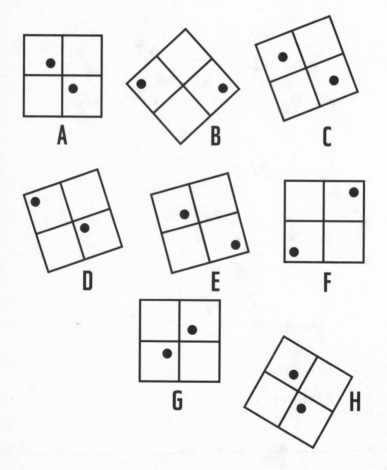

138 Which date does not conform with the others?

A 1584   B 1692   C 1729   D 1809   E 1980

139 Who has changed his expression?

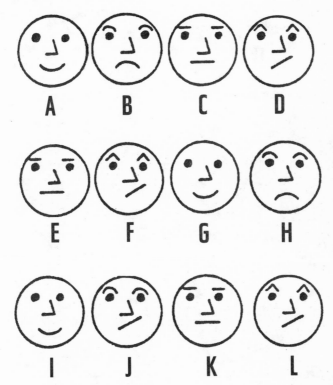

A   B   C   D

E   F   G   H

I   J   K   L

140 What goes into the empty brackets?

144 (3 6 2 5) 1 2 5

96 (1 6 1 8) 1 2 6

112 (   ) 1 4 4

141 Which two of these shields are identical?

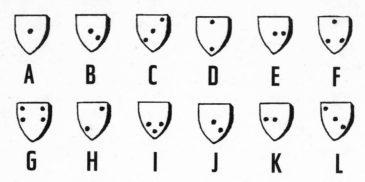

142 Arrange these patterns into four pairs.

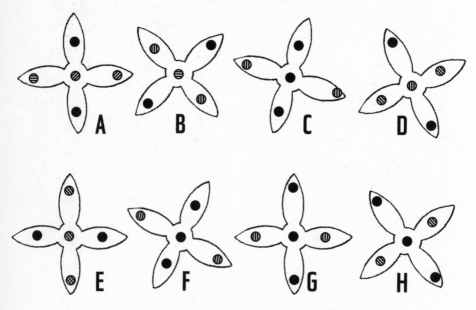

143 Which of these is the odd man out?

4 18 16 8 24

GAMBLING

144 Three husbands and wives visit a casino. The men are John, Ernie and Oswald. The women are Alice, Betty and Marjorie. Each of the six gamble independently but agree to stop whenever each couple's gain or loss reaches £200. All three husbands lose all the time but each couple wins the agreed £200. Each of the six had participated in as many single games as on average he or she had won or lost pounds per game. Ernie lost £504 more than John. Betty won £2,376 more than Marjorie. Who is married to whom?

THINK OF A NUMBER

145 A has thought of a number between 13 and 1300
B is trying to guess it

1 B asks whether the number is below 500
A says "yes"

2 B asks if the number is a perfect square
A says "yes"

3 B asks if the number is a perfect cube
A says "yes"

A says "only two of my answers are correct"

A says "the number starts with 5, 7 or 9"

B now knows the number.

What is it?

146 Assuming that the two top stars are correct, which of those below are wrong?

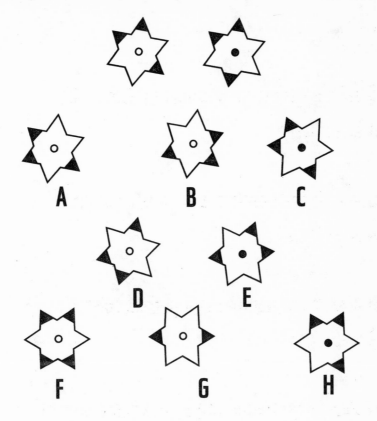

147 What are X and Y?

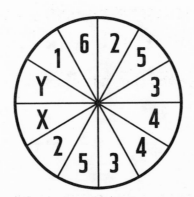

The Great Book of Brainteasers

148 If is superimposed on

Which of the OUTLINES below will result?

A

B

C

D

149 Which column does not conform?

A	B	C	D	E	F
17	14	22	31	29	33
9	13	15	22	19	8
13	11	17	17	31	19
24	7	2	13	5	20
2	29	8	4	2	17
10	6	21	3	10	3

150 Which row is wrong?

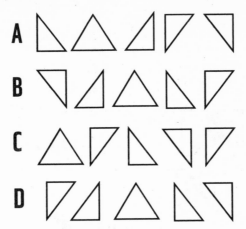

151 What is two days after the day after the day before yesterday?

152 What trellis is wrong?

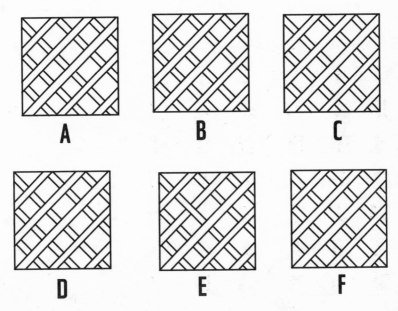

ODOMETER

153 The odometer in the car showed 15951 miles, a palindromic number. Two hours later the odometer once again was palindromic. How far had the car travelled?

ZOETROPE

154

Clue: Hanging about over the water? (10-6)

Find the (10-6) letter word. Find the 1st letter. Draw a straight line to the 2nd letter, then to the 3rd letter and so on. The enclosed areas have been filled in.

155 If 3 (76) equals 212
and 4 (320) equals 125
what is:
5 (6100)?

156 Which of the symbols at the bottom should take the place of X?

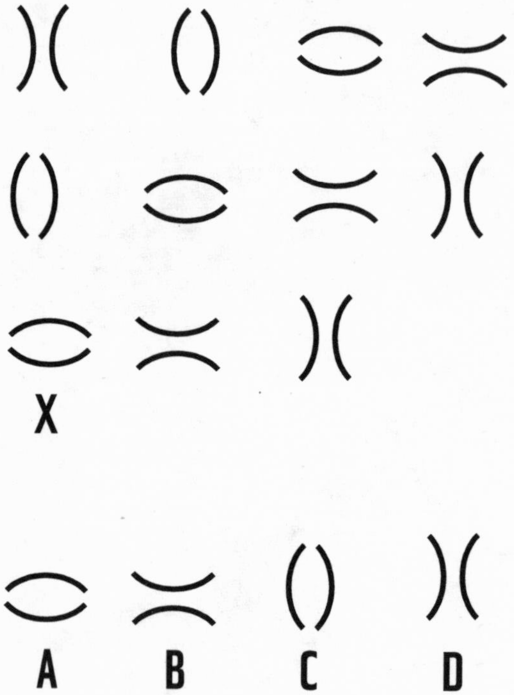

)(() ⌒⌣ ⌣⌒

() ⌒⌣ ⌣⌒)(

⌒⌣ ⌣⌒)(

X

⌒⌣ ⌣⌒ ())(

A   B   C   D

157 What is X?

21859

37262

4211X

158 Arrange these into six pairs:

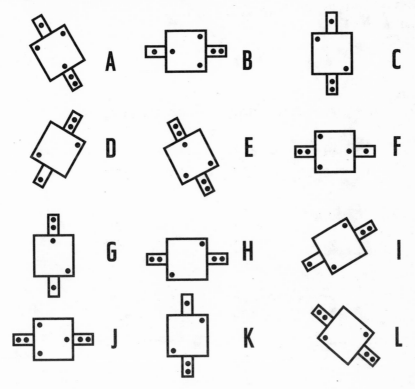

159 Which are the weak links?

160 What are X and Y

7 8 6 9 5 10 X Y 3 12

161 Arrange these shapes in order according to the number of sides, starting with the one with the least number:

A OCTAGON

B HEXAGON

C PENTAGON

D DECAGON

E TETRAGON

F NONAGON

G HEPTAGON

162 Which cross does not conform with the others?

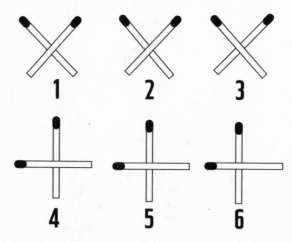

163 Which one is different from the others?

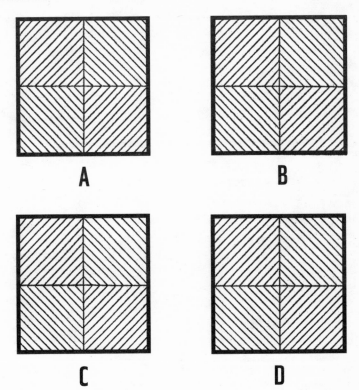

164 Which of the numbered figures at the bottom belongs to G?

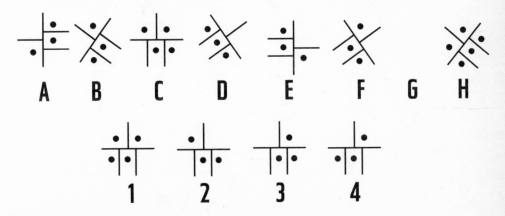

165 Which figure is wrong?

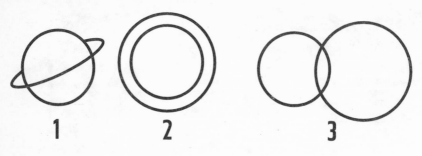

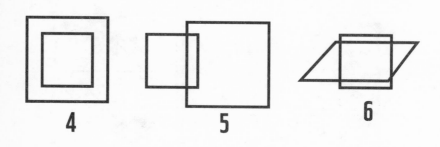

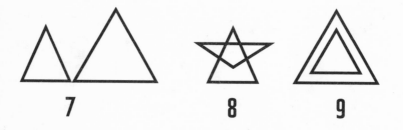

166 Which is the odd man out?

3	**11**	**17**
7	**15**	**29**

ALPHABET X-WORD

167 Place all of the letters of the alphabet in the grid to make a x-word. 9 letters have been placed for you.

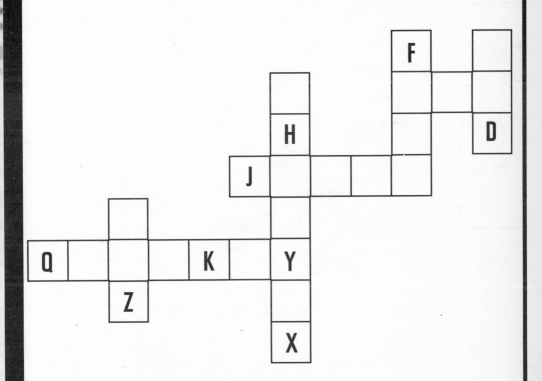

A B C D E F G H I J K L M N
O P Q R S T U V W X Y Z

CRICKET

168 The local cricket team used 16 players during the season and each players' total score for the season was a palindromic prime number. No two players had the same score for the season. If you sum the 16 players' total score and then find the average you arrive at a 3-digit number that contains the same 3 digits. The lowest total was 11.

What was the average total?

169 Which envelope should occupy the empty space?

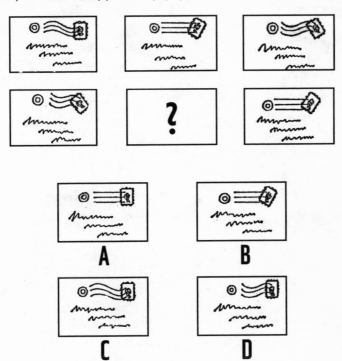

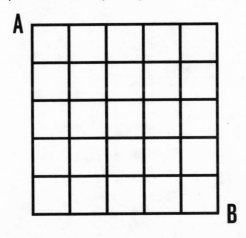

170 Using your eyes only, how many squares are there in the figure below and assuming that A and B were joined, how many triangles?

171 Which figure is wrong?

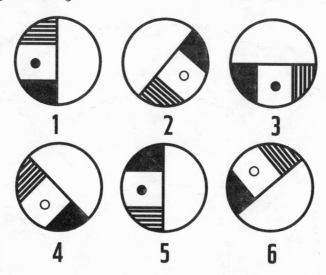

172 What is the value of X in each of the following three diagrams?

5	4	9
3	5	8
2	7	X

A

32	35	39
42	46	51
3	8	X

B

A	E	J
D	X	O
F	L	S

C

173 What number goes into the brackets?

64 (49) 144

85 (57) 119

144 (   ) 90

174 Give values for X and Y.

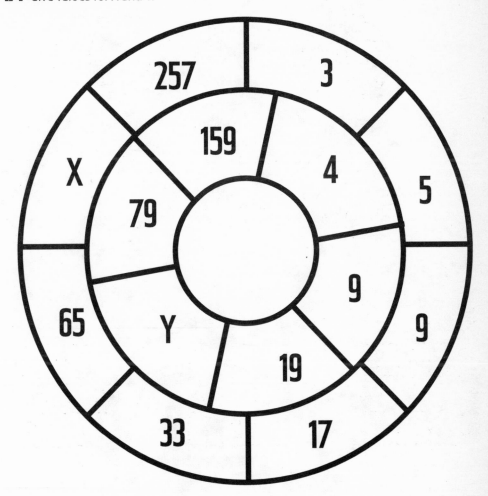

175 A heavy smoker, worried about the high cost of tobacco, decided to economise by saving his cigarette ends and making new cigarettes from them.
He found that each cigarette end accounted for one-sixth of the whole cigarette,
He smoked 36 cigarettes a day.
By using this method, how many EXTRA cigarettes was he able to obtain in a week?

HOUSE

176 Cyril lives in a road, the houses are numbered 8 to 100.

John asks "Is it greater than 50?"
Cyril answers "YES".
John asks "Is it a square number?"
Cyril answers "YES".
John asks "Is it an odd number?"
Cyril answers "YES".
John asks "Is the first digit an 8?"
Cyril lies.

What is the number of the house belonging to Cyril?

CASINO

177 The casino game called craps is played with two dice 1-6 standard.

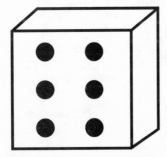 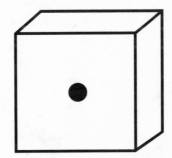

7 or 11 wins.

Which 3 numbers lose?

178 Arrange these patterns into four pairs.

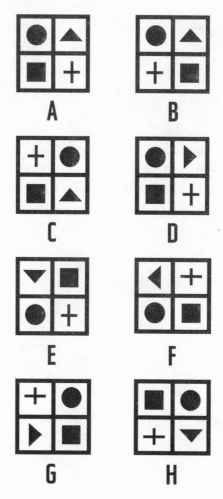

179 Sheffield is 100 miles from Worcester.

At 1pm train A leaves Sheffield for Worcester and travels at a constant speed of 30mph. One hour later train B leaves Worcester for Sheffield and travels at a constant speed of 40mph.

Each train makes one stop only at a station ten miles form its starting-point and remains there for fifteen minutes.

Which train is nearer to Sheffield when they meet?

180 Which car goes into which road?

243   136   567

A   B   C

1.7   81

1   2

27

3

181 What number should go into the blank space?

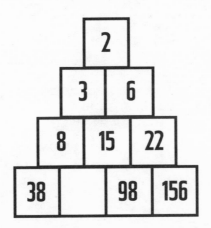

	2	
3		6
8	15	22
38		98	156

The Great Book of Brainteasers

182 Which of these patterns does not conform with the others?

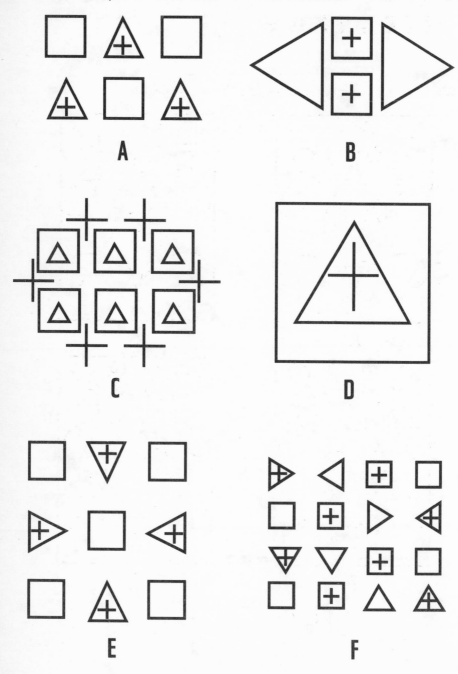

A

B

C

D

E

F

183 What two terms complete this series?

A 1 D 4 H 8 M 13 _ _

184 Which of these wrought iron gates differs from the others?

A

B

C

D

185 Which scroll is wrong?

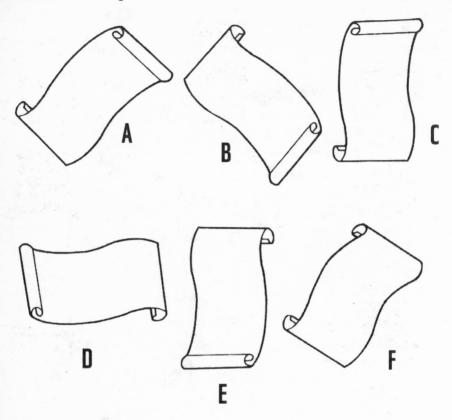

186 Assuming four of these dates are correct, which one is wrong?

A Saturday 7 January 1764

B Saturday 21 January 1764

C Saturday 11 February 1764

D Saturday 11 March 1764

E Saturday 14 April 1764

187 Which gentleman has changed his appearance?

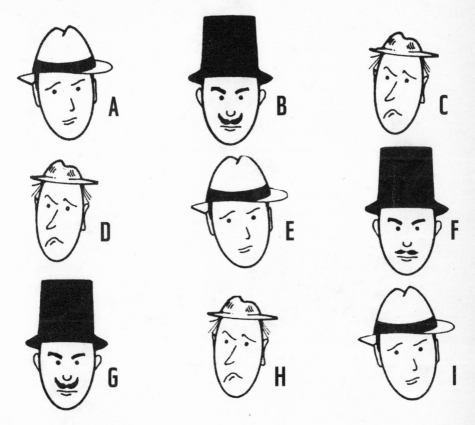

188 What are x and y?

7 8 6 9 5 10 X Y

189 Which of these moons are waxing (becoming larger)?

A B C D E F

TILES

190 Two square floors had to be tiled, covered in 12" square tiles. The number of tiles used was 850 total.

Each side of one floor was 10' more than the other floor.

What were the dimensions of the two floors?

BOXES

191	Boxes 1 + 2	weigh 12 KG
"	2 + 3	" 13.5 KG
"	3 + 4	" 11.5 KG
"	4 + 5	" 8 KG
"	1 + 3 + 5	" 16 KG

How much does each box weigh?

192 Which shield is wrong?

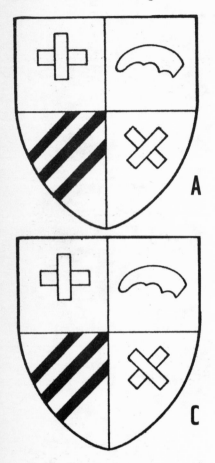 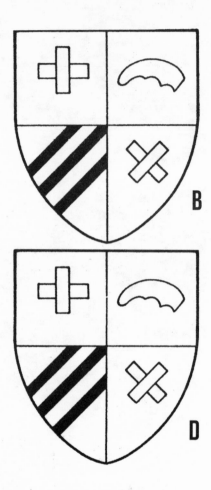

193 Add the difference between the two lowest numbers to the difference between the two highest numbers:

91 13 76 12   7 88 17 84

11 14 87 15 86 16 89 85

194 Assuming that the top two cars are correct, which of those below are wrong?

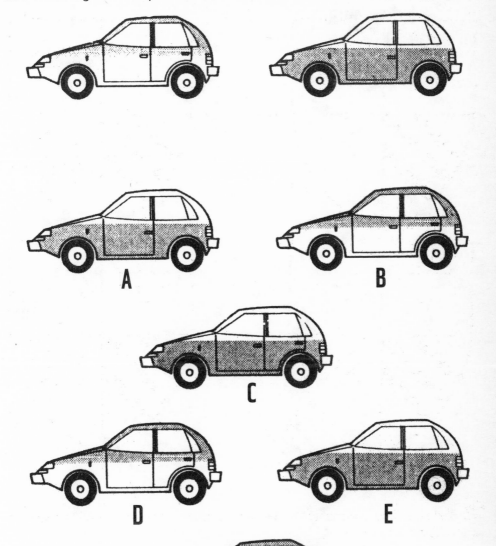

195 What are X and Y?

1 3 3 6 5 9 7 12 X Y

196 Which of these could NOT be drawn with a continuous unbroken line without crossing another line?

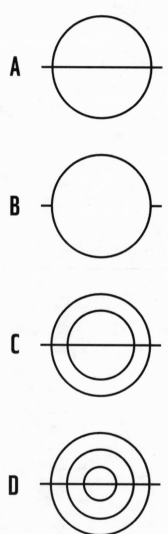

197 Subtract the sum of the three lowest numbers from the sum of the three highest numbers.

$$11 \quad 36 \quad 7 \quad 38 \quad 3 \quad 45$$
$$39 \quad 10 \quad 48 \quad 37 \quad 12 \quad 36$$

198 What is the last term in this series?

B 2 T 20 Q 17 G 7 C –

199 What is X ?

4 9 X 25

200 Whose face is wrong?

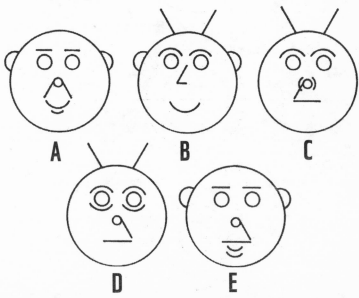

A   B   C

D   E

ARRESTS

201 At a demonstration, protesters outnumbered the police by 8 to 1. 84 arrests were made, averaging 3 for every 2 policemen.

How many demonstrations were there?

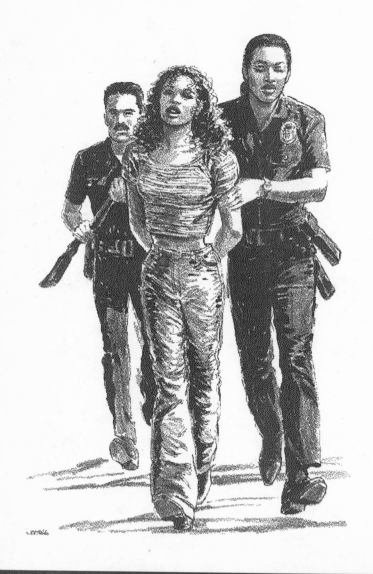

BRIDGE

202 A hand in bridge in which all 13 cards are a 9 or below is called a YARBOROUGH after the Second Earl of Yarborough (d. 1897) who frequented games schools and wagered 1000-1 against dealing such a hand.

Was he on to a good thing?

The Great Book of Brainteasers

203 Which keyboard is wrong?

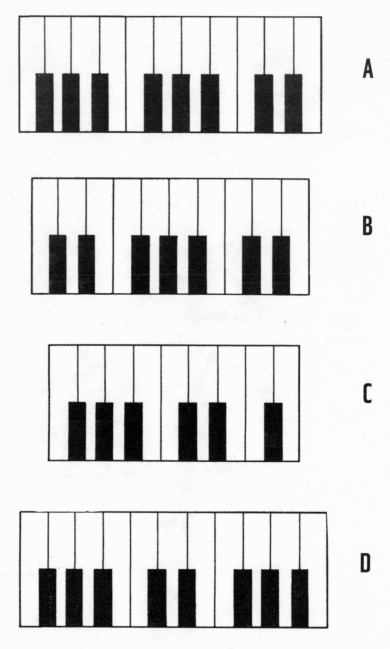

A

B

C

D

204 What comes next?

208   CIV   52   XXVI   –

205 Which one does not conform with the others?

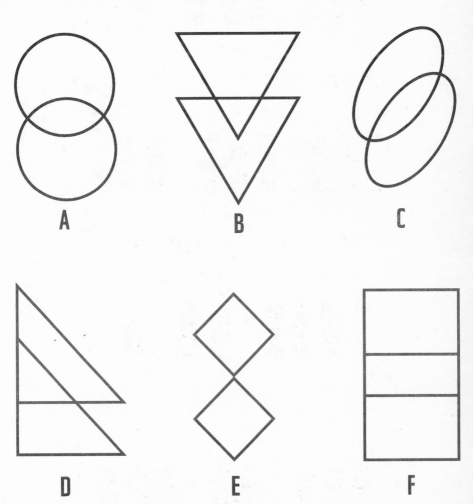

206 What knot is different?

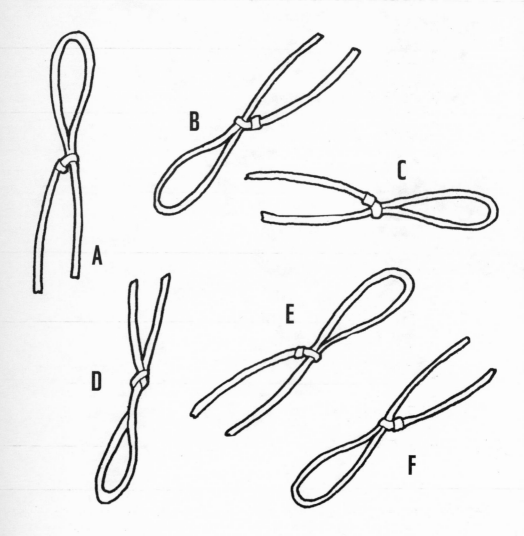

207 Which date does not conform with the others?

A 1417

B 1533

C 1605

D 1722

E 1812

F 1902

208 Which one is wrong?

A $\frac{9}{4} + 1.75 = 4$

B $\frac{9}{5} + 2.2 = 4$

C $\frac{6}{5} + 2.8 = 4$

D $\frac{6}{4} + 1.5 = 4$

E $\frac{9}{6} + 2.5 = 4$

209 Multiply the second highest number by the second lowest number and then divide the result by the third lowest number.

10	35	2	32	37	33	9
13	36	12	14	34	3	11

210 What is X?

3 6 10 15 X 28

211 Which of the circles at the bottom should take the place of number 2 at the top?

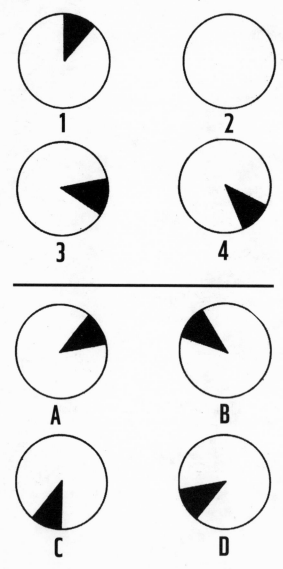

212 If the two figures at the top are correct, which of those below are wrong?

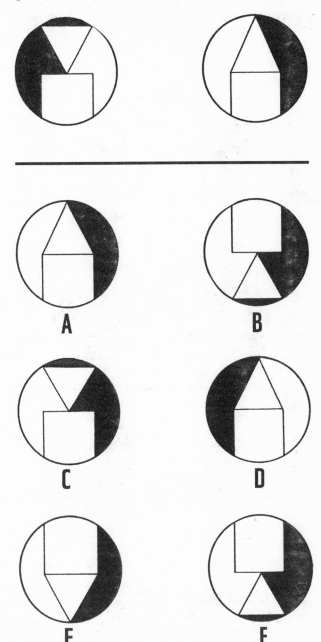

FRANKENSTEIN

213 For his latest creation Frankenstein takes half of CONNIE, part of NESTA, part of NELLIE, and part of AUNTIE.

What does Frankenstein call his creation?

REBUS

214 Solve the following rebus.

Section One

Answers

The Great Book of Brainteasers

1 D
The bottom figure is below the higher figure.

2 E is nearest, A is furthest away.

3 2 revolutions clockwise
C (24 teeth) rotates 4 revolutions. Therefore D also rotates 4 revolutions. Pulley B has twice the circumference of pulley D and so will rotate 2 revolutions. C rotates clockwise, as B does not change the direction of C. Pulleys D and E also rotate clockwise.

4 A 4, B4
When correctly spaced they are:
A. <u>4</u>   8   16   32   64   128
B. 19   38   76   152   30<u>4</u>

5 808
Multiply the first two numbers in the preceding line;
multiply the next two numbers in the preceding line;
multiply the last two numbers in the preceding line

6 B
A contains 7 triangles
B contains 11 triangles
C contains 10 triangles
D contains 6 triangles

7 A is 9, B is 11, C is 8, D is 12
If the four corners are numbered:

1	2
3	4

the numbers in the four corners of the second overall square in each pair are as follows:

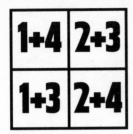

8 ANN
give each letter a number according to its position in the alphabet.
TED = 20 + 5 + 4 (29)
ANN = 1 + 14 + 14 (29)
(George and Mary each add to 57)

9 5
The numbers are the alphabetical positions of the letters:
6-F; 1-A; 3-C; 1-A; 4-D; 5-E.

10 D
D adds up to 36. The others add up to 33

11 Turn the numbers upside down
96
88
99
11
294

12 E
The knob is on the wrong side.

13 C
VIII has taken place of VII

14 40

15 E
The design consists of the letter S repeated 10 times, but in E one of them is the wrong way round.

16 105

17 25

18 5 men, 10 children and 20 women
If x + the number of men, then x + 2x + 4x =35
therefore 7x = 35
so x = 5

19 A-C, B-F, D-G, E-H

20

	EVEN	ODD	PRIME	SQUARE	2 DIGITS	6-12
1		✔		✔		
2	✔		✔			
3		✔	✔			
4	✔			✔		
5		✔	✔			
6	✔					✔
7		✔	✔			✔
8	✔					✔
9		✔		✔		✔
10	✔				✔	✔
11		✔	✔		✔	✔
12	✔				✔	✔
13		✔	✔		✔	
14	✔				✔	
15		✔			✔	
16	✔			✔	✔	

1 is not a prime number
Square numbers are 1, 4, 9, 16

Only 4 ticks means 4 truths

So, 11 is the winner

21 ZERO
He had 3 white socks and 1 black sock in his drawer.
His chances were

Pr white socks	Mixed Pair	Pr Black socks
$\frac{1}{2}$	$\frac{1}{2}$	ZERO

22 G
All the others can be paired A-J, B-E, C-L, D-N, F-I, H-K and M-O

23 B and C
They become:
5 4 1
3 1 6
2 5 3

24 55706065
In the first line multiplythe digits outside the brackets by 2 in this order: extreme left, extreme right, second left and first right. In the second line multiply by 3 and in the third line by 4, following the same procedure. Therefore in the fourth line multiply by 5 and follwo the same procedure.

25 B
The two strands should pass over and under each other alternately, as in the other examples.

26 D
They all rotate clockwise, first to the next vane, then missing one, then two and so on.

27 A is 9 or 6, B is 6 or 9, C is 6, D is 12
$9 \times 6 + 6 \div 12 = 5$

28 A is true; B is false (the majority are concave); C is false (a spider has eight legs); D is false (a stalagmite grows upwards, whereas as stalactite grows downwards).

The Great Book of Brainteasers

29

OBSERVATION	of	HERMITS
MELODY	of	HARPERS
EXALTATION	of	LARKS
SIEGE	of	CRANES
WATCH	of	NIGHTINGALES
PARLIAMENT	of	OWLS
COLONY	of	RABBITS
TRIP	of	SHEEP
HUSK	of	HARES
TRIBE	of	GOATS
KENNEL	of	RACHES
CRY	of	HOUNDS

30 A The lead flautist took $1/19 \times 37 = 1\,18/19$
Plus $1/19$ $= 1/19$ $= 2$ and so on
  B 37

31 128
The consecutive numbers are: 9, 10, 11; 17, 18; 20, 21 and 22

32 H
The centre stroke is shorter

33 D
Apart from D, each row contains one figure with one stroke, one with two strokes, one with three strokes, one with four strokes and one with five strokes. In row D there are two figures with four strokes and none with five strokes.

34 1 6 2 7 8 4
The numbers putside the brackets are transposed inside the brackets in the same order as in the top line.

35 52
The results are increased by one and decreased by one alternately:
$17 \times 3 = 51 + 1 = 52$

36 21
There are 15 small hexagons and 6 large ones. The last shape in the bottom row is a pentagon.

37 B
The figure is rotating clockwise.

38 C
The figures are transposed in the same way as in the example at the top.

39 A + ÷, B x ÷ or ÷ x or - +, C x -, D xx or + x

40 C
A, B and D all contain two circles, two squares, two straight lines and two triangles. In C there is only one triangle.

41 Nobody.
The Barber is a woman.

42 He tilted the butt until the water came up to the top edge without any running over. As the level of the water did not reach point X the butt was not half-full. If it had reached point X, it would have been exactly half full.
But if point X had been submerged it would have been more than half full.

43 5 6 2 5
The first number inside the brackets is the square root of the number outside the brackets. The remaining number inside the brackets is the square of the number outside the brackets.

44 N
There are two black balls instead of one white and one black.

45 Three sisters and two brothers
This can be solved by simple deduction, but if algebra is used let x be the number of sisters and y the number of brothers:

$$x + 1 = 2y$$
$$y + 1 = x$$

Therefore, $y + 1 + 1 = 2y$
so $y = 2$
or $x + 1 = 2x - 2$
so $x = 3$

The Great Book of Brainteasers

46 3 – C
Line 1 finsihes at 2, and line 2 finishes at 1.

47 59
The first 56 balls could be of all colours *except* red. This would leave 8 balls, all of which are red, so any three chosen would be red.

48 A - F, B - C. D - G and E - H

49 53
37 is midway between 3 (the lowest number) and 71 (the highest number); 53 is midway between 37 and 69 (nearest to the highest number).

50 A

51 2 8 9 4. The two numbers on the right of the *previous* brackets are the numbers on the left inside the brackets; the numbers on the left of the *previous* brackets are the numbers on the right inside the brackets.

52 F
Stripes go the opposite way when reflected in a mirror.

53 17 is the smallest segment; 14 is the largest segment

54 K, which is longer

55	100.00	Won by	Money in Wallet
	1st Hole	A	150.00
	2nd	A	225.00
	3rd	Tie	225.00
	4th	B	112.50
	5th	B	56.25
	6th	B	28.12
	7th	A	42.18
	8th	A	63.27
	9th	Tie	63.27
	10th	A	94.90
	11th	A	142.35
	12th	B	71.18

It is good way to wager if the 2 players are equal standard, B will always win money if he ties or loses by a few holes, but if A wins by a large number of holes, he will win a fortune.

B, if he won every hole, could only win £100, but A could win a fortune.

56 8

$$
\begin{array}{r}
70 \\
75 \\
85 \\
+\ 80 \\
\hline
310 \div 3 = 100 \text{ remainder } 10
\end{array}
$$

3 subjects each student, 10 at least 4

57 6+10+13, 8+9+12, 5+6+18, 4+12+13, 8+10+11, 19+4+6, 11+6+12

58 D
B is too big, A and C are too small

59 B
The position of the spots is repeated in every 4th sector.

60 87
The numbers are considered as moving clockwise in each successive large square. In each case they add to 100:
14 – 50 – 8 – 28
19 – 41 - 30 – 10
22 – 22 – 22 – 34
8 – 1 – 4 – 87 (X)

61 6380
The numbers inside the brackets are the squares of the numbers outside the brackets with 1 deducted. Alternatively, multiply 2, 4, 6 and 8 by 4, 6, 8 and 10 respectively and put the number at the end of the figure in the brackets, and multiply 3, 5, 7 and 9 by 1, 3, 5 and 7 respectively and put these numbers first.

62 12

	First face	Second face	Third face
1st move	1	2	6
2nd move	4	3	2
3rd move	6	5	1

63 36
The scores are: 1,7,1,7,1,2,1,5,1,4,1,4,and 1

64 B

65 42
There are 5 diamonds made with 9 squares, 12 diamonds made with 4 squares, and 25 diamonds made with 1 square.

66 Glass sign on glass door
PULL on one side
PUSH on opposite side

67 Start the 7 and 11 min. hour glasses when the egg is dropped into the water when it is boiling. When the sand stops running in the 7 glass, turn it over. When the sand stops running in the 11 glass, turn the 7 glass again. When the sand stops again in the 7 glass, 15 mins. will have elapsed.

68 1.2cm
The measurement is reduced by $\frac{1}{13}$ (four cards removed from 52).

69 A–D, B–L, C–H, E–G, F–J and I–K

70 X = G, Y = H

71 B
In the last white cross the diagonal from bottom left to top right should not pass over both vertical slats.

72 E
All the others contain three consecutive digits.

73 A 4, B 8

74 I is the second smallest. F is the second largest

75 0–0 and 5–2

76

SOLUTION 1	SOLUTION 2	
TANK	VEHICLE	TRACTOR
CASTLE	TURRET	TANK
BANK	SAND	CASTLE
RIVER	RIPARIAN	BANK
BRIDGE	SEVERN	RIVER
CARDS	YARBOROUGH	BRIDGE
WOOD	JACK	CARDS
BOW	YEW	WOOD
BULLS-EYE	ARROW	BOW
TRACTOR	FARM	BULLS-EYE

77 The three throws do not have the same chances, because if the 1st throw scores a 6, the other 2 throws do not occur. So the first throw has the best chance.

1st throw $\quad \dfrac{1}{6} \quad = \quad \dfrac{6}{36} \quad = \quad \dfrac{36}{216}$

2nd throw $\quad \dfrac{1 \times 5}{6 \times 6} \quad = \quad \dfrac{5}{36} \quad = \quad \dfrac{30}{216} \quad \dfrac{5}{6} = $ 1st throw losing

3rd throw $\quad \dfrac{1 \times 5 \times 5}{6 \times 6 \times 6} \quad = \quad \dfrac{25}{216}$

Total $\quad \dfrac{91}{216} \times \$100$

$\quad = \quad \$42.13$ stake

78 E

In E there are 4 white beads between the two black beads. In the others there are 5.

79 A is 3, B is 7, C is 4

There are several pointers to the solution; for example, in the last vertical column A cannot be 5, 6, 7, 8 or 9.

80 C

C results in 4; all the others result in 5.

81 A and F

82 26

Starting at the top left-hand corner and taking every fourth number, there are four series:

1, 2, 3, 4, 5, 6 (bottom left-hand square in centre section), 7, 8, 9; 2, 3, 4, 5, 6, 7 (bottom right-hand square in centre section), 8, 9, 10; 9, 8, 7, 6 (top left-hand square in centre section), 5, 4, 3, 2, 1; and 1, 3, 5, 7 (top right-hand square in centre section), 9, 11, 13, 15, 17.

83 P

It is the only arrow pointing to the left.

84 1020

Multiply the first two numbers in the right-hand column and place the result in the left-hand column; multiply the last two numbers in the right-hand column and place the result in the left-hand column.

85 A

86 A

87   OLIVE, SANDY, ISABEL (colours)

   MARTIN, ROBIN, MAVIS (birds)

   PRIMROSE, POPPY, MYRTLE (flowers)

   GARNET, DIAMOND, PEARL (gems)

88 A Either 239 cats killed 4,649 rats

B or 4,649 cats killed 239 rats. (A) is the most likely answer

89 6

The series is spaced incorrectly. When the spacing is correct it becomes: 2 4 8 16 32 64 128 256, which is an obvious doubling-up series.

90 J

It should be the same as C, E and P.

91 20

X, C and M are the Roman numerals 10, 100 and 1000 respectively. 1000 divided by 100 is 10; 100 divided by 10 is also 10.

92 E

There are only 7 off-shoots from the centre, instead of 8, as in all the others.

93 147

Add the first two numbers and place the total on the left inside the brackets, then place the difference between the other two numbers on the right inside the brackets.

94 A–C–H, B–E–L, D–G–M and F–I–J; K is the odd one out.

95 5

The numbers represent the alphabetic position of the letters; 1 is A, 4 is D etc. the word becomes ADUMBRATE with the addition of the final E. (One meaning of this word is 'to indicate faintly'.)

96 I

This man has no hands, as seen on his counterpart – E and M.

97 C and E

C goes on the right side of the piece already hung; E goes on the left side.

98 CLEFT

Turn the keys upside down and read the word formed by the lock ends.

99 A   6, 1, 8, 6, 1, 8
B   7, 5, 3, 7, 5, 3
C   2, 9, 4, 2, 9, 4

A beats B twice
B beats C twice
C beats A twice

100 Company C
Company A made £800,000,000
Company B made £850,000,000
Company C made £875,000,000
Company D made £700,000,000

101 A is a heart, B is a diamond, C is a heart
By simple elimination the following emerges:
a diamond is 1 (see third vertical column)
a club is 2
a spade is 3
a heart is 4

102 E and H
In both cases the minute and the hour hands have changed places.

103 1 and 7 are clefs– the G, or treble, clef, and the F, or bass, clef (indicating musical pitch). 3 and 9 are crotchets; 4 and 11 are minims; 5 and 10 are quavers; 6 and 8 are semi-quavers (all musical notes). 2 is a musical time signature, in this case indicating 'common' or 4/4 time. A sit has no counterpart, it is the odd one out.

104 F
There are 5 related pairs:
A (cricket bat) with J (cricket ball)
B (tennis ball) with E (tennis racket)
C (table tennis bat) with H (table tennis ball)
D (billiards ball) with K (billiards cue)
G (golf ball) with I (golf club)
F (football) is on its own

105 20

The black stripe is too narrow

106 b (BILL); c (TOM); d (JIM); e (FRED)

107 B

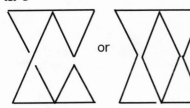

or

108 A

The figure is rotating clockwise, 45 degrees at a time. 6 and 7 indicate that the vane is shaded entirely on its blind side as compared with 1, 2 and 3.

109 £61

110 Their ages equalled 72

These are the possible ages:

72 – 1 – 1	The door number	74
36 – 2 – 1		39
24 – 3 – 1		28
18 – 4 – 1		23
18 – 2 – 2		22
12 – 6 – 1		19
12 – 3 – 2		17
9 – 4 – 2		15
8 – 9 – 1		18
8 – 3 – 3		14
6 – 6 – 2		14
6 – 4 – 3		13

The census taker did not know their ages because there were 2 totals of 14.

The door number was 14, so the total was 14

8 – 3 – 3   )   There was an oldest girl

6 – 6 – 2   )

so it must have been 8 – 3 – 3

111 A3, B5, C1, D6
In the first line the shading moves from top to bottom.
In the second line it moves from left to right.
In the third line it moves from bottom to top.
In the fourth line it moves from right to left.

112 6

113 B
From top to bottom, traffic lights are coloured red, amber and green. They change as follows: red and amber together – green – amber alone – red. As the amber light is showing, it will be followed by the red (B).

114 C

115 5040
Multiply each number by 2, 3, 4, 5 and 6 and (finally) 7.

116 X is 193; Y is 63
In the outer ring, starting with the lowest number, each number is doubled and 1 subtracted from the result. In the inner ring, starting with the lowest number, each number is doubled and 1 added to the result. (Alternatively, in the outer ring, the progression is 3, 6, 12, 24, 48 and 96; in the inner ring the progression is 2, 4, 8, 16, 32).

117 A is 4; B is 20; C is 5; D is 2
Add the numbers from top to bottom diagonally to the left of the bottom line for the first three positions on the bottom line, and to the right for the next three positions.

118 A is 2; B is 11; C is 5
The bottom line totals 19; the next line up totals 18; then 17. Hence 16, 15 and 14.

119 D
Examination of the previous globes shows that the globe is rotating anti-clockwise.

120 F
The right edge of the horizontal line forming the cross should not be shaded, as compared with C and K.

121 B
Other than in B, the designs are made up with a square, a triangle, a rectangle, a right angle and a line. In B, there are two squares but no rectangle.

122 One of the pockets, though not the one it started from.

123 4

124 29
The odd numbers in A total 39; the even numbers in B total 40. From this combined total of 79 is subtracted 50 – the total of the prime numbers in C.

125 X is 2; Y is 8

126 No number plate begins with 0, so whether a number plate contains 1, 2, 3, or 4 digits Freddie has an advantage.

127 AJ; BE; CD; GH; FI

128 A11; B2; C8; D10; E16

129 C is the shortest route; B is the longest route
The curves may have misled you, since it might appear that the biggest curve – in C – gives the longest route. In fact, the curves are semicircles, the length of which is estimated on the formula of 3.14 approx, multiplied by the radius.

130 N
The dots in the rectangle ar too close together as compared with those in the other rectangles – D, E and L.

131 B
The mast is too far forward.

132 A
When the diagonal line from the base-line of the square inclines to the right, as in C, E and G, the right half of the square is black.
Whenit inclines to the left as in B, D and F, the bottom half of the square is black.
In A the right half of the square should be black.

133 If at first you don't succeed, try, try, again, then quit. There's no sense being a damn fool about it.

134 $9 \times 8 \times 7 \times 6 \times 5$ $8 \times 7 \times 6 \times 5 \times 4 \times 3$
    $\dfrac{}{1 \times 2 \times 3 \times 4 \times 5}$ x $\dfrac{}{1 \times 2 \times 3 \times 4 \times 5 \times 6}$
    $= 3528$

135 17

136 D F B C E
The letters must be transposed in the same order as the numbers.

137 AG, BF, CH, DE

138 C
The digits add up to 19. In all the others the total is 18.

139 J
The mouth should be as in B and H.

140 1416
In the first example, divide the left-hand number by 4 and the right-hand number by 5. In the second example, divide the left-hand number by 6 and the right-hand number by 7. Therefore, in the third line, divide the left-hand number by 8 (14) and the right-hand number by 9 (16).

141 B and M

142 AE, BD, CG, FH

143 18
All the others are divisible by 4

144 Oswald   (lost £2401) is married
    to Betty   (won £2601)

    Ernie   (lost £529) is married
    to Alice   (won £729)

    John   (lost £25) is married
    to Marjorie   (won £225)

145 729

Squares 13-499	16, 25, 36, 49, 64, 81, 100, 121, 144, 169, 196, 225, 256, 289, 324, 361, 400, 441, 484
Squares 500-1300	529, 576, 625, 676, 729, 784, 841, 900, 961, 1024, 1089, 1156, 1225, 1296
Cubes 13-499	27, 64, 125, 216, 343
Cubes 500-1300	512, 729, 1000
Both	64, 729

Possible true answers:

No 1 and 2)
No 1 and 3)
   2 and 3 – Yes, over 500 there is a cube and a square (729)

146 F and H

147 X is 6; Y is 1
Starting at number 1 and moving to alternate segments clockwise:
1 2 3 4 5 6
Starting at number 6 and moving in the same way:
6 5 4 3 2 1

148 B

149 E
Adding up each column:
Column A = 75
Column B = 80
Column C = 85
Column D = 90
Column E = 96
Column F = 100

150 C

Except for C, each row contains 1 equilateral triangle, 2 right-angled triangles with the base at the bottom and 2 with the base at the top,
In C, there are 3 right-angled traingles with the base at the top and only 1 with the base at the bottom.

151 Tomorrow
The day before yesterday was two days ago; the day after the day before yesterday was yesterday; two days after that (yesterday) is tomorrow.

152 E
The diagonal slat from the top left to bottom right should pass under the other slats.

153 16061

154 Suspension bridge

155 3020
The first 2 digits on the right of the brackets are divided by the digit on the left to gve the first digit inside the brackets. The remaining number on the right of the brackets is multiplied by the digit on the left of the brackets to give the remaining number inside the brackets.

156 A
In each row the first symbol is the same as the second in the previous row and the other symbols continue in the same order.

157 2
The first column totals 9. The second column totals 10. This pattern continues, so the final column should total 13, by the addition of 2.

158 AG CI, BF, DK, EJ, HL

159 G and H

160 X is 4; Y is 11
Two alternate series
Starting with the first number: 7 6 5 4 3
Starting with the second number: 8 9 10 11 12
161

E – tetragon (4 sides)
C – pentagon (5 sides)
B – hexagon (6 sides)
G – heptagon (7 sides)
A – octagon (8 sides)
F – nonagon (9 sides)
D – decagon (10 sides)

162 2 When the head of the match points to the left, that match should lie on top of the other match. In 2 it lies underneath.

163 C
in the top right hand quarter there are only 14 hatchlines, whereas in all other quarters there are 15.

164 In the top row the figure is rotated — turn clockwise and the position of the dots changes. In the second row the figure is rotated — turn anti-clockwise and the position of the dots changes as in the first row. $\frac{1}{4}$

165 The triangles should overlap. In each row across there is a large and a small shape, with one figure encircling the other (1, 6 and 8); one outside the other (2, 4 and 9); and both figures overlapping (3, 5 and 7 – which <u>should</u> do so but doesn't).

166 15
All the others are prime numbers.

167

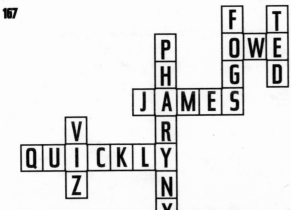

168 No player could have achieved a five digit total. There are no four digit prime palin-

149

dromic numbers. There are only 15 three digit prime numbers which are palindromic, and one two digit prime palindromic number 11. The total is 7104 divided by 16 equals an average of 444.

169 C

Each row contains one envelope with an upright stamp, one with the stamp sloping to the right and one to the left. The upright stamp (the missing one in the second row) should be cancelled with wavy lines to correspond with the first envelope in the top row, and C is the only one which so conforms.

170 55 squares and 30 triangles

171 1.

From 2 onwards the figure is rotated clockwise, 45 degrees at a time. In each movement the spot alternates from white to black, the heavy and light-shaded portions being alternately transposed in their positions. Number 1 should be as follows:

172

A $x = 9$. The figure in the third square across is the sum of the figures in the preceding two squares.

B $x = 14$. In the first row across the numbers increase by 3 and 4; in the second row by 4 and 5. Therefore, in the third row they should increase by 5 and 6.

C $x = I$. This is similar to the previous example, except that letters are used instead of numbers. In the first row the letters advance, skipping 3 and 4 places respectively. In the second row they should advance, skipping 4 and 5 places, so as to conform with the third row, in which the letters skip 5 and 6 places.

173 85

In the first row, the numbers outside the brackets are divided by 16 and the results placed inside the brackets. In the second row they are divided by 17. Therefore, in the third row they are divided by 18.

174 X = 129. In the outer ring, moving clockwise, each number is doubled and 1 subtracted from the result.

Y = 39. In the inner ring, moving clockwise, each number is doubled and 1 added to the result.

175 8— cigarettes.

176 81$^{6}_{1}$

177 2, 3, 12 – These losing numbers have been decided by the gambling authorities and apply world wide.

178 AF, BG, CE, DH

179 They are both the same distance from Sheffield *when they meet* !

180 Car 1 goes into road B, because 17 goes into 136;
Car 2 goes into road C, because 81 goes into 567
Car 3 goes into road A, because 27 goes into 243

181 59
Proceeding from top to bottom along the rows from left to right, add the two previous numbers and add 1, then add the two previous numbers and subtract 1, and so forth, adding 1 and subtracting 1 alternately. Thus the two numbers previous to the blank square are 22 and 38. These are added together, giving 60, and 1 subtracted from the total.

182 E
All of the figures except E consist of an equal number of squares, triangles and crosses. In E there are 4 triangles and crosses, but 5 squares.

183 S19
There are two separate series. The letters advance missing first two (A to D), then three (D to H) and so on. After M there must be five missing letters, bringing us to S. The numbers advance in the same way.

184 C
The middle scrolls do not conform with the others.

185 F
Both scrolls are turned the same way; in all the others one is turned inwards and the other outwards.

186 D $_1$
As 1764 was a leap year, there were 29 days in February, so it would be Saturday 10 NOT 11 March.

187 F
His moustache differs from B and G.

188 X is 4; Y is 11
There are two alternate series. One is:
7 6 5 4
The other is:
8 9 10 11

189 A, B and E
With regard to the shape of the moon, D comes before C: when the moon is in the shape of a D it is waxing and when it is in the shape of a C it is waning.

190 25' x 25'
   15' x 15'

191
   1 5.5 KG
   2 6.5 KG
   3 7 KG
   4 4.5 KG
   5 3.5 KG

192 C
The cross in the bottom right quarter is different from those in the other shields

193 6

194 C and F

195 X is 9; Y is 15
There are two separate series. Starting with the first number and taking the others alternately:
1 3 5 7 9
Starting with the second number and proceeding in the same way:
3 6 9 12 15

196 B
As can be seen below, all the others can be drawn with a continuous unbroken line:

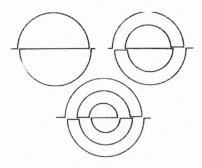

197 112

198 3
The numbers following the letters correspond with the position in the alphabet of the letters.

199 16
4 is the square of 2; 9 is the square of 3; 25 is the square of 5; x must be the square of 4 (16).

200 B
The face in B is composed of three circles, four straight lines and five curves. All the other faces have four circles, four straight lines and four curves.

201 448

202 Yes
True odds are $^1/_{1828}$

203 A
These are keys of a piano. It is not possible to have two groups of three black keys next to each other.

204 13
Change the Roman numerals into modern numbers:
208 104 52 26
Each one is half the previous number. therefore the next number is 13, expressed in modern numerals to conform with the established pattern.

205 E
In all the others identical shapes overlap:
A two circles
B two equilateral triangles
C two ovals
D two right-angled triangles
F two squares
In E there are two diamonds which do not overlap

206 D

207 A
With the exception of the digits in A, which add up to 13, the digits in all other dates add up to 12.

208 D
D equals 3; all the others equal 4

209 12

210 21
The numbers increase by 3, 4, 5, 6 and 7

211 A
The black section rotates 40° at a time.

212 C, D, E

213 CONSTANTINE

214 SCATTERBRAIN

Section Two

The Great Book of Brainteasers

1 Which of the figures at the bottom belongs to E?

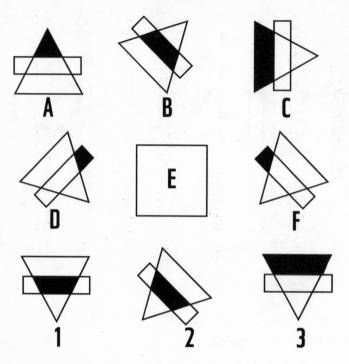

2 Which ladder is wrong?

3 Which of these is out of place?

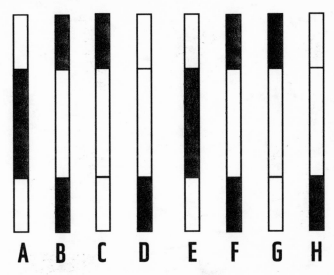

A B C D E F G H

4 Arrange these patterns into four pairs.

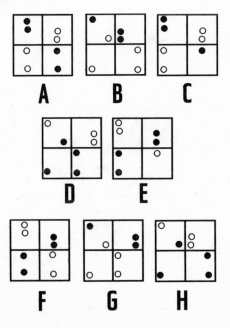

5 What numbers belong to a and b?

36 (35) 60

65 (58) 104

A (79) B

6 Which piece completes the jig-saw puzzle?

A

B

C

D

E

F

7 What numbers should take the place of A & B?

8 Murmansk, in Russia, is on a longitude 33 degrees east. Victoria Island, off Canada, is on longitude 110 degrees west. If you travelled due east from the North Pole, which would you reach first?

9 Assuming that house A, B, C and D are correct, which of the numbered houses below are incorrect?

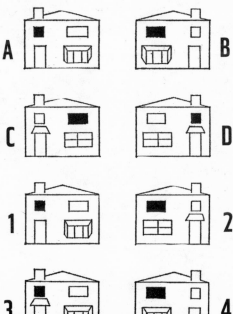

10 Can you compose music? Study the music below and decide which of the numbered symbols belong to A and B.

11 What numbers are represented by A and B?

4	5	6
7	8	1
5	3	A
B	9	7
9	9	1
7	6	7

12 Which of the numbered figures at the bottom belongs to X?

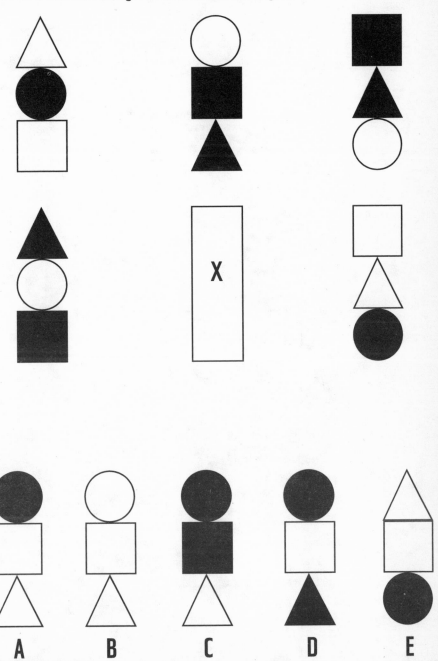

ERNIE

13 'ERNIE' is a random number producer. Pi could also be said to be a random number producer, because the decimal equivalent is known to only 2000 million decimal places. Nobody knows the million millionth decimal place, each digit has the same chance to be the one.

So if you had a transcendental number which consists of random digits, what would be the average difference between two random digits side by side?

It should be $\dfrac{0+9}{2} = 4.5$

But it isn't. What is it?

ZOETROPE

14

Clue: You need this to run before the wind (9)

Find the (9) letter word. Find the 1st letter. Draw a straight line to the 2nd letter, then to the 3rd letter and so on. The enclosed areas have been filled in.

15 Complete this sequence:

2 3 4 9 16 81 256

16 How many revolutions of 1 will take place in order to bring the black teeth into mesh with the other:

A If 1 rotates clockwise

B If 2 rotates anti clockwise?

17 Which signal is wrong? (The arrow indicates the direction of operation of the signal.)

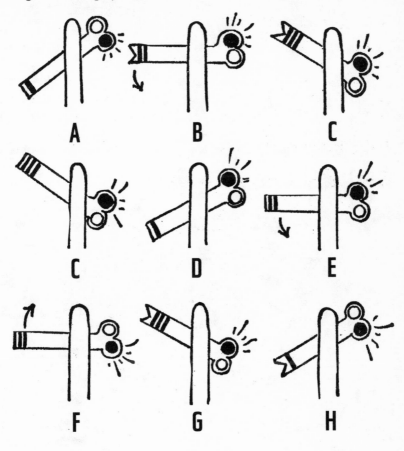

18 What number should replace the ?

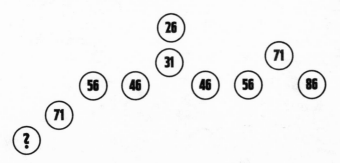

19 A man is walking down a street at 3mph. He notices that for every 40 buses that pass him travelling in the same direction, 60 pass him in the opposite direction.

What is the average speed of the buses?

20 Which hexagon fits the missing space?

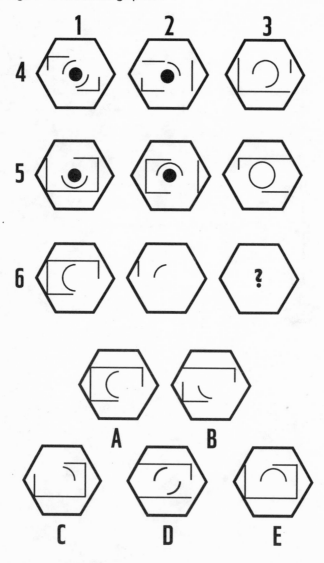

21 What number should replace the question mark?

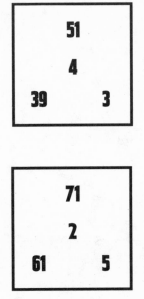

22 A man wagers £40.00 and wins back his original stake, plus £60.00. He spends $\frac{1}{10}$ of it on a meal and $\frac{1}{20}$ of it on a taxi fare home home. He then buys a present for his wife which cost $\frac{1}{2}$ of what he had left.

How much more money did he have since he started out?

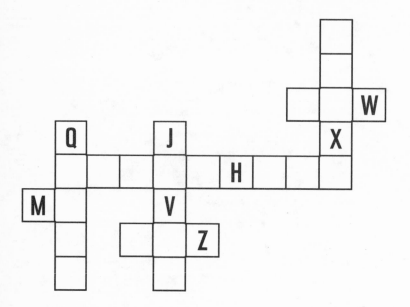

The Great Book of Brainteasers

ALPHABET X-WORD

23 Place all of the letters of the alphabet in the grid to make a crossword.

8 letters have been placed for you.

GOLF

24 Two professionals had no further teaching to do on the golf course, so they decided to have a match. They scored 79 and 81.

Amazingly, the 81 score won, they were not playing match play, how was that?

The Great Book of Brainteasers

25 What is the difference between the lowest number and the average of all the numbers?

3   9   12   15   18   25   30

26 Square the lowest even number and subtract the result from the third highest odd number:

9	**67**	**4**	**11**	**58**	**66**
2	**65**	**1**	**8**	**10**	**41**
6	**71**	**5**	**12**	**25**	**3**
7	**41**	**32**	**70**	**69**	**68**

27 What is X?

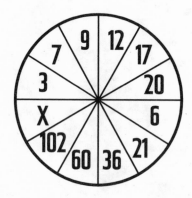

28 What comes next in the series?

16 72 38 94 50 –

29 The black ball moves one position at a time clockwise. The white ball moves two positions at a time anti-clockwise.

A In how many moves will they be together again?

B In what corner will they be?

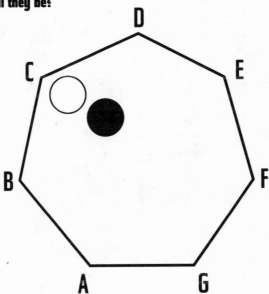

30 What is X?

1	2	3	4	5	6	7	8
7	14	1	2	2	1	8	7
10	3	4	18	2	1	8	6
8	5	11	12	2	21	3	4
2	11	6	3	13	1	2	10
2	5	5	1	6	10	2	X

31 What are X and Y?

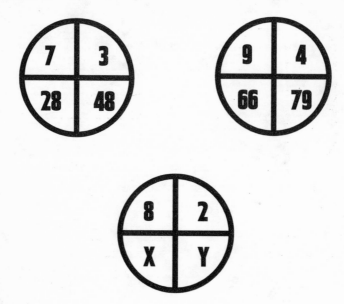

32 What are X and Y?

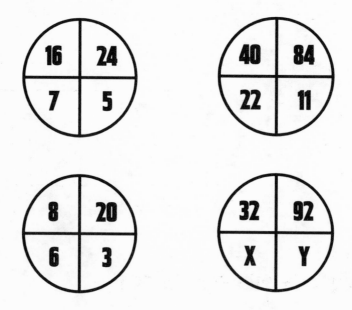

33 Which is the odd one out?

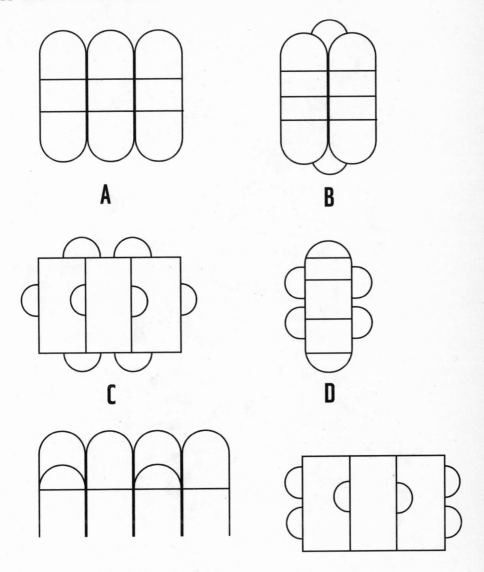

34 What comes next in the series?

1072 1055 1021 953 817 545 –

OWZAT

35 The village team were all out for 0, each man was out first ball. It was a 6 ball an over game.

Who was the last batsman left not out?

A SIX-HORSE RACE

36 In a 6 horse race the bookmaker needed to make a profit of 25% in order to cover his expenses, salary for his clerk, income tax and profit.

These were the prices, what price should be quote for No. 6?

Horse No.	Against	
1	2-1	"
2	3-1	"
3	4-1	"
4	5-1	"
5	6-1	"
6	?	"

37 What is X?

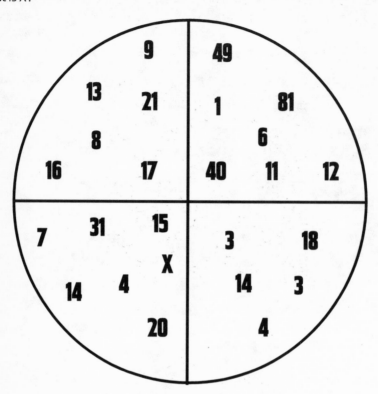

38 If : **4** equals **4**,

      9 equals **7 $\frac{1}{2}$**,

      16 equals **12**,

      25 equals **17 $\frac{1}{2}$**,

      36 equals **24**,

      49 equals **31 $\frac{1}{2}$**,

What does **64** equal?

39 On a chessboard how many sets of three black squares occur, horizontally, vertically or diagonally? (ie threes in each row and column, plus threes touching diagonally.)

You many use any square more than once.

40 What is X?

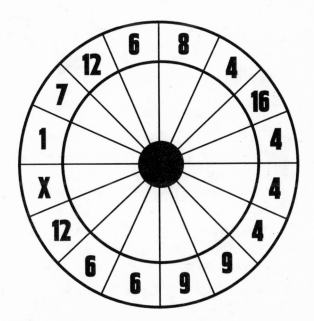

41 Group these into four matching pairs:

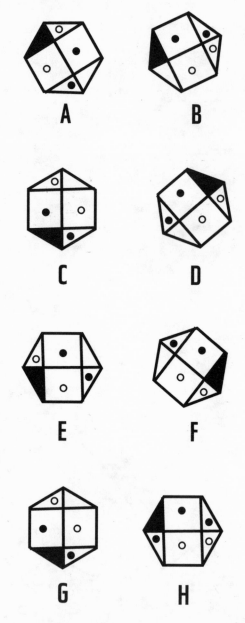

42 What word is represented by the seven cards at the bottom?

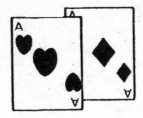

43 Give the time indicated at X?

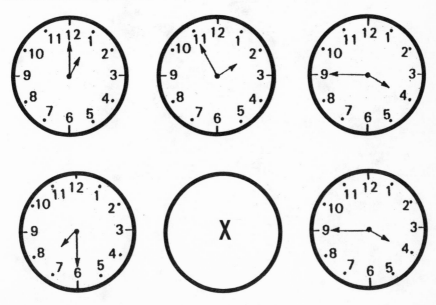

44 Insert arithmetical signs between these numbers to make the equation correct:

18 2 9 24 5 = 100

45 Which is the odd one out?

A.	K	N	Q	T	W	Z
B.	B	F	J	N	R	V
C.	A	F	K	P	V	Z
D.	3	6	9	12	15	18
E.	7	11	15	19	23	27
F.	13	18	23	28	33	38

46 What is the total of the square of the lowest number, the square root of the highest number, and the number that is midway between the results?

168	9	4	167	162
8	5	161	7	163
169	6	166	10	3
11	12	165	14	164

PLAYING FIELD

47 The grass in a school playing field had to be cut.
One man could mow the grass in 4 hours
One man could mow the grass in 5 hours
One man could mow the grass in 6 hours
One man could mow the grass in 8 hours

If they all joined forces to cut the field and they all worked at their individual rates, how long would it take to cut the grass?

CLOTH

48 A factory was cutting rolls of cloth into 1 metre lengths, from a 200 metre roll. How long would it take for the machine to cut the roll if each cut took 4 secs?

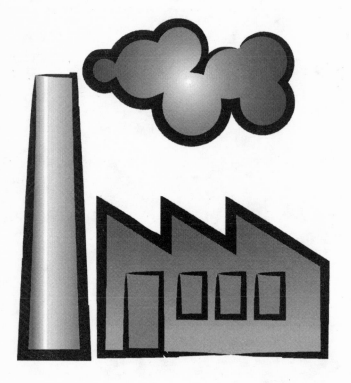

49 In a road with 20 houses:

Tom lives at number 4;
Bill lives four houses from Tom;
Jim lives opposite Bill's next door neighbour;
Fred lives four houses from Jim.
What is the number of Fred's house?

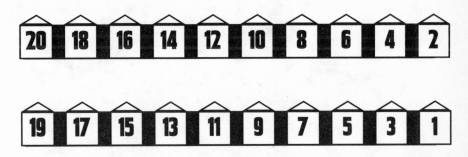

50 Reading across, down or diagonally, which three consecutive numbers give the highest total?

6	8	10	10	8	10
10	11	7	7	1	18
9	9	10	7	12	1
7	9	10	8	7	8
12	10	7	9	11	8
9	8	12	7	10	10

51 Which die is wrong?

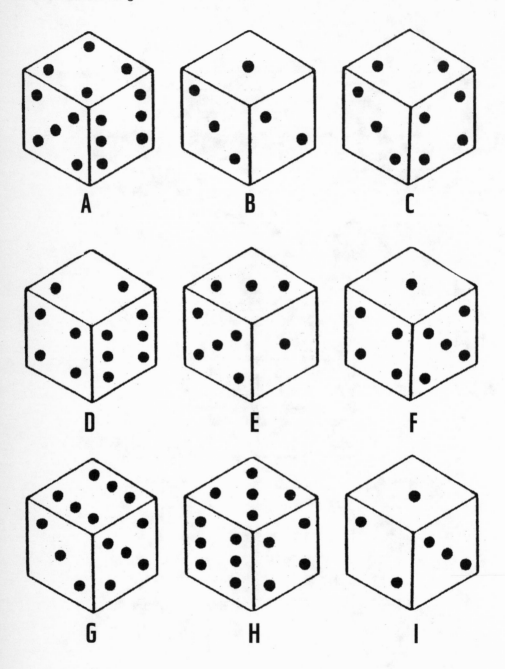

52 The black blocks each weigh 3 kilograms. The white blocks each weigh 2 kilograms. which of these see-saws is wrong?

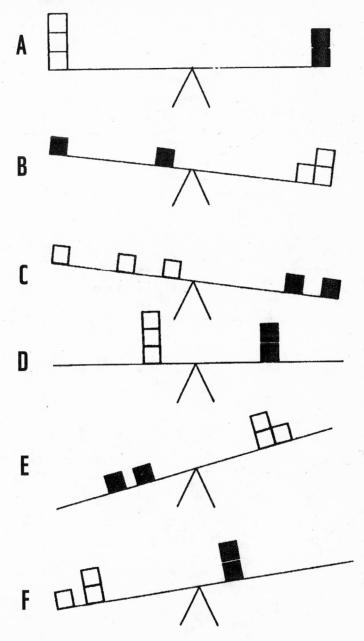

53 Think of the numbers from 1 to 10 and decide which domino is missing:

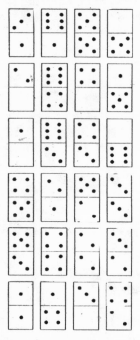

54 Given that the area of a circle is 3.14 times the square of its radius, and without using a pocket calculator, which of the figures below has an area nearest to that of the circle?

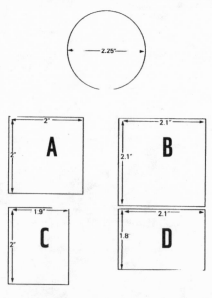

55 What are X and Y?

3 7 4 6 21 12 12 84 36 24 420 X Y

56 If this clock were turned upside-down and held in front of a mirror, which of those below would be reflected?

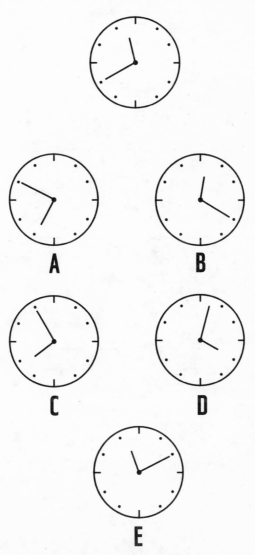

A

B

C

D

E

'A FRIENDLY STREET'

57 5 friends live in the same road A, B, C, D, E.

The numbers of B, C, D when multiplied together equals 1260. The numbers B, C, D when added equal twice E's number, and is even.

A's number is half as much again as E's. The road numbers run from 2 to 222.

What are the 5 house numbers?

CHILDREN

58 A woman has 7 children.

On multiplying their ages together one obtains the number 6591.

Given that today is the birthday of all 7, what are their seven ages? There are two sets of triplets

59 Match these into four pairs:

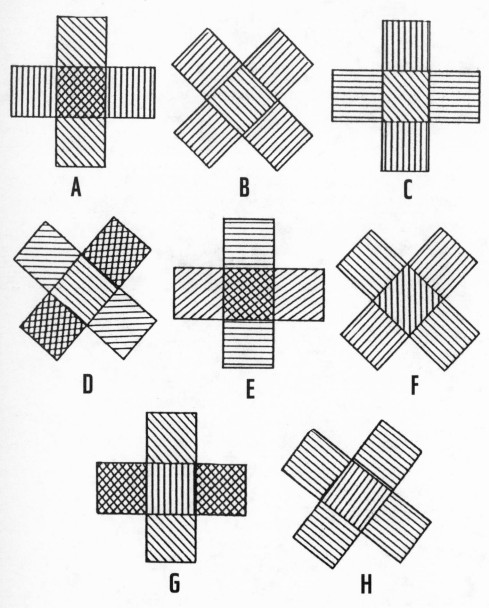

60 Which triangle is the odd one out?

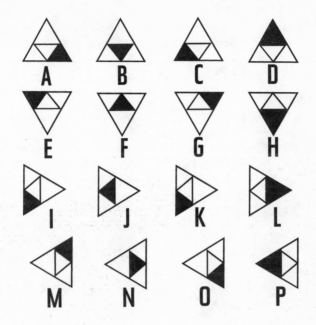

61 Which two pieces will make the hexagon?

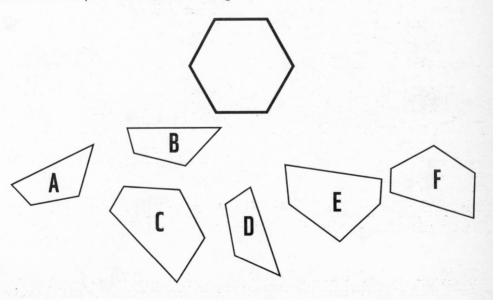

62 When the die shows an even number on top, the counter moves two places forward in addition to the number on the die.

When the die shows an odd number on top, the counter moves one place back in addition to the number on the die.
On what number will the counter be after seven throws of the die, producing the following numbers on top.

6 4 3 1 2 6 5

63 What goes into the empty brackets?

12 (27144) 3
13 (64169) 4
14 (125196) 5
15 (   ) 6

64 Which key will not fit the lock?

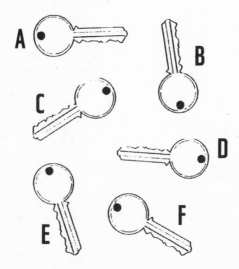

65 Which of the heptagons below follows number 5?

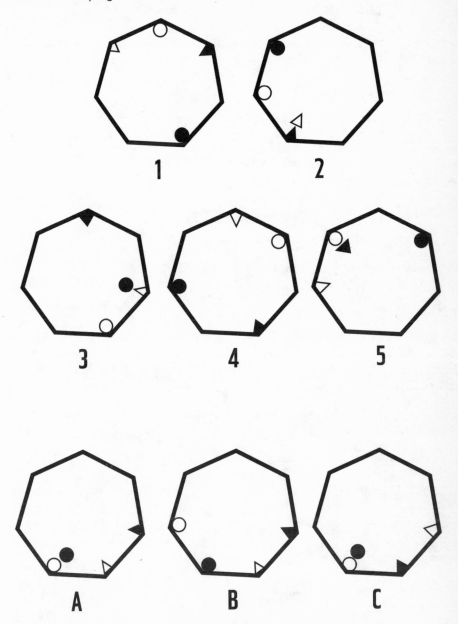

66 Give values for x and y:

$$2X - Y = 5$$
$$X + Y = 16$$
$$Y - X = 2$$

67 How much does it weigh if its weight is:

A 999 lbs plus half its own weight
B 999 lbs minus half its own weight
C 999 lbs times half its own weight
D 999 lbs divided by half its own weight

68 Each of the nine squares in the grid marked 1A to 3C, should incorporate all the lines and symbols which are shown in the squares of the same letter and number immediately above and to the left. For example, 2B should incorporate all the lines and symbols that are in 2 and B.
One of the squares is incorrect.
Which one is it?

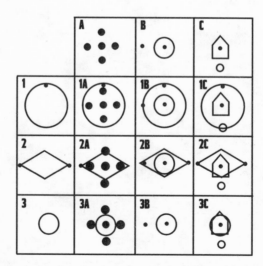

WHAT'S THE SCORE

69 Three cricketers were discussing their scores:

GEORGE: "I scored 9, I scored 2 less than HENRY, I scored 1 more than MALCOLM".

HENRY: "I did not score the lowest, the difference between my score and MALCOLM's was 3, MALCOLM scored 12".

MALCOLM: "I scored less than GEORGE, GEORGE scored 10, HENRY scored 3 more than GEORGE".

Each man had made one incorrect statement out of 3.

What were the scores?

The Great Book of Brainteasers

HALF 'N HALF

70 Given two numbers, if we subtract half of the smaller number from each number, the result with the larger number is three times as large as the result with the smaller number.

How many times is the larger number as large as the smaller number?

160

407

80

66

97

11

132

1013

396

3

71 What number should replace the question mark to a definite rule?

147   **159**   **174**   **186**   **?**

72 A farmer told his labourer to pick 896,809 apples and pack them into as few boxes as possible, each having the same number of apples.
How many boxes did he use?

73 Which of these is the odd one out?

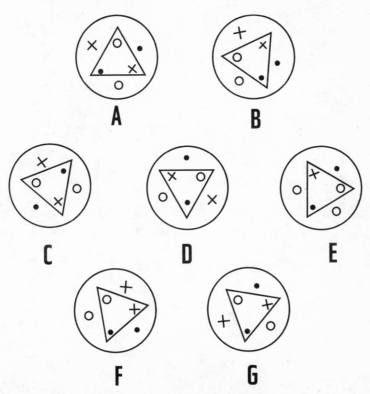

A   B

C   D   E

F   G

74 A driving school claims an average test pass rate of 76.8 per cent. What is the least number of pupils required to achieve this result?

75 Which row does not conform with the others?

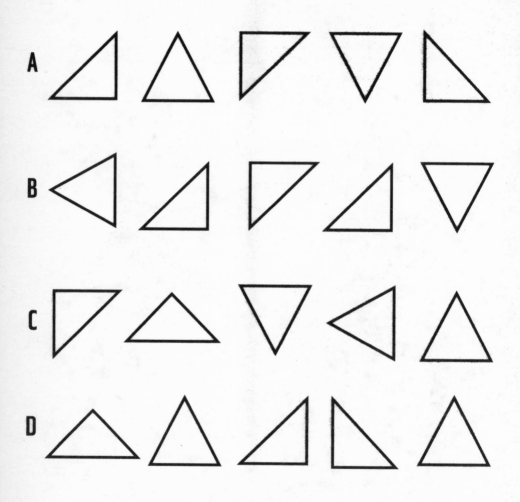

76 How many combinations of three or four of these numbers will add up to 50?

2 4 6 8 10 17 19 21 25

ENVELOPES

77 A correspondent writes 7 letters and addresses 7 envelopes, one for each letter. In how many ways can all of the letters be placed in the wrong envelopes?

ALPHAMETICS

78 Replace the letters with numbers.

```
      COPS
     CLOSE
    CELLAR
    CORPSE
      CASE
 +  COLLAR
    RECTOR
```

79 Which of the rows below will form three perfect circles when line 1 – 2 is superimposed on line X – Y at the top?

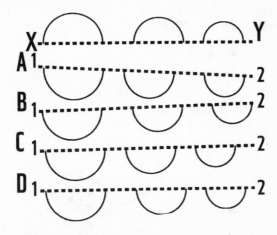

80 Six of these patterns can be arranged into threee pairs. Which two will not make a matching pair?

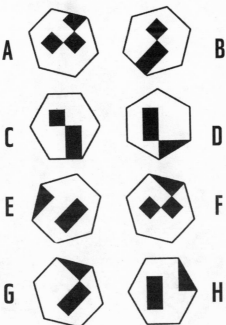

81 Which number in the bottom line belongs to the top line?

2　3　5　6　8　9　10　13

1　4　7　11　13　14　17　77

82 If the two clocks at the top are right, which of those below are wrong?

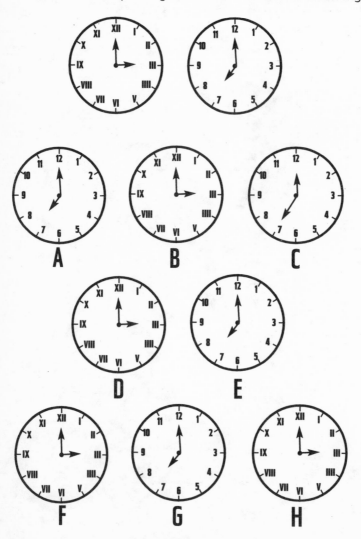

83

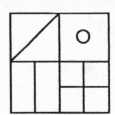

is to

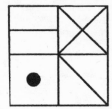

as

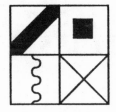

is to

A

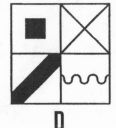

B

C

D

84 Which number in the bottom line comes next in the top line?

9   8   10   18   21   16   –

14   15   20   27

85 Give values for X and Y

86 Which is the odd one out?

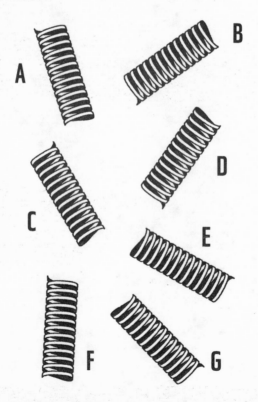

NEW STATIONS

87 Every station on the railway system sells tickets to every other station.

Some new stations were added. 46 sets of additional sets of tickets were required.

How many new stations have been added? How many stations were there originally?

HOLE IN ONE

88 My friend had scored a hole in one.

There were 5 witnesses. Here is a list of their statements about which hole produced the amazing feat. It was an 18 hole course.

A Not an even number

B It had double digits

C The number was made up of only straight lines

D Not a prime number

E Not a square number

But only one statement was a true one.

Which hole was it?

89 What comes next in this series?

1 7 8 15 23 38 61 –

90 Which is the odd one out?

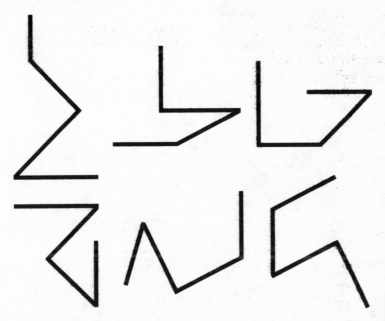

91 What number goes into the empty brackets?

98 (79) 126

105 (79) 135

48 (35) 80

34 (   ) 85

92 What are A, B and C?

$$
\begin{array}{cccc}
 & 3 & A & 6 \\
 & C & 4 & B \\
\hline
B & 2 & B & A \\
\end{array}
$$

93 What is X?

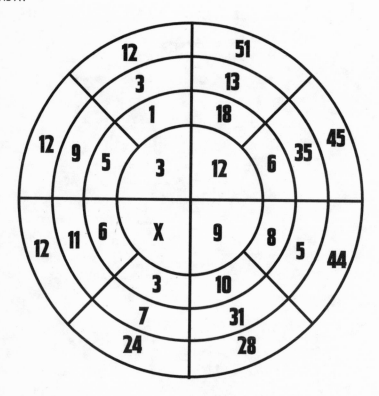

94 What is X?

25 22 15 X 10 19 24

95 What are x and y?

72 7 36 14 18 28 9 56 X Y

96 Which is the odd one out?

A.	1	6	3	4	9	2
B.	6	14	3	8	1	2
C.	19	7	5	23	3	4
D.	1	9	4	7	3	2

97 Which leaves obviously came from the same plant?

98 What is X?

X 11 1098 76 5 43 21

99 What are X, Y and Z?

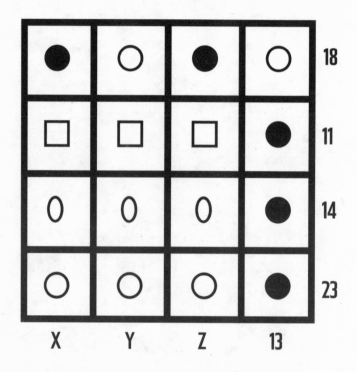

100 Among these dominoes how many double-sixes are there?

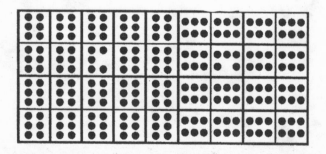

HIGH SCHOOL REUNION

101 Barbara visited her High School friend, Natasha after their 25th school reunion. "What a nice pair of children you have, are they twins?", Barbara asked.

"No my sister is older than I", said Natasha's son Philip. "The square of my age plus the cube of her age is 7148".

"The square of my age plus the cube of his age is 5274", said Matilda.

How old were they?

A PASSING MOVE

102 A train moving at 49 mph meets and is passed by a train moving at 63 mph. A passenger in the first train noted that the second train took 4.5 seconds to pass him.

How long is the second train?

103 Which slice has been cut out from the cake?

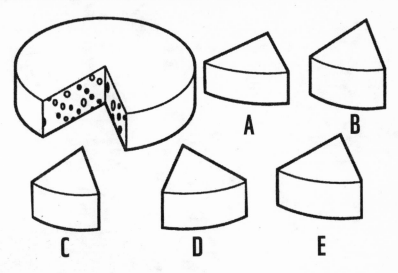

104 what is the ratio between A and C?

A. 2 to 1

B. 4 to 1

C. 1 to 1

D. 5 to 1

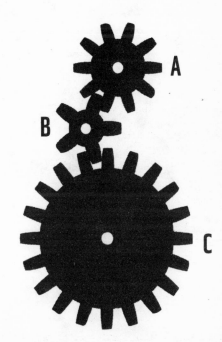

105 A card player holds 13 cards of four suits, of which seven are black and six are red. There are twice as many hearts as clubs and twice as many diamonds as hearts. How many spades does he hold?

106 What is X?

131 517 192 X

107 Arrange these into four matching pairs.

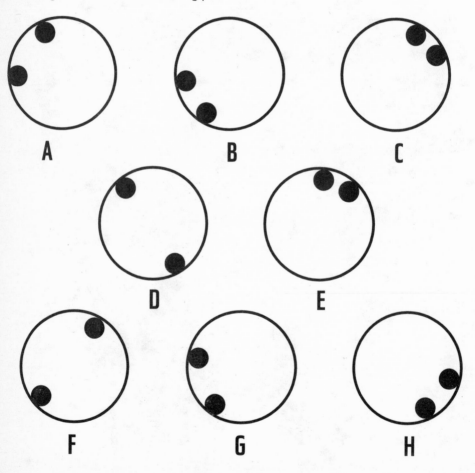

108 Group these symbols into five sets of three.

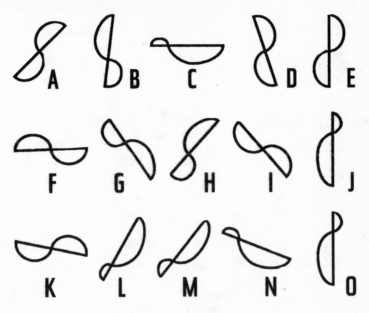

109 Group these six figures into three pairs.

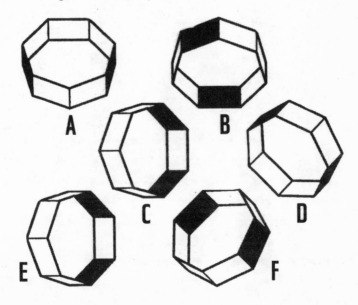

110 Multiply the numbers that are midway between the lowest and highest numbers in A and B and subtract the midway number in C.

5	4	97
6	95	99
3	98	96

A

77	8	75
9	76	10
79	7	74

B

10	9	76
75	77	12
73	11	74

C

111 What goes into the empty square?

0	7	2	4	12	6	3
	7	9	6		18	9

JEWELS

112 The 1st man has 16 sapphires
The 2nd man has 10 emeralds
The 3rd man has 8 diamonds

Each man gives the other two, two of his gems and then all 3 have the same value of wealth.

What are the individual values of the three types of jewels?

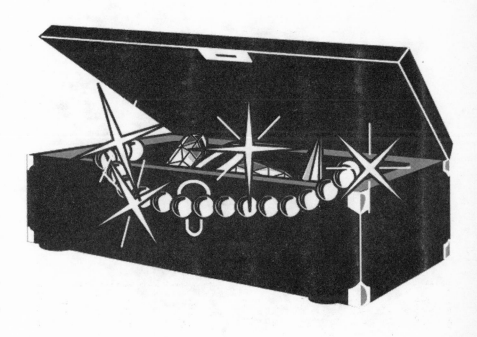

APPLES

113 A man had to pack apples in packets, but as each packet has to have exactly the same number of apples, he was having difficulty.

If he packed 10 apples in a packet, one packet had only 9
"   9   "   "   8
"   8   "   "   7
"   7   "   "   6
and so on, down to
"   2   "   "   1

How many apples did he have?

114 Add the numbers that are squares of whole numbers to the prime numbers.

$$12 \quad 16 \quad 7 \quad 180 \quad 31$$
$$225 \quad 81 \quad 23 \quad 56 \quad 64$$
$$35 \quad 15 \quad 72 \quad 48 \quad 14$$

115 Which, if any, of these is wrong?

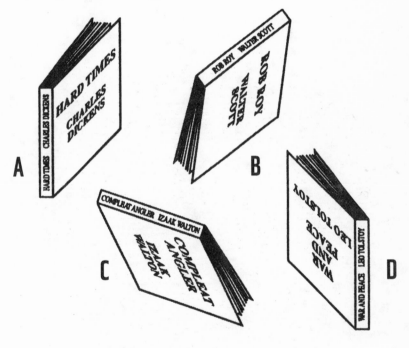

A — HARD TIMES, CHARLES DICKENS

B — ROB ROY, WALTER SCOTT

C — COMPLEAT ANGLER, IZAAK WALTON

D — WAR AND PEACE, LEO TOLSTOY

116 Which number in the top row belongs to the bottom row, and which number in the bottom row belongs to the top row?

$$9 \quad 25 \quad 49 \quad 81 \quad 96$$
$$8 \quad 12 \quad 121 \quad 18 \quad 14$$

117 What are X and Y?

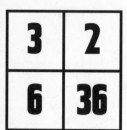

3	2
6	36

1	4
4	16

1	2
X	Y

118 Simplify:

$$\frac{3}{4} \div \frac{27}{32} = \ ?$$

119 Find the missing numbers.

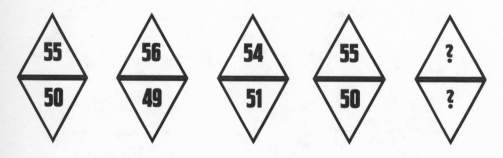

120 Which is the odd one out

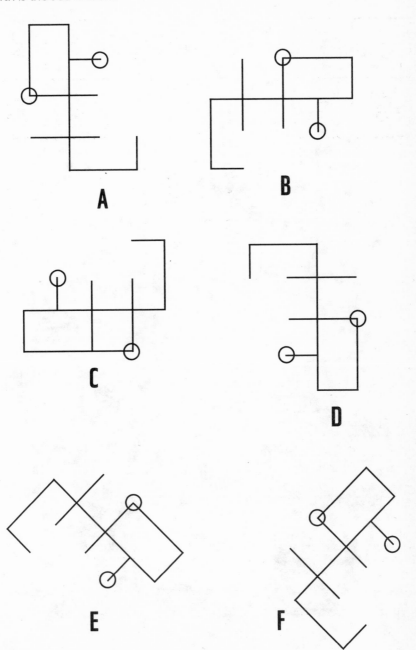

A

B

C

D

E

F

KEYS

121 The porter had mixed up the room keys. There are 20 rooms. What is the maximum number of trials required to sort out the keys?

ZOETROPE

122

Clue: Spindrift skimmers! (4-7)

Find the (4-7) letter words. Find the 1st letter. Draw a straight line to the 2nd letter, then to the 3rd letter and so on. The enclosed areas have been filled in.

123 Which hexagon fits the missing space?

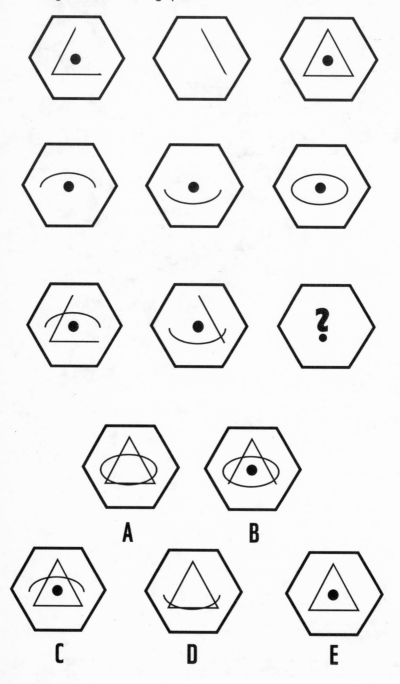

124 Which is the odd one out?

A

B

C

D

E

125 Multiply the second highest number by the second lowest number and then divide the result by the third lowest number.

10 35 2 32 37 33 9

13 36 12 14 34 3 11

126 Which of the circles at the bottom should take the place of number 2 at the top?

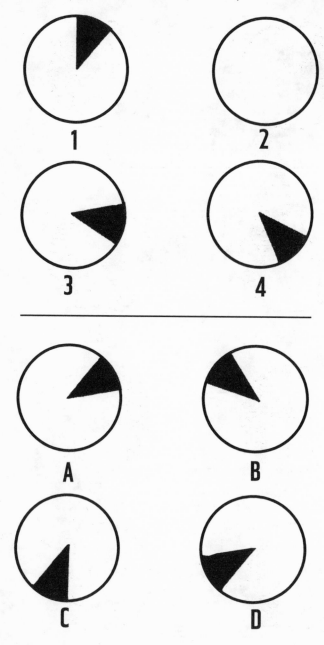

127 If the two figures at the top are correct, which of those below are wrong?

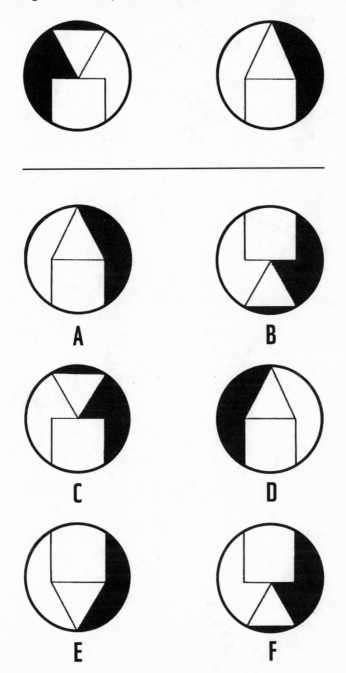

128 Which one is wrong?

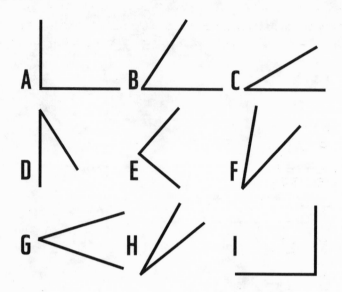

129 Which tumbler is wrong?

130 From a certain station a northbound train ran every ten minutes throughout the day; a southbound train also ran every ten minutes throughout the day. A man went to the station every day at random times and caught the first train that arrived. On average he caught the northbound train nine times out of ten. Why was this?

131 What is x?

3	4	13
8	8	56
1	5	24
9	7	40
2	2	2
6	4	10
7	5	18
4	9	77
5	3	X

132 What are x, y and z?

76 69 52 65 60 45 54 51 38

43 42 31 32 33 24 X Y Z

ALPHABET X-WORD

133 Place the 26 letters of the alphabet in the grid to make a crossword. 9 letters have already been placed.

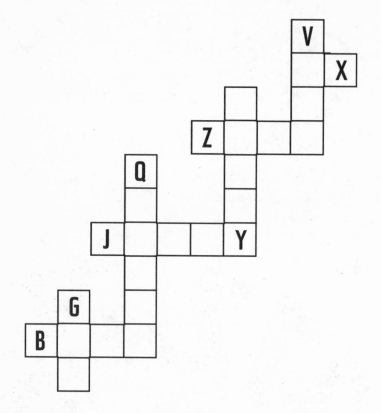

A B C D E F G H I J K L M N
O P Q R S T U V W X Y Z

ALPHAMETICS

134 Replace the letters with numbers.

```
    TWELVE
    TWELVE
    TWELVE
    TWELVE
    TWELVE
  + THIRTY
    ──────
    NINETY
```

135 What are X and Y?

S	20
8	J
W	25
16	T
A	4
5	K
C	7
X	L
A	Y
4	N

136 A rotates clockwise all the time, one position at a time. If it stops on an odd number, ball B moves one place anti-clockwise; if A stops on an even number, B moves three places clockwise. If ball B stops on an even number, ball C moves three places clockwise; if B stops on an odd number, C moves five places anti-clockwise.
At the end of six moves what place will be spelled out by ball C?

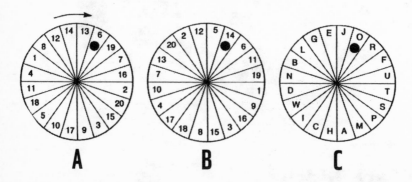

A   B   C

137 Which of the figures at the bottom should come next?

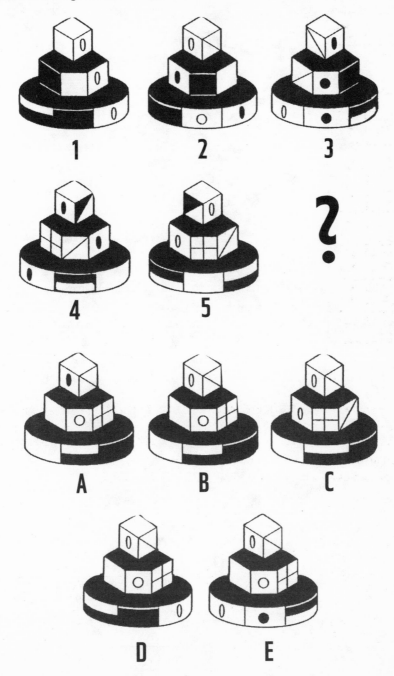

The Great Book of Brainteasers

138 What time will this clock show in 3½ hours' time, assuming it loses four seconds in every hour? (State the exact time.)

139 A turns clockwise, two positions at a time. B turns anti-clockwise, three positions at a time. After six moves, what will be the total of the two front faces? (The concealed numbers progress in the same way as the visible numbers: 7, 9 and 11 on A and 8, 10 and 12 on B.)

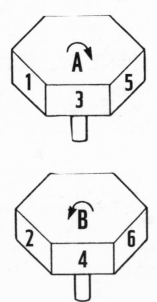

140 Assuming that the top two houses are correct, which of those below are wrong?

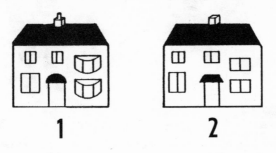

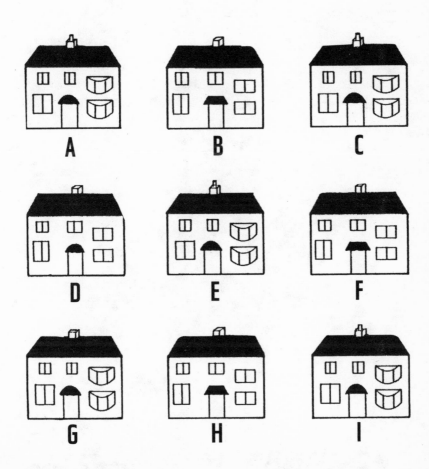

BLOCKS

141 I have 11 blocks

4 of them are 8" thick
2 of them are 4" thick
3 of them are 3" thick
2 of them are 1" thick

Pile them in a column 51" high with a 3" block at the bottom so that individual blocks or combinations of adjacent blocks can be used to measure every thickness in exact inches from 1" to 48".

In which order should they stand?

REBUS

142 Solve the rebus

NILE

HO   HO   HO

143 Which of the figures at the bottom should follow number 3 at the top?

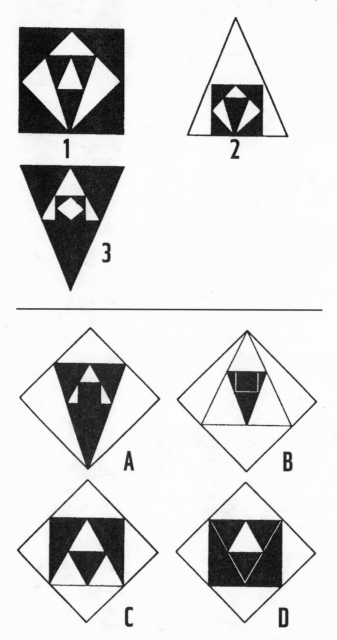

144 Which number from 1 to 9 is X?

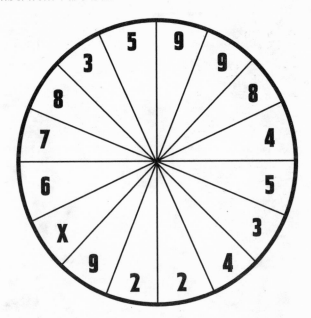

145 What is X?

1	2	3	2	10	12
2	5	12	10	16	13
1	2	1	x	10	24

146 Multiply the square root of the highest number by the square of the lowest number.

144	6	169	7	152
5	166	9	158	8
3	168	4	167	10

The Great Book of Brainteasers

147 A chimney breast has been removed from a room, leaving the hearth-space bare of carpet. The rest of the floor is carpeted, and fortunately there are some pieces of carpet left over. Which two pieces will fit the hearth-space and exactly match the existing carpet?

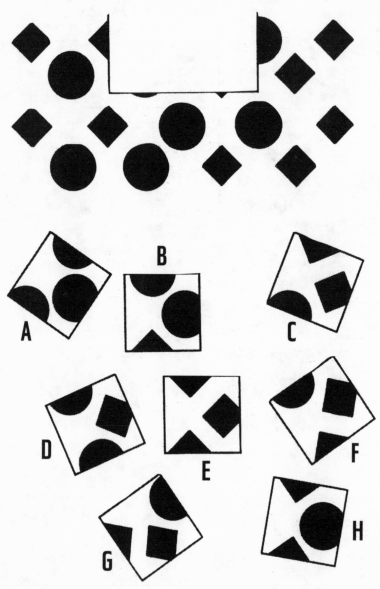

148 What is X?

4 9 1 3 2 2 3 5 5 7 9 X

149 Here is part of a jigsaw puzzle on which a triangle is marked. Which is the missing piece?

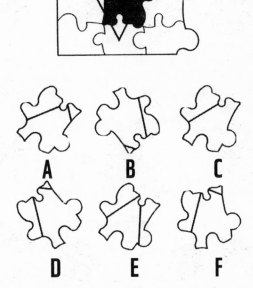

150 What number goes into the empty brackets?

916 (160) 916

971 (177) 879

245 ( ) 511

The Great Book of Brainteasers

151 What comes between 16 and 4 in this series?

6561   256   81   16   –   4   3

152 Six of these keys will open the door. Which one won't?

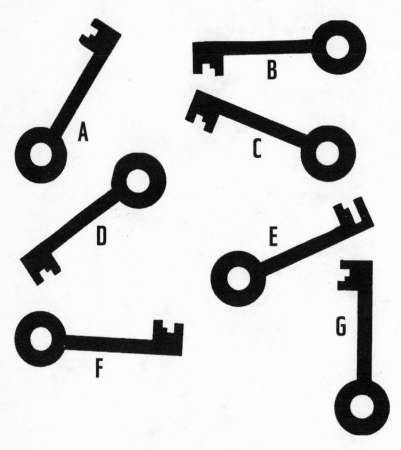

HOW MANY CHILDREN?

153 Smith has a number of children.
Brown has a smaller number of children.
Green has an even smaller number of children.
Black has the smallest number.
The total is less than 18
The product of the children is the door number of Smith's house (120).
I asked Smith: "Is there more than one child in the Black family?"
When he replied, as I know the house number, I also knew the number of children in each family.

How many children were there in each family?

The Great Book of Brainteasers

A PRIME COMBINATION

154 In a lottery a gambler has to select 6 numbers between 1 and 49. The order of the numbers is immaterial.

Assuming that he only selects prime numbers, how many tickets would he have to purchase in order to cover every combination?

155 Pair these words to make nine titles of books by Charles Dickens:

A	LITTLE	1	RUDGE
B	PICKWICK	2	COPPERFIELD
C	EDWIN	3	TIMES
D	BARNABY	4	CHUZZLEWIT
E	NICHOLAS	5	PAPERS
F	HARD	6	HOUSE
G	BLEAK	7	DROOD
H	DAVID	8	DORRIT
I	MARTIN	9	NICKLEBY

156 Which screw is different?

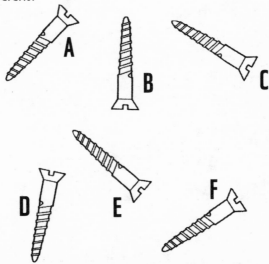

157 Which of the figures below should occupy the vacant space?

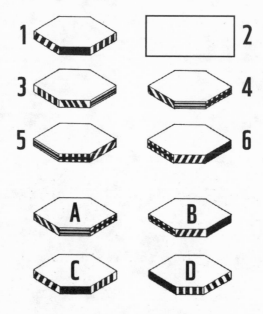

158 Here is a roulette wheel. When the ball stops at zero all the stakes go to the casino. The ball travesl anti-clockwise. At the first spin it stops at the next number. Then it misses one and stops at the next. After that each spin brings the ball one extra number along (missing two, then three, and so on). At what spin will the stakes go to the casino?

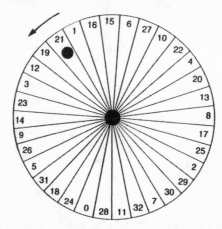

BILL & BEN

159 Bill and Ben have a combined age of 91 years. Bill is now twice as old as Ben was when Bill was as old as Ben is now.

How old are Bill and Ben?

BEAMS

160 Which is the strongest beam?

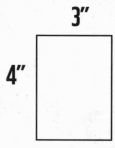

3"

4"

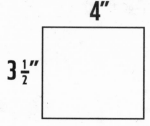

4"

3 $\frac{1}{2}$"

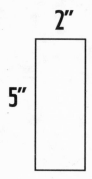

2"

5"

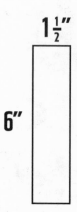

1 $\frac{1}{2}$"

6"

161 Arrange these into four pairs.

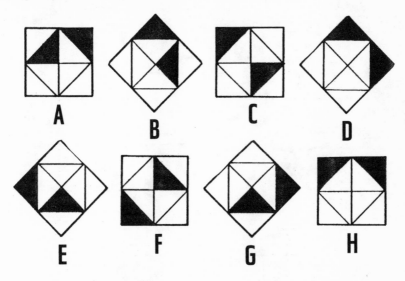

162 What goes into the empty space?

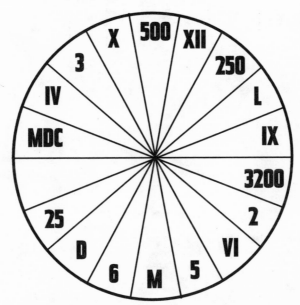

The Great Book of Brainteasers

163 Which of the cubes at the bottom should follow the two at the top?

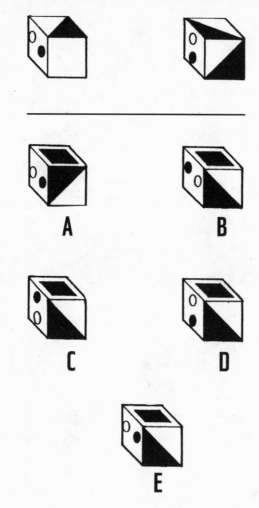

164 Complete this series, giving a value for X.

11 13 17 25 32 37 47 58 X 79

165 If A were placed on top of B which of the outlines below would result?

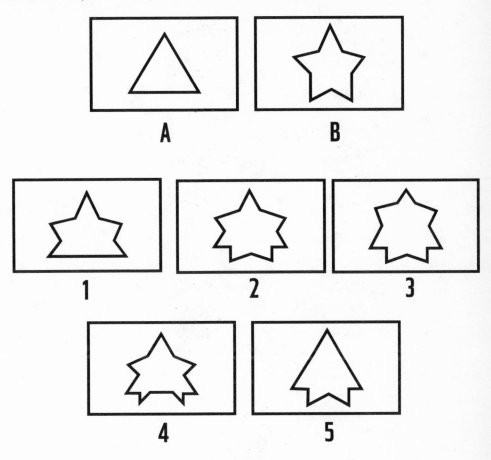

166 What number should replace the question mark?

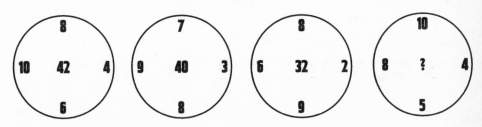

167 Simplify $(x-y)^2 = x$

Choose from

A. $-x^2 - 2xy + y^2$

B. $x^2 - 2xy + y^2$

C. $x^2 - 2xy - y^2$

D. $x^2 + 2xy - y^2$

E. $-x^2 + 2xy + y^2$

168 Which of these is the odd one out?

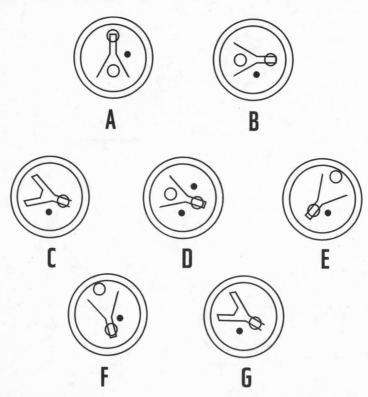

169 What number comes next in this sequence?

1 8 70 627 5639 ?

170 Which figure is the odd one out?

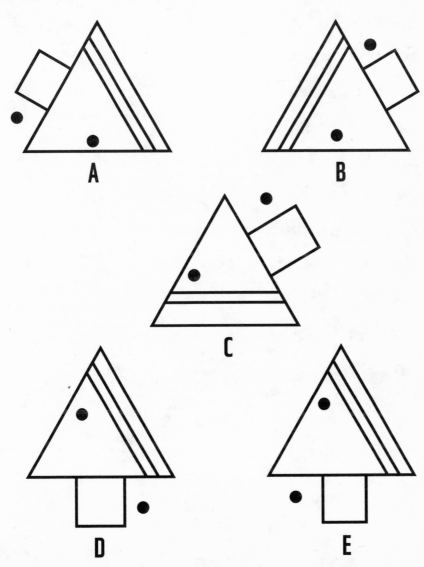

ALL MIXED UP

171 These are the recognised names given to groups of creatures, but they have been mixed up. You have to re-arrange them correctly.

Colony of Birds

Horde of Spiders

Den of Wild Pigs

Clutter of Crows

Nest of Snakes

Park of Elks

Doylt of Ferrets

Gang of Machine Guns

Business of Swine

Volery of Artillery

Hover of Gnats

Drift of Frogs

ZOETROPE

172

Clue: Place where the duds hang out? (7-4)

Find the (7-4) letter words. Find the 1st letter. Draw a straight line to the 2nd letter, then to the 3rd letter and so on. The enclosed areas have been filled in.

173 What number should replace the question mark?

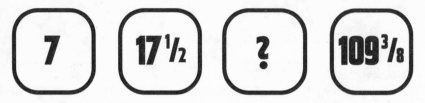

174 What number should replace the question mark?

175 Which of A, B, C, D or E fits into the blank circle to carry on a logical sequence?

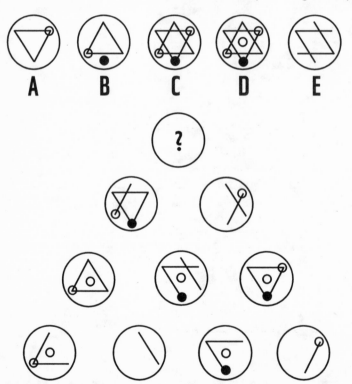

176 You don't have to be a motorist to solve this. Minimum stopping distances are as follows:

at 20mph ... 40 feet
at 30mph ... 75 feet
at 40mph ... 120 feet
at 50mph ... 175 feet
at 60mph ... 240 feet
at 70mph ... 315 feet

When following another vehicle a gap of one yard (three feet) for every mile per hour MAY be sufficient.

At what speed would this gap exactly correspond with the minimum stopping distance.

177 What is the total of the spots on the rear sides of these dice?

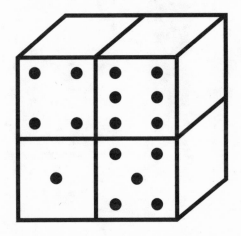

The Great Book of Brainteasers

178 Which of the four squares at the bottom should follow square 4?

8	2	3	6
2	6	7	4
7	6	4	2
2	5	5	7

1

4	9	1	4
3	6	6	3
7	1	8	2
4	2	3	9

2

3	8	1	5
5	3	5	4
4	2	9	2
5	4	2	6

3

3	9	3	1
4	3	4	5
6	1	5	4
3	3	4	6

4

4	7	1	4
5	6	4	1
3	1	6	6
4	2	5	5

A

7	1	4	3
3	8	2	2
1	4	4	6
4	2	5	4

B

3	4	5	2
4	1	6	3
3	7	2	2
4	2	1	7

C

1	2	7	7
8	6	1	2
4	3	5	5
4	6	4	3

D

ALPHABET X-WORD

179 Place the 26 letters of the alphabet into the grid to make a x-word.

7 letters have already been placed for you.

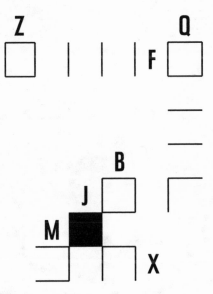

A B C D E F G H I J K L M N
O P Q R S T U V W X Y Z

BIRTHDAYS

180 If there were twenty-four people in a room and you bet that at least one coincidence of birth dates existed would you have a better chance of winning or losing your bet

181 Using the example set in the top grid, what are X and Y in the bottom grid?

6	7	■	3	9	3
■	6	6	3	■	7
6	■	2	4	6	5
2	4	5	7	1	■
5	9	1	■	8	5
4	■	5		2	

4	1	4	8	■	6
■	11	2	■	6	7
3	3	X	7	1	■
■	■	3	Y	8	2
2	9	5	1	■	7
■	4	■	5	4	6

182 What is X in the last circle?

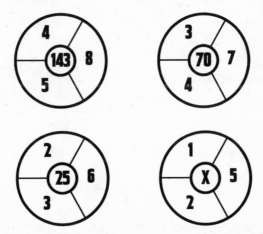

The Great Book of Brainteasers

183 Which of the clocks at the bottom should take the place of the last one in those above?

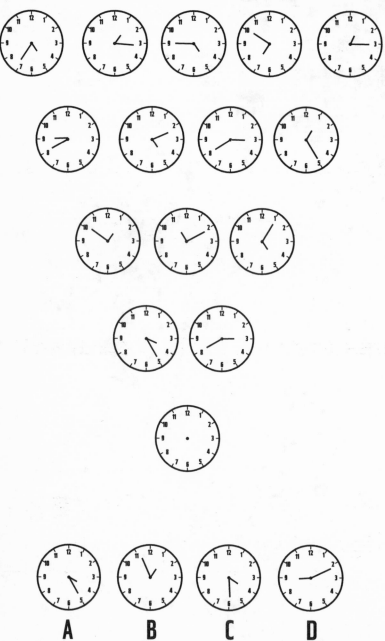

264

184 What numbers are represented by A, B, C and D

$$\frac{\frac{A}{B}}{6} \qquad \frac{\frac{C}{B}}{8} \qquad \frac{\frac{A}{D}}{8} \qquad \frac{\frac{D}{C}}{10}$$

185 What is the only weight from 1 kilogram to 14 kilograms that cannot be weighed with the weights available?

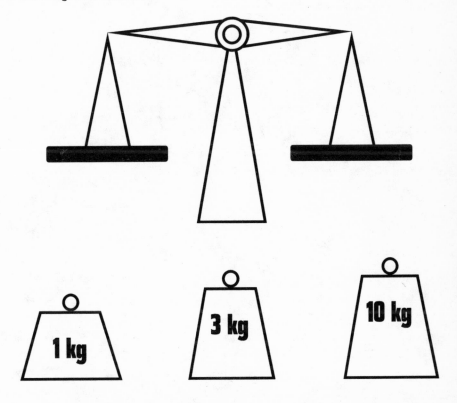

186 What is X?

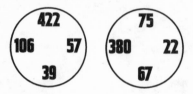

187 What number should replace the question mark?

BATH

188 You have left out the plug in the bath, and you are filling the bath with both taps on.

The hot tap takes 6 minutes to fill the bath.

The cold tap takes 4 minutes to fill the bath.

The bath empties in 12 minutes.

In how many minutes will the bath be filled?

BUTCHER

189 A butcher had a number of legs of lamb to chop up. He chopped each leg into 11 pieces. He chopped at the rate of 45 strokes per minute. How many legs would he chop in 22 mins?

190 Simplify:

$$\frac{11}{12} \div \frac{33}{48} = X$$

191 What circle should replace the question mark?

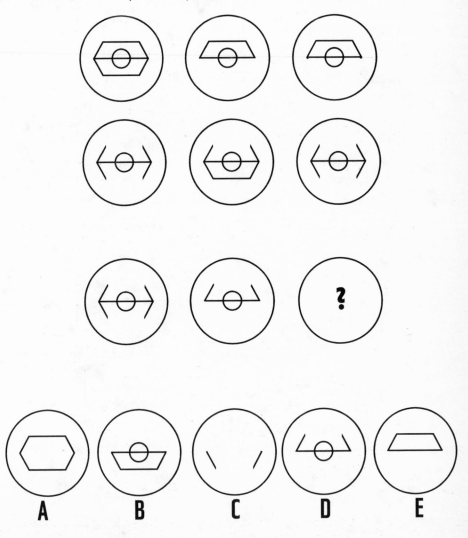

192 What number should repalce the question mark?

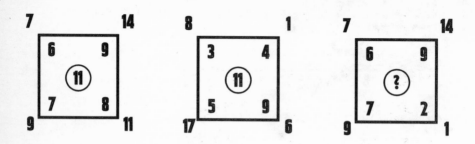

193 If a stone is dropped from a cliff and takes 5 seconds to hit the water, how high is the cliff?

194 How many boxes 2.5 cm cube can be placed in these three boxes?

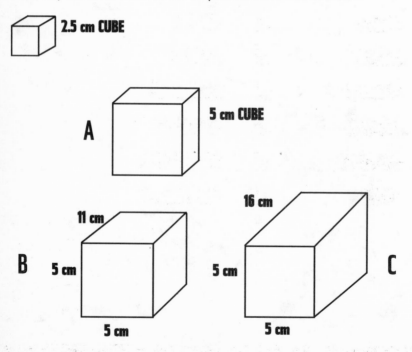

ALL MIXED UP

195 These names of groups of objects have been mixed up. Your task is to re-arrange them.

STALK	of	**HUNTERS**
BUILDING	of	**SWANS**
CLOUD	of	**MAGPIES**
SKULK	of	**FORESTERS**
COVERT	of	**LAPWING**
HERD	of	**BAGDGERS**
CONVOCATION	of	**FRIARS**
SORD	of	**COOTS**
BLAST	of	**ROOKS**
DESERT	of	**MALLARD**
TIDING	of	**EAGLES**
COLONY	of	**SEAFOWL**
NIDE	of	**PHEASANT**

COUNTERS

196 A bag contains one counter, it is either white or black. A white counter is put into the bag, and a counter is drawn out, which proves to be white.

What are the chances of drawing out a white counter?

Section Two

Answers

The Great Book of Brainteasers

1 The figure is turned 45 degrees clockwise each time the black shaded portion moves first from top to bottom (in the first row) and then from left to right (in the second row).

2 E, which has an even number of rungs. All the others have an odd number.

3 E, which should be moved slightly to the left, so that they are all equidistant. (The design is quite in order, but probably diverted your attention from the spacing.)

4 AF, BH, CE, DG

5 A = 98
B = 126
In the first row the numbers outside the brackets are divided by 12 and the results placed inside the brackets; in the second row they are divided by 13; thus, in the third row the numbers inside the brackets are multiplied by 14 to obtain a and b.

6 A

7 A:12 (Each number doubles its opposite lower number and adds two.)
B: 25 (Each number doubles its opposite lower number and adds three.)

8 You can only travel south from the North Pole!

9 Examination of the four correct houses gives the following information:

A The front door is on the same side as the chimney.
B If the front door is on the left, the lower window is a bay window if there is no porch over the door.
C Also, if the front door is on the left, there is a black window over the door if there is no porch and a white window if there is a porch.
D If the front door is on the right, again there is a bay window if there is no porch over the door and a rectangular window if there is.
E If the front door is on the right, however, the window over the door is reversed from previously, that is, if there is no porch there is a white window over the door and if there is a porch there is a black window.

Comparing the four numbered houses with this information we find:
i) House number 1 is correct (front door on left, black window over door and lower bay window).

ii) House number 2 is incorrect because the window over the porch should be black and that over the lower window should be white.

iii) House number 3 is incorrect becasue not only is there a bay window in addition to a porch, but the upper windows are also wrong.

iv) House number 4 is correct and conforms with house B.

Therefore, 2 and 3 are incorrect.

10 A = 7

B = 8

From the music shown the following can be deduced:

after ♩　　　comes

after ♩　　　comes

after ♪　　　comes

after ♭♩　　comes

11 A = 9

B = 2

The first row across totals 15; the second row 16; the fifth row 19 and the bottom row 20. Thus, the total increases by one in each successive row.

12 1

The shapes are moved progressively upwards, the top shape becoming the bottom shape with each move. The top row indicates the manner in which the black and white shapes are varied and the bottom row conforms to this, except that black takes the place of white and vice versa.

13 Take any 100 digits in a random number sequent. Write down all the differences between every pair of digits, you will have 99 digits. Take every possible difference in the digits, you will find 100.

Such as

0-0	1-0	0-3	1-3
0-1	1-1	0-4	1-4
0-2	1-2 etc.		

Add the differences = $\dfrac{330}{100}$ = 3.3

14 SPINNAKER

15 6,561
There are two sequences arranged alternately. In each sequence the number is the square of the previous number in that sequence. 6,561 is the square of 81.

16 A 1/2 revolution
B 21/2 revolutions.

17 E
The light should be in the lower glass, since, when the signal-arm goes up there will be no light showing.

18 86
Add five straightdown; Add ten sideways; Add fifteen diagonally

19 50mph

$$X+3 = 60$$
$$X - 3 = 40$$
$$X = 63$$
$$\underline{X = 37}$$
therefore $\quad 2X = 100$
$$X = 50$$

20 B

21 11
$(6 \times 11) - 24 = 90$

22 2.50

23

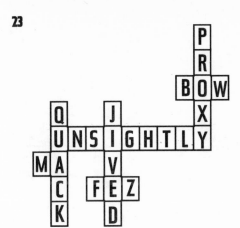

24 They were playing darts in the Club House.

25 13

26 31

27 140
Starting with 3 in the upper half, the number in the opposite segment multiplies it by 2. The next number (7) is multiplied by 3; then by 4, and so on.
Therefore 20 is multiplied by 7 to give 140.

28 16
each number reverses the previous number and adds 1 to each digit. Thus, in the first two terms, 16 reversed is 61, which then changes to 72. In the penultimate term, 50 reversed becomes 05, which in turn becomes 16 – by adding 1 to each digit.

29 A 7; B C

	Black ball	White ball
1st move	D	A
2nd move	E	F
3rd move	F	D
4th move	G	B
5th move	A	G
6th move	B	E
7th move	C	C

30 5

Columns headed by an odd number add up to 30. Columns headed by an even number add up to 40. The last column adds up to 35, to which must be added 5 to bring it up to 40, as this column is headed by an even number.

31 x is 11; y is 61

In the first circle the number in the top left quarter is squared and then reduced by 1 in the opposite diagonal quarter; the number in the top right quarter is cubed and then 1 added to give the number in the opposite lower quarter.

In the second circle the same procedure is followed except that 2 is deducted from the squared number and 2 is added to the cubed number.

Therefore, in the third circle 3 is deducted from the square of 8 (64 becomes 61 – the value for Y), while 3 is added to the cube of 2 (8 becomes 11 – the value for X).

32 x is 9 or 24; y also is 9 or 24

In each case the numbers at the top are divided by 4 in the opposite quarter and 1 is added.

An alternative solution is that the numbers in the lower quarters are miltiplied by 4 in their opposite quarters and 4 is deducted from the result.

33 C

In C there are 8 curves and 6 straight lines. In all the others there are 6 curves and 6 straight lines.

34 1

The numbers reduce by 17, 34, 68, 136, 272 and hence – 544 thus reducing the previous number – 545 by 1. (The terms reduce in multiples of 17.)

35 No. 8

	1st over – other end			2nd over – other end	
Batsmen out	1	2	Batsmen out	2	8 not out
	3			9	
	4			10	
	5			11	
	6				
	7				

36 Horse No. 6 5-1 Against

		Amount to be staked to recover 100 including stake	
2-1	1	£ 33.3	
3-1	2	25	
4-1	3	20	
5-1	4	16.6	
6-1	5	14.3	
	6	?	
		109.3	
5-1	6	16.6	Add horse No. 6
		125.9	

Whichever horse wins he gains 125.9% as long as he has balanced his books. (He receives £125.90 and pays out £100.00. His profit is, therefore, £25.90.)

37 9
The totals in the bottom quarters are half those in the opposite top quarters.

38 40
Add half the number on the left to its square root and arrive at the number on the right. Alternatively, the left hand column from top to bottom follows the progression of adding 5, 7, 9, 11, 13 and 15, while the right hand column adds $3^1/_2$, $4^1/_2$, $6^1/_2$, $7^1/_2$ and finally $8^1/_2$, bringing the last number to 40.

39 68

40 8
Starting with the two segments above x, the sum of each part in the upper semicircle is the same as its corresponding pair in the lower semicircle.

41 AE, BH, CG, DF

42 ABANDON
The two cards at the top represent the letters of the alphabet, as there are 13 in each suit. Thus hearts represent A to M, and diamonds N to Z. Therefore:

Ace of hearts	A
2 of hearts	B
Ace of hearts	A
Ace of diamonds	N
4 of hearts	D
2 of diamonds	O
Ace of diamonds	N

43 Ten minutes past eleven
The hour hand advances first 1 hour, then 2, then 3 then 4 (11 in X) and finally 5. At the same time, the minute hand goes back first 5 minutes, then 10, followed by 15, 20 (to 10 minutes past), and finally 25.

44 $18 \div 2 \times 9 + 24 - 5 = 100$

45 C
In A two letters are missed out
In B three letters are missed out
In C four letters are missed out with the exception of V, which should be U.
The numbers in D, E and F follow the same pattern.

46 33

47 Take reciprocal, i.e. divide into 1

4 hrs	=	1/4	= .25
5 hrs	=	1/5	= .20
6 hrs	=	1/6	= .166
8 hrs	=	1/8	= .125
			.741

Take reciprocal again $\dfrac{1}{.741} = 1$ hr 21 mins

48 200m would only take 199 cuts not 200.
199 x 4 sec = 13.27 mins

49 Number 1

50 18, 12 and 8

51 C
As opposite faces of a die add up to 7 it would not be possible for a 4 and a 3 to be on adjacent faces.

52 D
As the black blocks are farther from the fulcrum the see-saw should go down on the right.

53 6/2 or:

Apart from this domino, which equals 8, all combinations of numbers from 1-10 are accounted for:
1/0
2/0 and 1/1
3/0 and 2/1
4/0, 3/1 and 2/2
5/0, 4/1 and 3/2
6/0, 5/1, 4/2 and 3/3
6/1, 5/2 and 4/3
5/3 and 4/4
6/3 and 5/4
6/4 and 5/5

54 A
The area of the circle (based on the formula: multiply the square of the radius by 3.14 approx) is 3.97 square inches.
A is 4 square inches (the nearest)
B is 4.41 square inches
C is 3.80 square inches
D is 3.78 square inches

55 X is 108; Y is 48.

There are three series, taking every third term:

3 6 12 24 48 (Y) (multiply by 2)

7 21 84 420 (multiply by 3, 4 and 5)

4 12 36 108 (X) (multiply by 3)

56 A

57 A 36

B 4

C 9

D 35

E 24

58 6591

    1

x 1

x 1

x 3

x 13

x 13

x 13 = 6591

59 AE, BH, CF, DG

60 K

Each row follows the same pattern of shading as in the first row, except for K, which should appear as in C, G and O.

61 B and C

They fit together like this.

62 14

The results are as follows:

1st throw 6 8
2nd throw 4 14
3rd throw 3 10
4th throw 1 8
5th throw 2 12
6th throw 6 20
7th throw 5 14

63 216225

Square the number on the left outside the brackets and place the result on the right inside the brackets, then cube the number on the right outside the brackets and place the result on the left inside the brackets. Repeat this procedure throughout, so the last line is 225 (15 squared) and 216 (6 cubed).

64 C

65 A

- ● moves 3 places clockwise
- ○ moves 2 places anti clockwise
- ▲ moves 3 places clockwise
- △ moves 2 places anti clockwise

66 X is 7; Y is 9

Although this can be solved by elimination, it can also be solved by algebra:
from the bottom line:
$y = 2 + x$
substituting this in the first line:
$2x - (2 + x) = 5$
hence:
$2x - 2 - x = 5;$
or
$x - 2 = 5,$
therefore
$x = 7$
substituting this in the second line:
$7 + y = 16$

therefore:
y = 9

67 i) 1998
ii) 666
iii) Not possible
iv) Not possible

68 2A. There is a dot missing

69 GEORGE   10
    HENRY   12
    MALCOLM   9

70 Twice as large

71 201 (add digits to previous number)

72 947 x 947 apples

73 E
B is the same as F
D is the same as C
A is the same as G

74 125
96 passes out of 125 give an average of 76.8%

75 C
In C there are 2 right-angled triangles. In the other rows there are 3 right-angled triangles and 2 isoceles triangles.

76 Here are nine possible combinations:
6   19 25;
8   17 25;
10 19 21;
4   21 25;
2   6 17 25;
2   4 19 25;

2 10 17 21;
4 10 17 19;
4   8 17 21.

77 1854

According to this mathematical formulai: $7!\left(\frac{1}{2}! - \frac{1}{3}! + \frac{1}{4}! - \frac{1}{5}! + \frac{1}{6}! - \frac{1}{7}\right) = 1854$

78

$$
\begin{array}{r}
2730 \\
29704 \\
249918 \\
278304 \\
2104 \\
+\ \underline{279918} \\
\underline{842678}
\end{array}
$$

79 D

80 A and F

81 13

All the numbers in the top line contain curves. The only one in the bottom line is 13, as all the others consist of straight strokes.

82 C and F

In C the hour and minute hands have been transposed; in F the Roman numeral for 4 is IIII instead of IV.

83 A

The figures in the quarters are transposed as in the top example and their shading or patterns are transposed in the same way.

84 27

In the top line the first number, 9 is divisible by 3; 8 is divisible by 4; 10 is divisible by 5; 18 is divisible by 6; 21 is divisible by 7; 16 is divisible by 8. hence the next number must be divisible by 9, and the only number that complies with this is 27.

85 X is 15; Y is 11

In th eouter ring, going clockwise from 7, each number doubles the previous number and subtracts 1. hence x (coming before 29) must be 15. In the inner ring, each number doubles the previous number and adds 1. Hence y is 11 (double 5 plus 1).

86 C
the spiral turns the opposite way from the others.

87 2 new stations
11 existing stations

88 Analyse the statements.

Hole No.	A	B	C	D	E
14	✔		✔	✔	✔
2					✔
3	✔				✔
4			✔	✔	
5	✔				✔
6				✔	✔
7	✔		✔		✔
8				✔	✔
9	✔			✔	
10		✔		✔	✔
11	✔		✔		✔
12		✔		✔	✔
13	✔				✔
14		✔		✔	✔
15	✔			✔	✔
16		✔		✔	
17	✔		✔		✔
18		✔		✔	✔

Only one tick means a true statement.
Hole No. 2

89 99
After the first two terms each subsequent term is the sum of the two previous terms.

90 D
All the others contain one acute angle, one obtuse angle and one right angle. D contains two acute angles and on obtuse angle.

91 25

In the first row divide the numbers outside the brackets by 14 and put the results inside the brackets. Continue in th esame way, but next dividing by 15 and then by 16. In the last row divide by 17.

92 A is 7, B is 1, C is 8

With a four-figure total, the calculation is obviously addition and not subtraction. In order to reconcile the units with the tens. B must be 1 (the units total 7), so that 7 added to 4 in the tens gives 11, confirming that B is 1 (also confirmed in the final total). to give 2 in the final total, C must be *, so that the hundreds came to 12.

93 $4^1/_2$ or 4.5

In each quarter halve each total of the rings up to and includiong the centre. Thus, in the bottom left quarter: 24 plus 12 = 36, 11 plus 7 = 18, 6 plus 3 = 9. Therefore x = 41/2 or 4.5.

94 4

The first term is follwed by the last term; the second term is followed by the penultimate term, and the third term follows the same procedure. Thus the series becomes: 25 24 22 19 15 10 4(x) – ie, decreasing by one more each time: -1 -2 -3 -4 -5 -6(x)

95 x is 41/2 or 4.5, y is 112

Halve the terms alternately from the first term: 72 36 18 9 41/2 or 4.5(x). Double the terms alternately from the second term: 7 14 28 56 112(y).

96 D

Add the numbers and then add the remaining digits: A – total of numbers is 25, 2 plus 5 = 7; B – total of numbers is 34, 3 plus 4 = 7; C – total of the numbers is 61, 6 plus 1 = 7; D – total of the numbers is 26, 2 plus 6 = 8.

97 C and H

98 12

The series must be read backwards and spaced correctly: 1 2 3 4 5 6 7 8 9 10 11 12(X).

99 X is 16; Y is 21; Z is 16

To justify the right hand vertical row with the top row, • must be 2. Substituting this in the remaining horizontal rows, it becomes obvious that (DIAGRAM) must be 3, (DIAGRAM) must be 4 and, in the bottom row (DIAGRAM) must be 7. The values for X, Y and Z now become clear.

100 16

The spots on two of the dominoes total 11, not 12

101 Matilda 19
    Philip   17

102 $\dfrac{5289 \times (49 + 63) \times 4.5}{60 \times 60}$

$= \quad 739.2$ ft

103 E

104 A

Pinion A has 10 teeth. Pimion C has 20 teeth. Therefore the ratio between them is exactly 2:1, which is obtained by dividing the larger by the smaller. In other words, pinion A will make two revolutions while pinion C makes one. The number of teeth on the intermediate pinion does not in any way alter the ratio between the other two.

105 6

The player holds 1 club, 2 hearts and 4 diamonds. As he holds 13 cards (or seven black cards), it follows that there must be 6 spades.

106 1

Spaced correctly, the series becomes 13 15 17 19 2(1)

107 AG, BH, CE, DF

108 AIK, BGH, CLN, DEF, JMO

109 AD BF CE

110 2,150

51 is midway between 3 and 99; 43 is midway between 7 and 79; 51 x 43 = 2,193, less

43 (midway between 9 and 77) = 2,150

111 16
each number in the bottom row is the sum of the number above it and the previous number.

112 Sapphire (2)
 Emerald (5)
 Diamond (10)

113 2519 apples

114 447
The square numbers are: 16 (4 squared), 225 (15 squared), 81 (9 squared) and 64 (8 squared), which equal 386. The prime numbers are: 7, 31 and 23, which equal 61. 386 + 61 = 447.

115 A, B and C are wrong
The titles on the spines are printed the wrong way round. You can check by looking at the spine on this book!

116 96 and 121
In the top row the numbers are square numbers (3, 5, 7 and 9) except 96; in the bottom row the numbers are even numbers (8, 12, 18 and 14) except 121 (which is th esquare of 11).

117 X = 3, Y = 4
The lower left hand number is the product of the two top numbers; the bottom right hand number is the square of the bottom left hand number.

118
$\underline{3} \times \underline{32} = 8$
4 27 9

119 Top 47; Bottom 52 (-6, -5, -4, -3) (+6, -5, +4, -3)

120 C
The others are all the same

121 190

122 Wind-surfers
(spindrift = spray)

123 A

124 C
It contains only one white dot, the rest contain two

125 12

126 A
The black sexction rotates clockwise 40o at a time.

127 C, D E

128 B
The angle is 60°. the others are 90°, 45° or 30°.

129 F
The design round the top should consist entirely of diamond shapes, as in B and L. In F one of the diamonds has become a square.

130 The southbound train ran one minute after the north bound train.

131 X is 4
Square the middle number in each horisontal row and subtract the left-hand number to give the right-hand number. So, in the bottom row:
3 squared is 9
Subtract 5
      X is 4

132 x is 21; y is 24; z is 17
There are three separate series. Start with the first term and take every third term thereafter:
76 65 54 43 32
As they reduce by 11 each time, the next term (X must be 21.

133

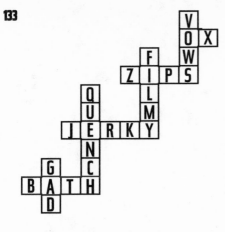

134

```
    130760
    130760
    130760
    130760
    130760
+   194215
    848015
```

135 X is 4; Y is 6

Expressing each letter as a number according to its position in the alphabet, the table appears as below, with what were originally letters circled:

(19)	20	+1	
8	(10)		-2
(23)	25	+2	
16	(20)		-4
(1)	4	+3	
5	(11)		-6
(3)	7	+4	
x	12	(x is 4)	-8
(1)	y	+5	(y is 6)
4	(14)		-10

136 BERLIN

The moves are as follows:

	Ball A	Ball B	Ball C
1st move	19	5	B
2nd move	7	12	E
3rd move	16	6	R
4th move	2	1	L
5th move	20	3	I
6th move	15	16	N

137 B

The cube rotates clockwise; the hexagon rotates anti-clockwise; the circle rotates clockwise.

138 6 hours, 19 minutes, 52 seconds

The present time shown is 2 hours, 50 minutes, 6 seconds. Ignoring the seconds, the time in 31/2 hours will be 6.20.

In the meantime, the second hand will have lost 14 seconds. Instead of showing six seconds AFTER the hour it will show eight seconds BEFORE the hour – that is, 52 seconds. This means that the minute hand will not have reached the 20-minute mark, but will have passed the 19-minute mark.

139 7

The moves result as follows:

	A	B
1st move	7	10
2nd move	11	4
3rd move	3	10
4th move	7	4
5th move	11	10
6th move	3	4 (Total: 7)

140 D and G

D (a house with an even number) should have a flat porch. G (a house with an odd number) should have a chimney stack.

141 3 – 1 – 1 – 4 – 8 – 8 – 8 – 8 – 3 – 4 – 3

142 Nylon hose

143 A

The smallest figure in the centre becomes the largest figure on the outside, while the other figures remain in the same order.

144 2

Starting at 7 and working clockwise, two adjacent numbers in the top semicircle are added. In the opposite segments are factors of that total:

$7 + 8 = 15;$ $3 \times 5 = 15$

$3 + 5 = 8;$ $2 \times 4 = 8$

$9 + 9 = 18;$ $9 \times 2 = 18$

Hence:

$8 + 4 = 12;$ $6 \times 2 = 12$

145 13

The totals of the columns are:

4 9 16 25 36 49

In other words, 2 squared, 3 squared, 4 squared, etc.

146 117

147 B and D

148 2

Spaced correctly the series becomes:

4 9 13 22 35 57 9 (2)

After the first two numbers, each subsequent number is the total of the previous two. The sum of 35 and 57 is 92.

149 B

150 114

The two numbers on the left inside the brackets are the sum of the digits on the left of the brackets. The number on the right inside the brackets is the difference between the sums of the digid on either side of the brackets.

151 9

There are two separate series here. starting with the first term and taking alternate terms thereafter: 6561 81 9 3. Each number is the square root of the previous number. Starting with the second term:

256 16 4
Again, each number is the square root of the previous number.

152 E
The wards (the projections at the end) which turn the lock are different from those in the other keys.

153 Black 2, Green 3, Brown 4, Smith 5
120 is made up of 2 x 3 x 4 x 5

154 5005

155 A 8; B 5; C 7; D 1; E 9; F 3; G 6; H 2; I 4

156 C
The thread turns the opposite way from the others.

157 D
the figure is rotating clockwise

158 the 9th spin

1st spin	19
2nd spin	3
3rd spin	9
4th spin	18
5th spin	32
6th spin	17
7th spin	27
8th spin	3
9th spin	ZERO

159 Bill 52
   Ben 39

160 6" x 1 " is the strongest beam
The strength of a beam is measured

bd   where b = breadth and d = depth

So,   4 x 3 is measured   4 x 4 x 3   = 48
        3 x 4   3 x 3 x 4   = 49
        5 x 2   5 x 5 x 2   = 50
        6 x 1   6 x 6 x 1   = 54

161 AE; BG; CF; DH

162 18
each modern number in any one segment has a number in Roman numerals in its opposite segment. Starting with MDC (1600), this is doubled in th eopposite segment to give 3200. Moving clockwise, IV is halved, to give 2 in the opposite segment. This doubling and halving continues, so by the time we get to IX (9), this must be doubled in the opposite segment to give 18, expressed in modern digits.

163 B
Examination of the top cubes reveals that they atre rotating forwards (confirmed by the changed positions of the two spots on the side). As far as the facing side is concerned, B C, D or E could be correct, but only in B have the two spots changed their positions in keeping with the forward rotation.

164 71
each number is increased by adding the total of its digits to the number itself. So, 11 (1 + 1 = 2) becomes 13, 13 (1 + 3 = 4) becomes 17, etc.
Following this procedure, 58 (5 + 8 = 13) becomes 71.

165 2

166 38 (5 x 4) + (10 + 8)

167 B

168 D
A is the same as B; C is the same as G; E is the same as F

169 50746

(1 x 9) - 1	= 8
(8 x 9) - 2	= 70
(70 x 9) - 3	= 627
(627 x 9) - 4	= 5639
(5639 x 9) - 5	= 50746

170 E

B is the same as D; A is the same as C

171 Colony of Frogs

Horde of Gnats

Den of Snakes

Clutter of Spiders

Nest of Machine Guns

Park of Artillery

Doylt of Swine

Gang of Elks

Business of Ferrets

Volery of Birds

Hover of Crows

Drift of Wild Pigs

172 Washing line

(duds – slang word for clothes)

173 43.75 (x $2^1/_2$)

174 17

There are 2 series of numbers: In the first series +6 (17 + 6 = 23). In the second series - 6 (35 - 6) = 29

175 C

176 40mph

177 12

Opposite faces of the dice add up to 7. Therefore, moving horizontally from left to right and starting in the top row, opposite faces are: 3 1 6 2.

178 B

All the rows, horizontally and vertically add as follows:

Square 1   19
Square 2   18
Square 3   17
Square 4   16

In square B all the rows, horizontally and vertically, add to 15.

Alternatively, the numbers in square 1 add to 76. Those in square 2 add to 72. Those in sqyuare 3 add to 68, and in square 4 they add to 64. Therefore (decreasing by 4 each time) square H (60) must follow square 4.

179

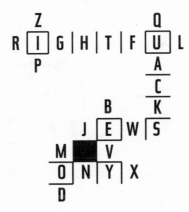

180 With 24 people in the room you would in the long run lose between 23 and 27 out of each 50 bets. (This ignores February 29th).

181 X = 5; Y = 4

From the top square:
2 numbers total 13
3 numbers total 15
4 numbers total 17
5 numbers total 19
In the bottom square:
X is in a row of five and must be 5 to bring the total (14) up to 19;
Y is in a row of four and must be 4 to bring the total (13) up to 17.

182 X is 2

The number in the inner circle is the difference between the product and the sum of the three numbers in the outer circle.

183 C

In the top row the total of the hours to which the hands point is 50 (12, 4, 13, 17 and 4); in the second row the total is 40 (17, 6, 11 and 6); in the third row the total is 30 (11, 13 and 6); in the fourth row the total is 20 (9 and 11). Hence, in the bottom clock the total must be 10, and C (4 and 6) is the only one that gives this.

184

A is 5		A is 1
B is 1	OR	B is 5
C is 7		C is 3
D is 3		D is 7

By elimination the sums are:

5	7	5	3
1	1	3	7
6	8	8	10

1	3	1	7
5	5	7	3
6	8	8	10

185 5 kilograms

1 kilo	weight available
2 kilos	3kg on one side; 1kg on the other side
3 kilos	weight available
4 kilos	3kg and 1kg on one side
5 kilos	not possible
6 kilos	3kg and 1kg on one side; 10kg on the other side
7 kilos	3kg on one side; 10 kg on the other side
8 kilos	3kg on one side;10kg and 1kg on the other side
9 kilos	1kg on one side; 10kg on the other side
10 kilos	weight available
11 kilos	10kg and 1kg on one side
12 kilos	10kg and 3kg on one side; 1kg on the other side
13 kilos	10kg and 3kg on one side
14 kilos	10kg, 3kg and 1kg on one side.

186 222

In each pair of circles the sum of the numbers in the second circle should be 80 less than the sum of the numbers in the first circle. In the last pair the sum of the numbers in the first circle is 1546, so x must be 222 to bring the sum of the numbers in the second circle to 1466

187 $3\,^1/_4$

There are 2 series. The first series is: $+\,1^1/_4$ $(9 + 1\,^1/_4 = 10\,^1/_4)$. The second series is $-\,1^1/_4$ $(7 - 1^1/_4 = 5\,^3/_4)$.

188 3 minutes

Take reciprocals

$$6 = \,^1/_6 = \quad .166$$
$$4 = \,^1/_4 \;= \quad \underline{.25}$$
$$+ \qquad\qquad .416$$

$$12 = \,^1/_{12} = \underline{.083}$$
$$- \qquad\qquad .333$$

$$\underline{1\quad} \qquad = 3 -$$
$$333$$

189 99 legs

Each leg requires 10 chops

190 $1\,^1/_3$

$$\underline{11}\; \times\; \underline{48}$$
$$12 \qquad 33$$

191 D

192 7

$(7 + 14 + 9 + 1) - (6 + 9 + 7 + 2)$

193 $52 \times 16 = 400$ feet

194 A 8
B 16
C 24

195

STALK	of	HUNTERS
BUILDING	of	SWANS
CLOUD	of	MAGPIES
SKULK	of	FORESTERS
COVERT	of	LAPWING
HERD	of	BADGERS
CONVOCATION	of	FRIARS
SORD	of	COOTS
BLAST	of	ROOKS
DESERT	of	MALLARD
TIDING	of	EAGLES
COLONY	of	SEAFOWL
NIDE	of	PHEASANTS

196 The probability is $2/3$.
Let B and W stand for the counters.
After removing one white counter there are three equal states:

IN BAG	OUTSIDE BAG
W1	W2
W2	W1
B	W2

in two out of three cases a white counter remains in the bag.

Section Three

The Great Book of Brainteasers

1 Which of the circles at the bottom should take the place of X?

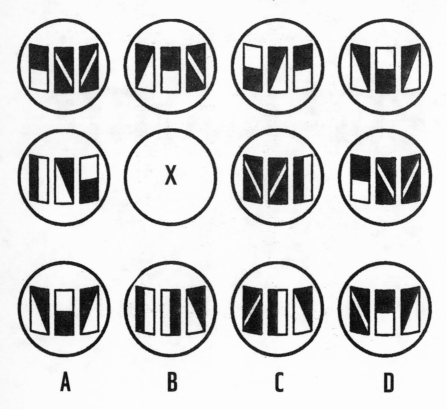

A   B   C   D

2 Which bar code is wrong?

A   B   C

D   E   F

3 Which cross is wrong?

4 What is X?

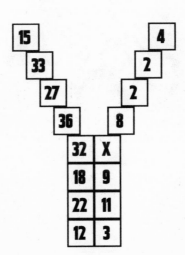

5 Match these into eight pairs.

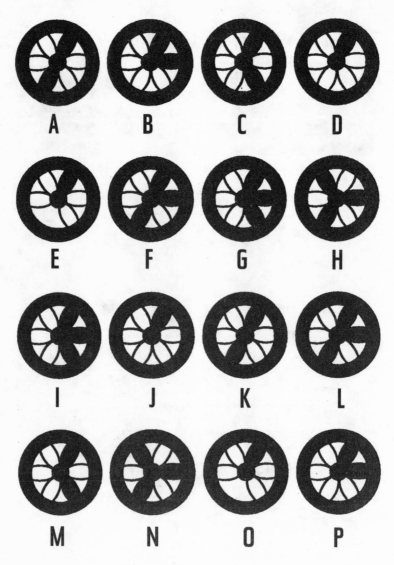

6 Multiply the highest prime numbers by the lowest even number and subtract the result from the total of the numbers remaining.

14 20 13 7 16 11 3 10 17 18 8 12 5 6

7 Which circle has been drawn by the compass? (Do not use any artificial guides.)

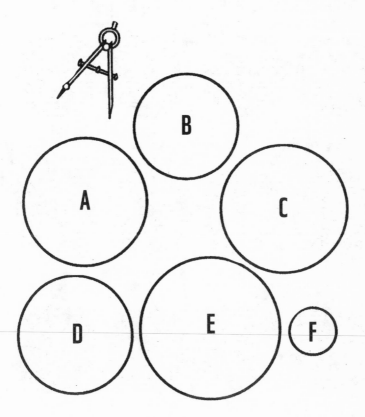

8 What is x?

4	7	9	11	8	15	21	6	5
7	6	1	19	11	7	17	8	4
3	11	15	2	9	8	13	10	9
15	8	3	10	4	9	1	3	9
3	13	10	5	1	10	1	6	19
2	12	11	14	5	6	8	3	X

9 The numbers on the dartboard are arranged as shown below. Add the sum of 10 consecutive numbers that will give the highest total to the sum of 10 consecutive numbers that will give the lowest total.

The Door Number Puzzle

10 Two workmen, Bob and Frank, were putting the finishing touches to a new door they had fitted to house number 7461. All that was left to do was screw the four metal digits to the door.

"Here's a puzzle for you", said Bob, "is it possible to screw these four digits on the door in such a way that the four-figure number thus produced cannot be divided by 9 exactly, without leaving a remainder?"

"I don't even have to think about that one", said Frank, "It simply is not possible".

Why did he reply so quickly, and was he correct?

Scratch Card

11 At a local fund raising effort our local Rotary Club ran a competition where each person who donated received a card with a number of rub-off pictures.

Just one picture has on it the Devil's Head, and only four pictures are identical.

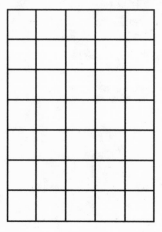

If the four pictures which are identical appear before the Devil's Head appears, then the competitor wins a prize. If, however, the Devil's head is uncovered, then the competitor loses.

There were a total of 35 pictures on the card.

What are the chances of winning?

12 Which row is different?

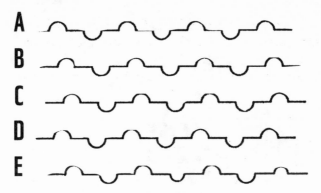

A

B

C

D

E

13 Which is the odd one out?

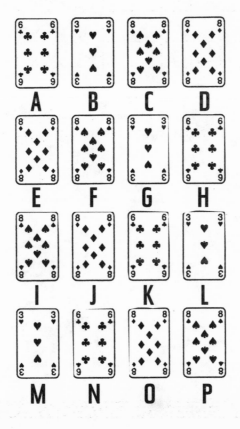

309

14

> **1 ANOTHER**
> **1 ANOTHER**
> **1 ANOTHER**
> **1 ANOTHER**
> **1 ANOTHER**
> **1 ANOTHER**

15 A woman has seven children. Half of them are boys. Explain?

16 Which of these is the odd one out?

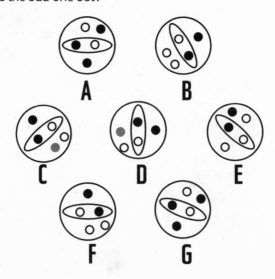

17 If is to

Then

is to

is to

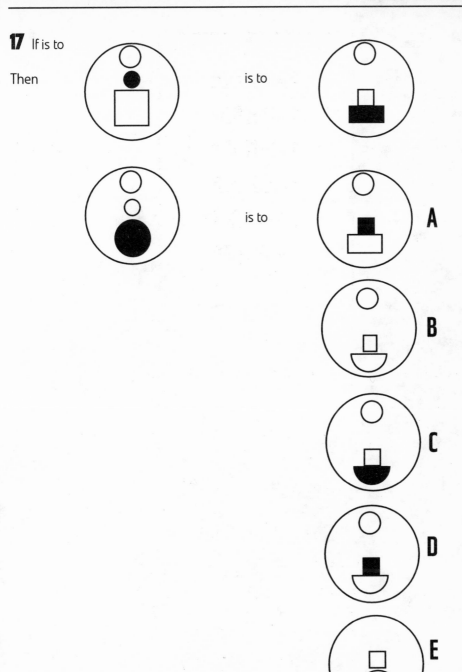

A

B

C

D

E

The Great Book of Brainteasers

Hot Shots

18 Susan, Helen and Dave reckon that they are the best three archers in the Archery Club and decide once and for all to hold a contest to see who is the best of the best.

At the halfway stage of the competition the three hot shots had a total of seventeen shots on target as marked on the target below.

At this stage Dave was the leader as he had scored half as many again as Helen and Helen had scored half as many again as Susan. In total they had scored 133 between them.

What were the total scores for each player, and what were their individual scoring shots?

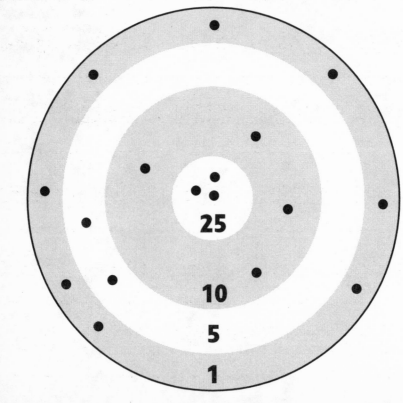

Racing Cars

19 The British Motor Racing Grand Prix was proving even more eventful than usual, and the commentator was getting even more excited than normal.

"The order of the leading five cars has changed yet again", he shrieked, "it changed during lap 3, then again in lap 8, and lap 10, and lap 15, and they way it is going I think I know what the order will be next time there is a change".

What pattern had he seen emerging, and what do you think the order will be next time there is a change?

LAP

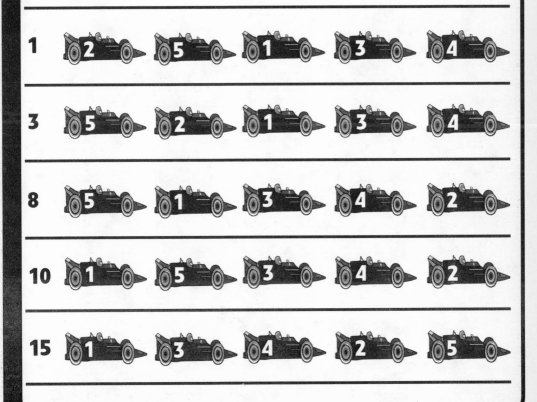

20 Give values for x and y in the third square.

6	7
42	1764

3	2
X	Y

8	3
24	576

21 Which of the numbered triangles belongs to X?

22 (i) Which globe in the second line should be placed at X?

(ii) Which globe in the bottom line should be placed at Y?

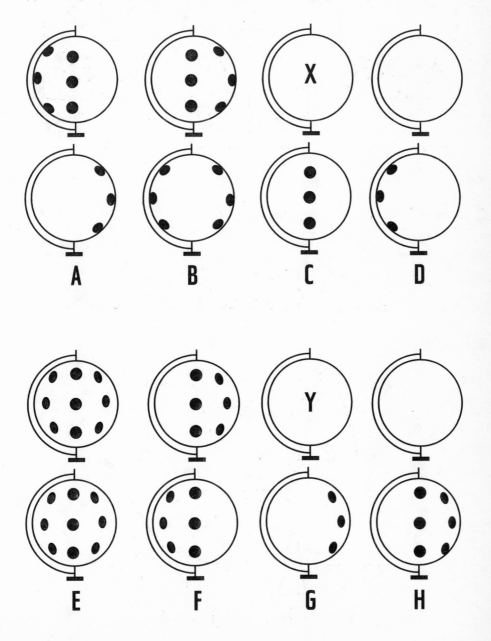

23 Complete this sequence:

7   91   11   143   16   208   –   –

24 Which figure is wrong?

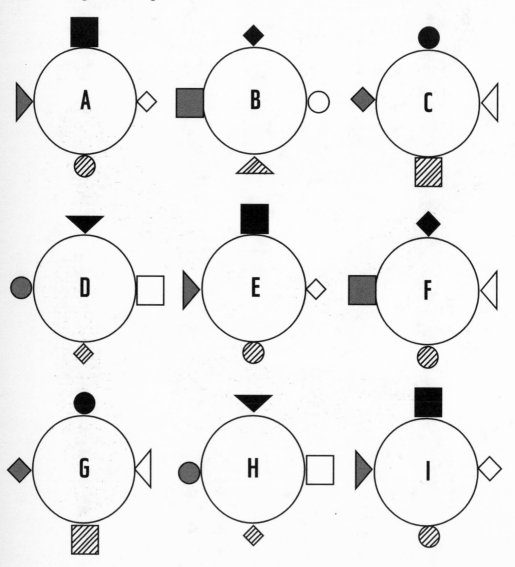

25 Which shape will complete the hexagon?

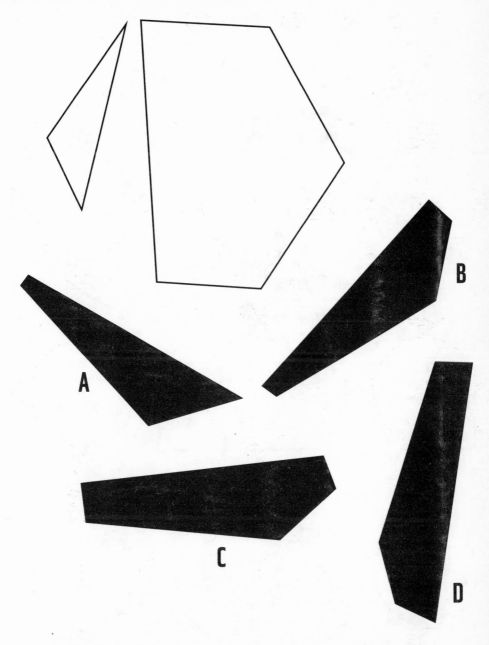

26 Give values for X, Y and Z

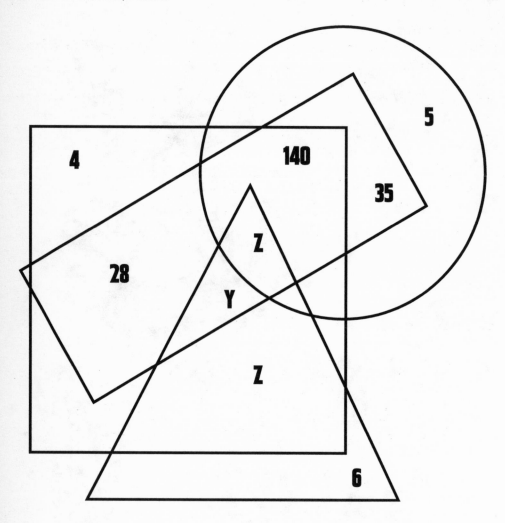

27 This octagonal-shaped figure has its faces numbered consecutively from 1-8.\

Imagine that it is turned anti-clockwise.
In the first move its position is changed by one face, in the second move by two faces, in the third move by three faces, and so on.

At the end of EIGHT moves what number will be in the present position of number 1?

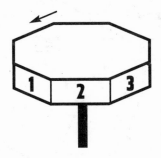

28 Which is the odd face out?

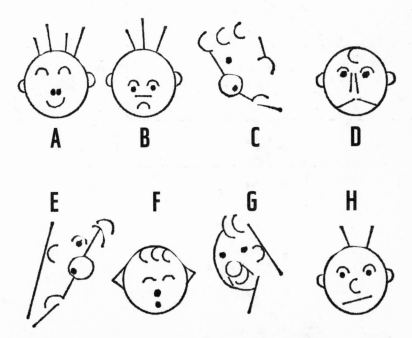

A B C D

E F G H

Crazy Columns

29 These columns are indeed crazy, and at first glance there does not appear to be rhyme nor reason in the way the numbers are distributed.

However, on closer inspection can you see a pattern emerging, and can you fill in the bottom row of numbers?

2	2	1	3
4	6	5	5
8	6	9	9
8	12	11	13
14	10	17	15
12	18	17	21
20	14	25	21
16	24	23	29
26	18	33	27
20	30	29	37
32	22	41	33
24	36	35	45
38	26	49	39
?	?	?	?

Eleven

30 Many people will be aware that when the sums of the alternate digits of a number are equal, that number is always divisible by 11 exactly, for example, the number 3685 is divisible by 11 exactly because:

$$3 + 8 = 6 + 5$$

It, therefore, follows that if the first three digits of a number are, for example, 256, then the addition of a 3 to the end of that number - 2563 - will make it divisible by 11 because $2 + 6 = 5 + 3$.

However, it does not necessarily follow that every number which is divisible by 11 exactly has the sums of its alternate digits equal. As an example, take the number 987652413. This number is exactly divisible by 11, even though its alternate digits are unequal.

There is, however, a further simple rule which will show that this number is divisible by 11 exactly, without the use of multiplication or division.

Can you determine what this simple rule is?

31 Which is the odd man out?

49 91 37

112 133 154

32 What are the two missing digits?

11131216131914221–2–

33 What numbers are represented by A, B and C?

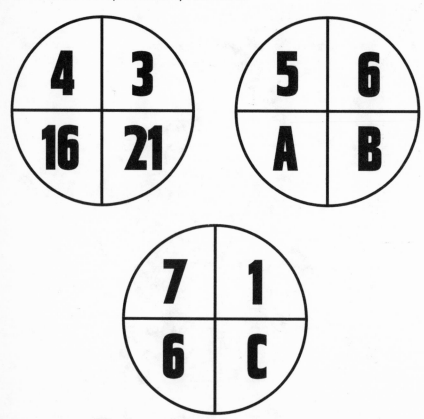

34 Which one does not conform?

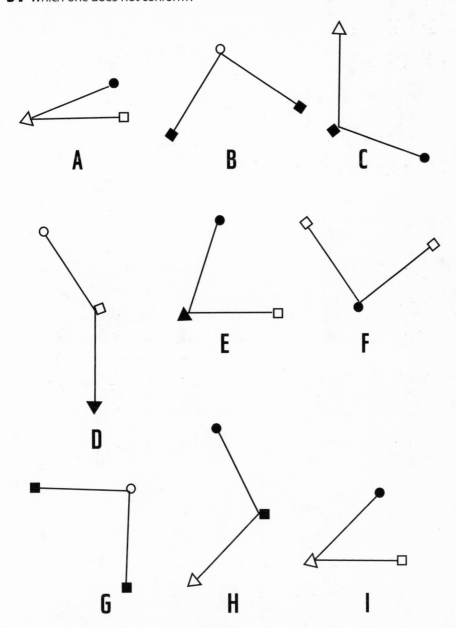

The Great Book of Brainteasers

35 Examine the first four diagrams below and then decide which of the numbered diagrams at the bottom should complete the third row.

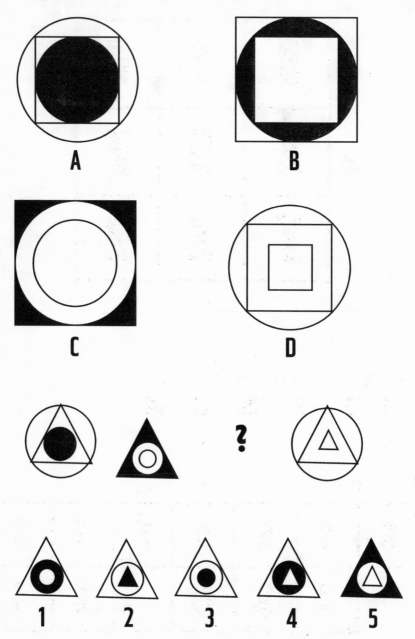

36 Which numbers belong to X, Y and Z?

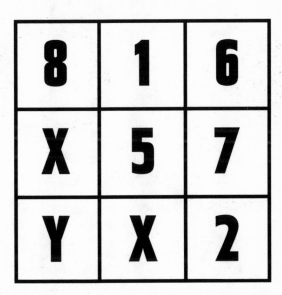

37 What is the next number in this sequence?

1   3   8   19   42   89   –

38 What number goes into the empty square?

0	4	5	8	7	1	3
	4	9	13		8	4

39 What number is missing in this sequence?

4   16   8   64   32   –   512

40 Which of the numbered symbols at the bottom belongs to x?

41 Supply the missing number:

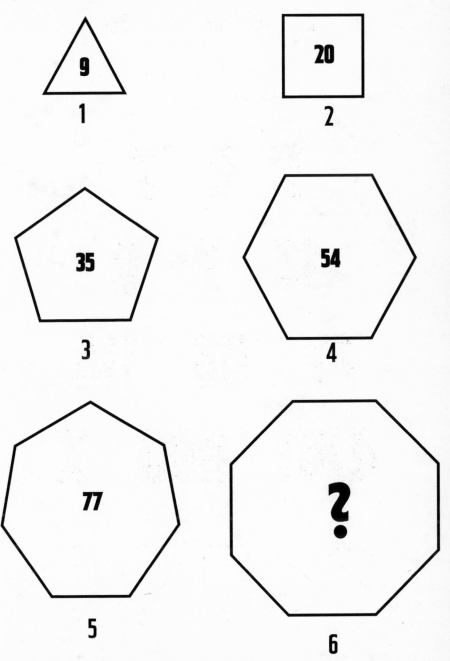

The Great Book of Brainteasers

Calendar Dice

42

By using two wooden cubes placed side by side and by numbering each side of each cube with one digit only, what is the highest number which can be displayed by starting at 1 then working upwards and not omitting any subsequent numbers?

Both cubes must be used for each number but can be switched around as desired.

A Magic Word Square

43 Magic Squares can be very intriguing, whether they use number in which each line, column and diagonal adds up to the same number, or whether they use words.

Usually a magic word square consists of a number of different words which can be read both across and down as in the example:

K	I	N	D
I	D	E	A
N	E	A	T
D	A	T	A

However, below is a magic word square with a difference.

Can you fill in the three missing letters so that this is, indeed, a magic word square?

S		I	D
E	I	O	I
R		N	G
P	A		I

44 Which vase is wrong?

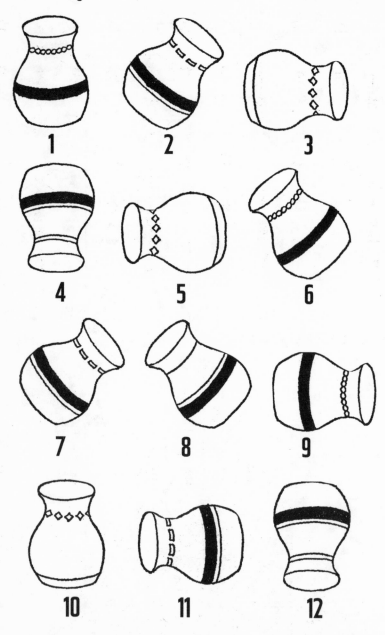

45 Which one is wrong?

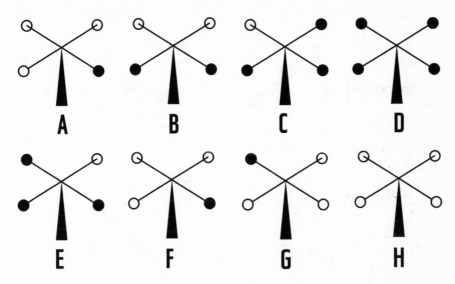

46 What should take the place of X?

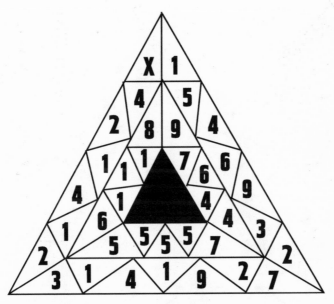

47 What is X?

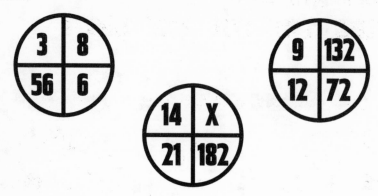

48 Which pattern does not conform with the others?

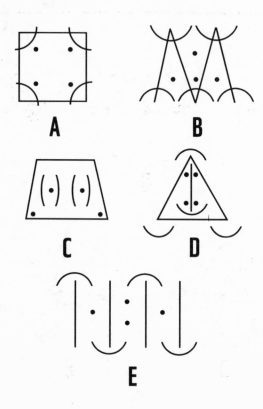

A

B

C

D

E

49 What comes next in thsi sequence/

1,000, 1,414, 1,732, 2,236 2,449, ?

50 Which option below should logically follow in the above sequence?

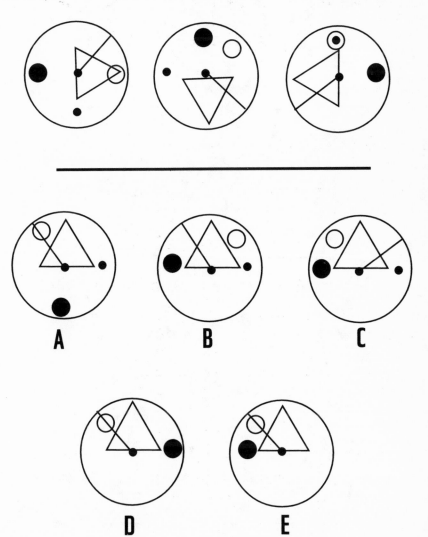

51 Which hexagonal shape is the odd one out?

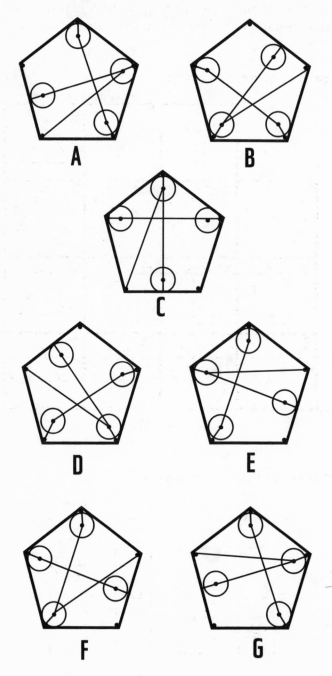

52 Each of the nine squares in the grid marked 1A to 3C, should incorporate all the lines and symbols which are shown in the squares of the same letter and number immediately above and to the left. For example, 2B should incorporate all the lines and symbols that ar ein 2 and B.

One of the squares is incorrect. Which one is it?

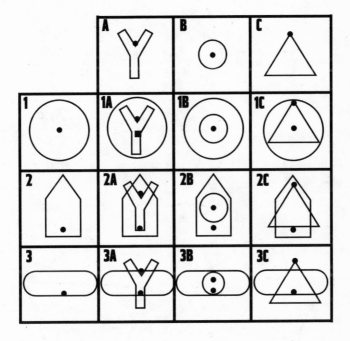

53 Arrange the four strips into a perfect square.

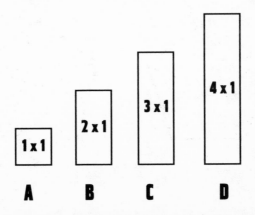

The Great Book of Brainteasers

Strange Markings

54 Charlie and Bob were demolishing an old house.

When they reached the children's bedroom they found three stones containing very strange markings.

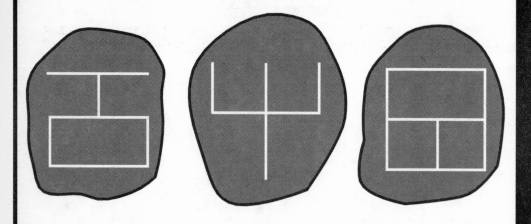

"Must be some sort of hieroglyphics", said Charlie.

"Possibly", said Bob, "but more likely it was one of the children setting a puzzle for one of his brothers or sisters".

"Aha", said Charlie, "and I think I have just solved the puzzle, here's another brick with some more markings, which must be the answer".

What markings did the fourth brick have on it?

Stop-Watch

55

My watch is terribly unreliable.

Although it was correct at noon, it then began to lose 30 minutes each hour. It now shows 4 pm, but it stopped 5 hours ago.

What is the correct time now?

56 If is to

then   is to

is to

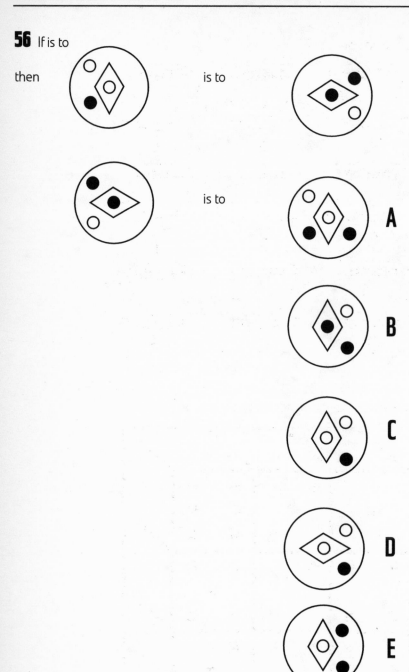

57 Which cup is the odd one out?

58 What is the total of the spots on the rear side?

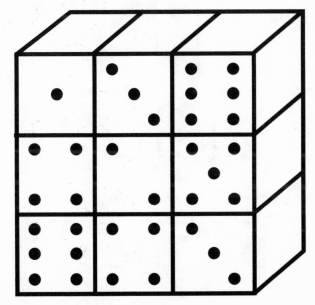

59 What comes next?

124   81   6   32   641   2   –

60 What are A, B, C and D?

3	27	1	32	4	26	3	29
5	25	5	26	6	A	B	C	D

61 If this shape were folded along the dotted lines it could be made into a cube:

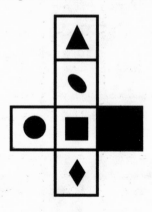

like this:

If this cube is turned upside-down, which of these faces will appear at the top?

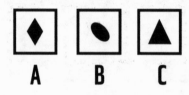

A   B   C

62 What are X, Y and Z?

A	1	3	L	12	6	M	13	9
O	15	12	S	19	X	Y	Z	

63 What are X, Y and Y

3	42	40
7	52	53
12	63	68
18	75	85
25	88	104
X	102	125
42	Y	148
52	133	Z

Lucky Punters

64 Tom, dick and Harry each win on the horses for three days running. The following are the nine amounts paid out by the bookmaker, starting with the largest amount through to the smallest amount.

£130

£104

£94

£78

£52

£46

£42

£30

£24

Tom won twice as much as Dick, but £40 less than Harry. What was the total winning amount for each man over the three days?

Snooker

65 The game of snooker is played with 15 red balls, a black ball, a pink, a blue, a brown, a green, a yellow, and a white ball, which is the cue ball.

Apart from the reds, which form a triangle at the top of the table, and the white, each of the remaining coloured balls must be placed on its own spot on the table prior to the commencement of a game.

Two novices were setting up their first ever game. They knew where to place the 15 red balls and that the white was the cue ball, and of the remaining seven balls knew where to place the black and pink balls, but hadn't a clue which of the remaining four balls went on which spot, so decided to guess and spot the four balls anywhere.

What were the chances that they would spot all four balls in the correct position?

Also what were the chances they would spot just three of the four balls in the correct position?

66 If this design were turned 90° anti-clockwise and held in front of a mirror, which of the designs below would be reflected?

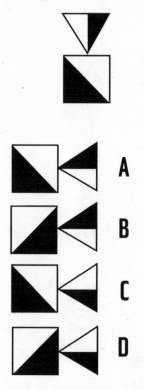

67 What is X?

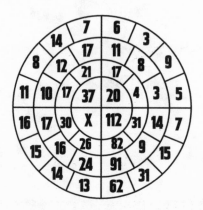

68 Which one is wrong?

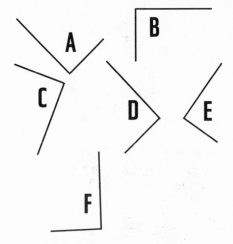

69 Which of the figures at the bottom should follow the six figures at the top?

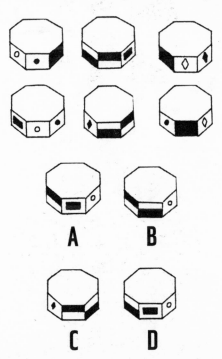

70 What comes next in the series?

I   III   VI   X   XV   XXI

XXVIII   -

71 All of these shapes – except one – are of the same area. Which is the exception, and is it of greater or lesser area?

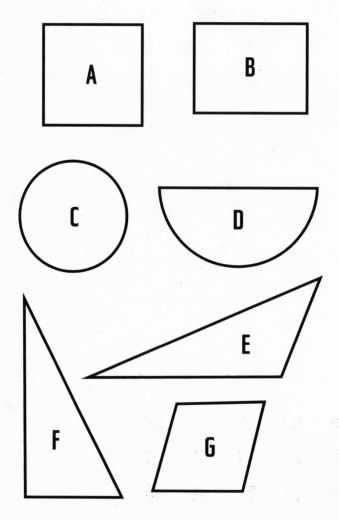

72 What does the third clock show?

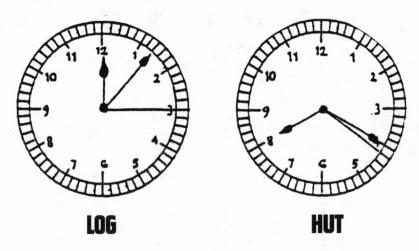

LOG   **HUT**

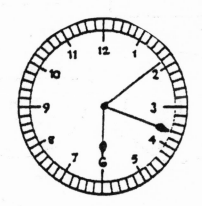

73 Which number is nearest to the number which is midway between the lowest and highest number?

11	84	41	9	79
81	7	36	51	47
88	12	8	89	10

74 Which piece completes the jigsaw puzzle?

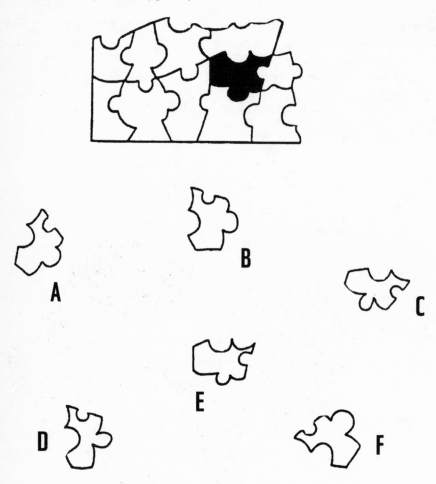

75 What comes next?

$$1\,^2/_3 \quad 2.75 \quad 3.8 \quad 4\,^5/_6$$
$$5\,^6/_7 \quad 6.875 \quad -$$

The Excited Dog

76 A man is walking his dog on the lead towards home at a steady 4 mph. When they are 10 miles from home the man lets the dog off the lead. The dog immediately runs off towards home at 6 mph. When the dog reaches the house it turns round and runs back to the man at the same speed. When it reaches the man it turns back for the house. This is repeated until the man gets home and lets in the dog. How many miles does the dog cover from being let off the lead to being let in the house?

The Great Book of Brainteasers

The Early Arrival

77 My wife usually leaves work at 5.30pm, calls at the supermarket, then catches the 6pm train which arrives at our home town station at 6.30pm. I leave home each day, drive to the station and pick up my wife at 6.30pm just as she gets off the train. One day last week my wife was able to finish work about 10 minutes earlier than usual, decided to go straight to the station instead of calling at the supermarket and managed to catch the 5.30pm train which arrived at our home town station at 6pm. Because I was not there to pick her up she began to walk home. I left home at the usual time, saw my wife walking, turned round, picked her up and drove home, arriving there 12 minutes earlier than usual. For how long had my wife walked before I picked her up?

78 In four years' time I shall be five times as old as I was sixteen years ago. How old am I?

79 All these vanes move 90° at a time. The longer ones rotate clockwise, first one move. then missing one and moving two (that is through 180°), then missing two and moving three, and so on.
At the same time, the shorter ones rotate anti-clockwise in the same way.
What will be their position after six moves?

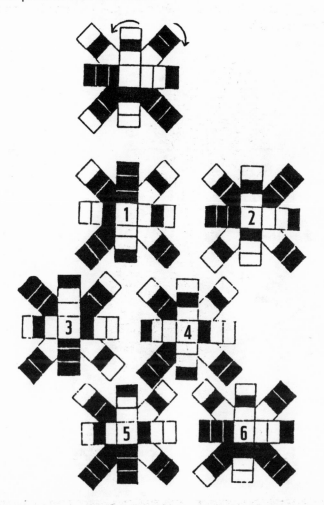

80 The black ball moves one position at a time clockwise.

If it stops on an even number the white ball moves one position clockwise.
If it stops on an odd number the white ball moves two positions ant-clockwise.
On what number will both balls be in the same position?

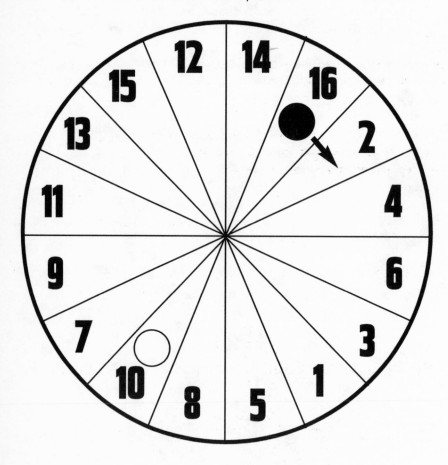

81 What comes next?

13   122   83   314   305   3   163

82 A colour is concealed in each of these sentences:

A Temper or anger are signs of weakness.

B The money is for Edward.

C You'll find I got it elsewhere.

D One dancer, I see, is out of step.

E 'I'm a gent and a lady's man,' he said.

83 Here are six clocks turned upside down. Which shows the nearest time to 2.25 if held in front of a mirror (Don't use a mirror or turn the page.)

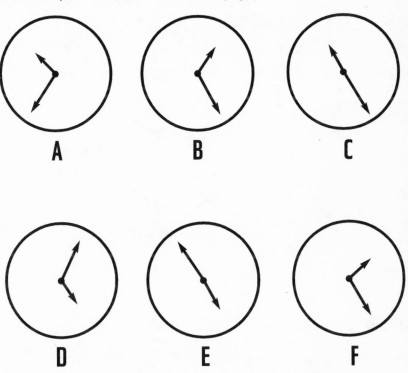

A   B   C

D   E   F

84 Complete the last line:

17 (35) 19

22 (46) 26

31 (65) 37

44 (92) 52

–   (–)   –

85 My mirror is flat. The wall is plumb and the floor horizontal. I can see myself in the mirror from top to toe. I am 5' 5" tall. How long is the mirror?

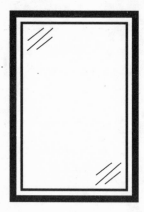

86 The Pharoah asked: "Who is the greatest of the gods?"
'I am not" said Horus.
"Anubis is" said Isis.
"Isis is lying", said Anubis.
Only one god was telling the truth, the other two were lying.
Who is the greatest?

Number Logic

87

	10	7	3
1	4	15	11
8		2	6
16		5	9

Apart from the numbers 12, 13 and 14, the numbers 1-16 have been inserted into the grid almost, but not quite, at random.

Following just two simple rules, where would you place the numbers 12, 13 and 14 in the grid?

Crocodile

88 The crocodile had a tail that was three times as long as its head and its body was half as long as its tail.

Its body and tail measured 171 inches.

How long was its head?

89 What number should replace the question mark?

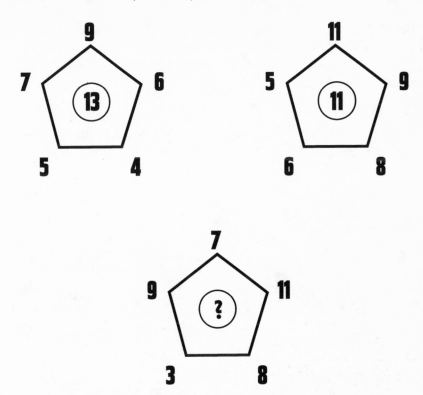

90 The tennis ball has fallen down a mole hole. How do you geet the tennis ball out?

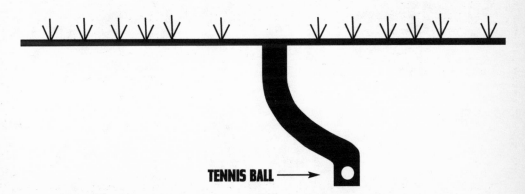

TENNIS BALL →

91 Simplify:

$$\frac{13}{24} \div \frac{26}{96} = X$$

92 What number should replace the question mark to make symmetry?

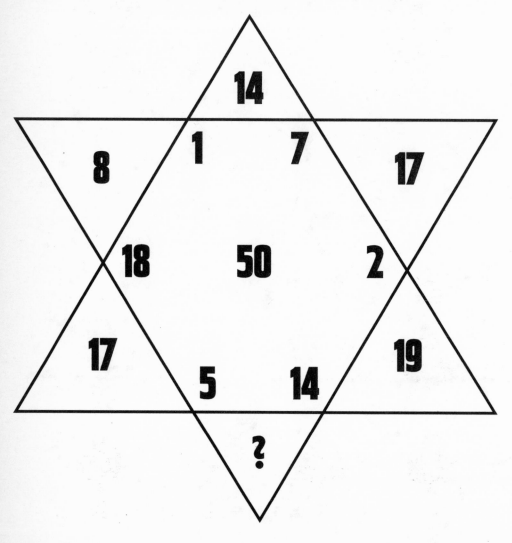

93 Which is the odd one out?

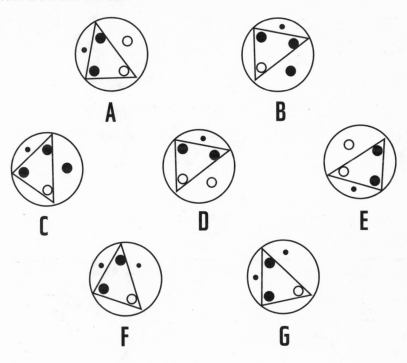

94

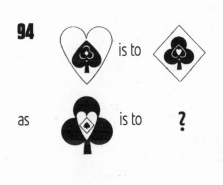

as

 is to **?**

95 What set of numbers comes next?

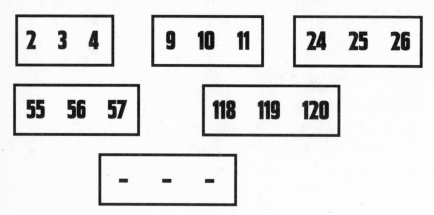

2	3	4
9	10	11
24	25	26
55	56	57
118	119	120
-	-	-

96 What goes into the empty brackets?

34 (3916) 102

26 (4436) 104

14 (   ) 70

97 Can you discover six male forenames in the outer ring and six female names in the inner ring.

98 How many totals of 50 can you find, using consecutive numbers and moving clockwise from the starting point?

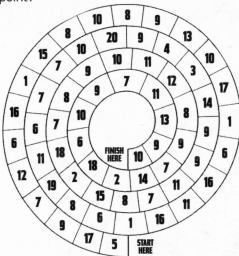

99 The dials on the electricty meter at the bottom show the consumption of electricty 13 weeks after those at the top.

A. How many units were used during the 13 weeks?
B. What was the total cost at 3.40p per unit?

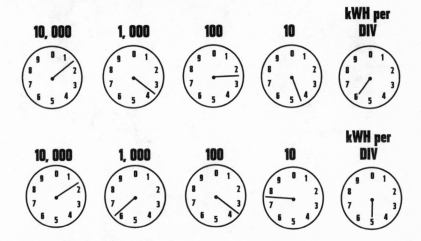

Guilty Party

100 At the scene of a heinous crime, five suspects, one of whom is the guilty party, are being interrogated by a detective. Each of the suspects gives one statement and it later transpires that just three of these statements are correct.

These are the statements:

Uncle Jack : Uncle Jim committed the murder
Aunt Mary : I did not do it
Cousin Stewart : It was not Cousin Margaret
Uncle Jim : Uncle Jack is lying when he says I did it
Cousin Margaret : Aunt Mary is telling the truth

Who committed the murder?

Rat-A-tacks!

101 In the rat-infested village of Cattatackya last month each cat killed the same number of rats as every other cat. The total number of rat fatalities during the month came to 2117.

Less than 50 cats achieved this remarkable feat. How many cats were there in Cattatackya, and how many rats did each kill?

102 In the game of snakes and ladders the counter is moved according to the throw of the die. When it lands on the foot of a ladder, it moves to the top of the ladder; when it lands on the head of a snake it moves down to the tail. What will be the total of the numbers reached after the following throws of the die? (Do NOT include the squares at the bottom of the ladders or the tops of the snakes in the total, i.e. the first throw = 15, NOT 20):

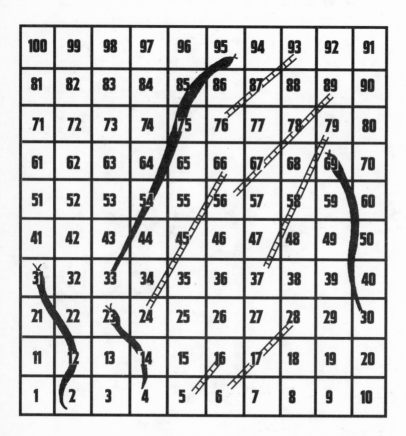

103 Which of the cubes at the bottom should be placed at A, B and C?

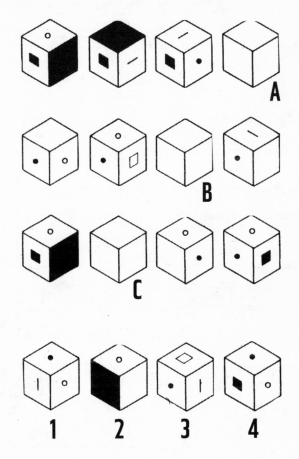

104 Which is the greater in each of these?

A 3¼ miles or 25 furlongs

B 4 quarts or 4.2 litres

C 3 inches or 78 millimetres

D 3¾ gills or 1 pint

105 A Which of these has the largest area?
B Which has the smallest area?

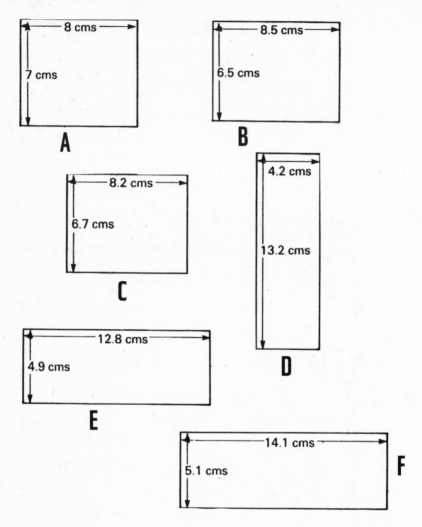

106 The square of a digit, when deducted from 100, leaves the square of another digit. Two different digits have this characteristic. You must give both.

107 What is x?

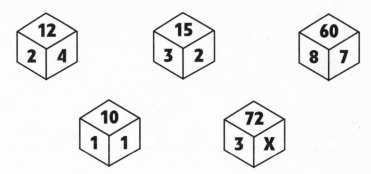

108 Give values for x and y.

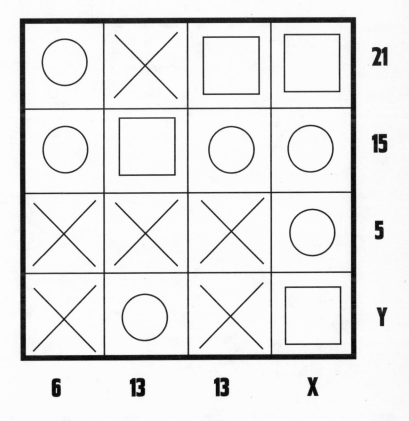

Logical Square

109

	15					
				21		**24**
?			**31**			
				12	**42**	
			11			

What number logically should replace the question mark?

The Mind Boggles

110 A boggle puzzle is where a word or a number can be read by moving from square to square horizontally, vertically or diagonally, as distinct from a conventional word search puzzle, where all the words or numbers are read in a straight line. Examples of each are shown below:

BOGGLE

WORD SEARCH

In the puzzle below consecutive years of the 20th-century are written boggle style, starting with the year 1901 and continuing with subsequent years 1902, 1903, 1904 etc. How many consecutive years of the 20th-century can you find before you get to a missing year? You cannot use a square twice for the same year, however, every square may be used as many times as you wish for different years.

3	8	7	6	4
4	3	2	4	9
9	2	9	0	8
0	1	5	1	7
6	3	9	4	1

111 Which of these statements are true and which are false?

A When a car is driven forwards the wheels rotate anti-clockwise.
B If a clock is put forward 1¼ hours the minute hand moves through 450⁰.
C When a clock reads 4.10 the acute angle between the hands is exactly 60⁰.

112 Which is the odd one out?

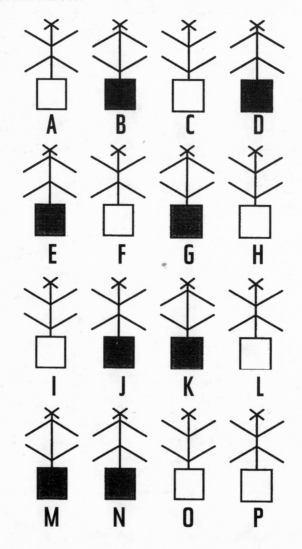

113 Which is the odd one out?

A. 119   B. 153   C. 136   D. 147   E. 102

114 Which is the odd one out?

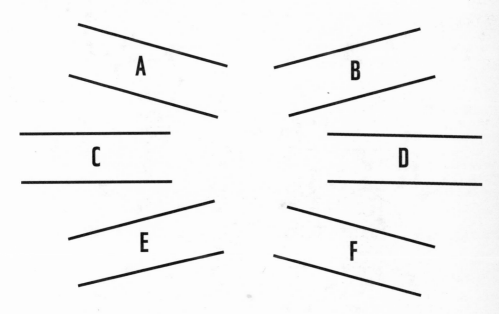

115 Which is the odd one out?

A   B   C   D

116 A Which route gioves the highest total?

B Which route gives the lowest total?

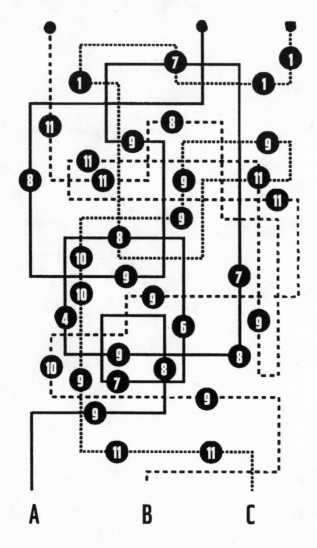

A   B   C

117 What is X?

3	4	6	5
2	15	105	4
7	480	X	8
8	9	6	7

118 What will be the result if the hands of this clock are moved as follows:

    A. forward 3 hours, 15 minutes

    B. back 4 hours, 25 minutes

    C. back 1 hour, 30 minutes

The Great Book of Brainteasers

119 Three players each throw three darts that, starting from X, score as follows:

A clockwise: the first three numbers divisible by 3 – all doubles;
B anti-clockwise: the first three numbers divisible by four – all doubles
C clockwise: the first three numbers divisible by four – all trebles.

What did each player score?

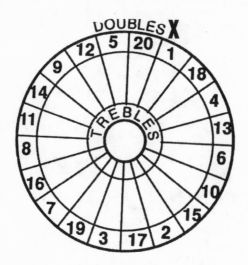

120 Insert arithmetical signs between these numbers to justify the equation. There are two different solutions.

$$1 \quad 2 \quad 3 \quad 4 \quad 5 \quad 6 \quad 7 \quad = \quad 3$$

Sum and Product

121 I went to our local hardware store this morning for a few bits and pieces and was able to obtain exactly what I requires, a bag of nails, some new blades for my hacksaw, a tin of grease and a new hammer, all very reasonably priced at £7.11

When I arrived home and checked the till receipt I discovered something quite unusual. When I added the individual prices of the four items together it checked at £7.11 as expected, however, I thin multiplied the price of the four items together and the result was still £7.11.

What did each article cost?

The items are listed below from least expensive to most expensive? Can you fill in the gaps?

Nails   £?.20

Grease   £1.??

Blades   £?.?0

Hammer   £3.??

Dice

122 What is the total of the spots on faces 1,2,3,4 and 5?

123 The ball in A moves clockwise, first one letter, then missing one and going onto the next, then missing two, and so on. If it lands on a consonant the ball in B moves to one number clockwise; if it lands on a vowel the ball in B moves to the third number ant-clockwise. If the ball in B lands on an even number the ball in C moves three letters clockwise; if it lands on an odd number the ball in C moves four letters anti-clockwise. What word will be spelt by the ball in C after seven moves?

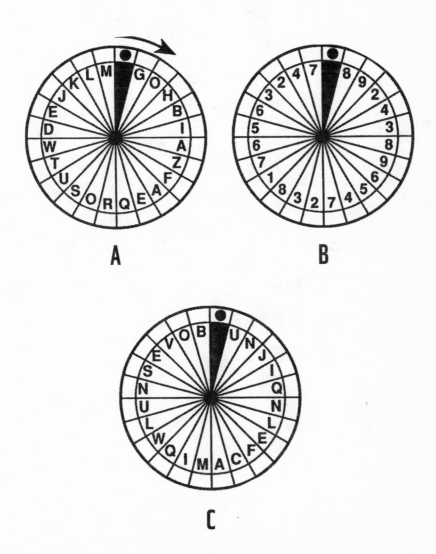

A

B

C

124 This wall has been demolished by a careless driver. Can you reconstruct it from four of the pieces below?

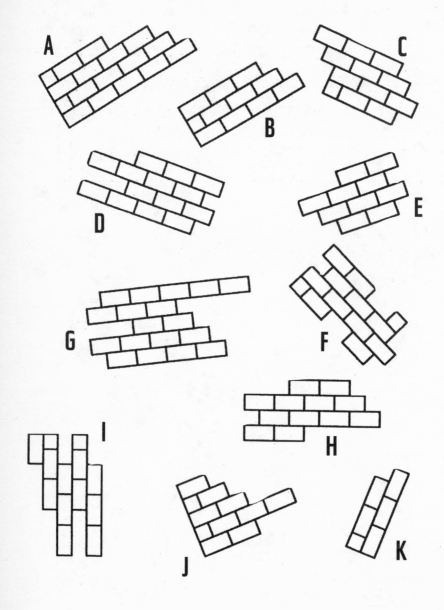

125 In a terrace of five house, numbered 1, 3, 5, 7 and 9, Charles lives next door to Alf; Ernie lives next door to Bert; Dave lives next door but one to Charles; Charles lives at number 9. Where does each man live?

126 Which circle is nearest in content to A?

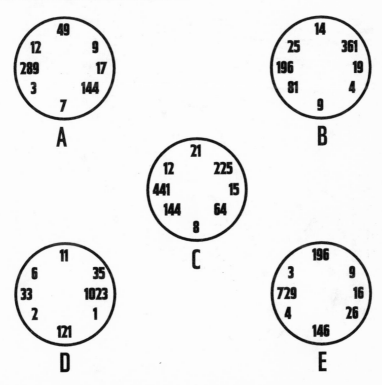

A
49
12
9
289
17
3
144
7

B
14
25
361
196
19
81
4
9

C
21
12
225
441
15
144
64
8

D
11
6
35
33
1023
2
1
121

E
196
3
9
729
16
4
26
146

127 Make this equation true with one stroke of the pen.

6 + 6 + 6 = 652

128 Which of A, B, C D or E, fits into the blank circle to carry on a logical sequence?

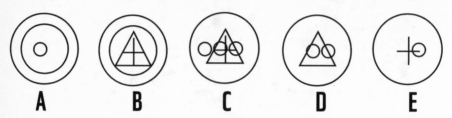

A   B   C   D   E

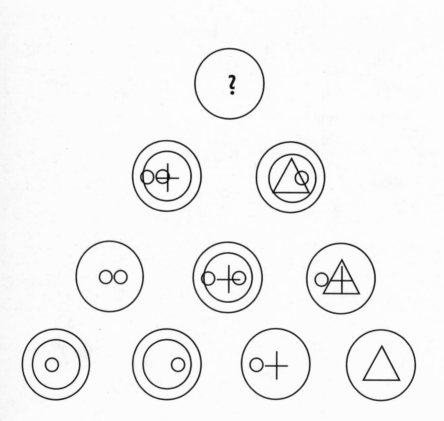

Swimming Pool

129 My wife and I were filling the swimming pool with two hosepipes, but unknown to us we were making very little headway as I had left the drainage valve open.

My wife could normally fill the swimming pool with the hosepipe she was using in 9 minutes, however, the hosepipe I was using would normally take 24 minutes, however, the drainage valve would normally empty the pool in 36 minutes.

To the nearest minute, how long would it take us to fill the swimming pool?

Conundrum Chase

130 The following are the runners for the Conundrum Chase at Sandown Park. The form shown is the position finished by each horse in its previous 8 races. Unfortunately the form for the 6th runner has been omitted. Can you work out what its form should be?

3 miles	Conundrum Chase Sandown Park	2.30

Number	Horse	Form
1	Little Snapper	14623256
2	Touchwood	22546316
3	Desert Storm	34126625
4	Water Cress	62245631
5	Summerset	64321562
6	Heathcliffe	?

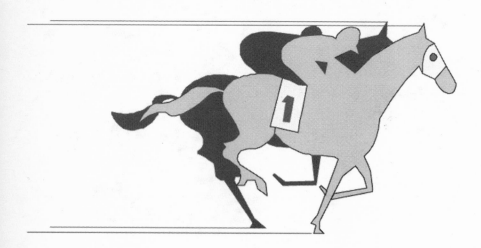

131 A biased coin is tossed a large number of times and gives heads 3 times out of 5. What is the chance that in 4 throws, 2 heads and 2 tails appear?

132 In a 6 horse race, the following odds appeared:

1   2 to 1 against

2   3 to 1 against

3   5 to 1 against

4   6 to 1 against

5   10 to 1 against

What should be the odds on the 6th horse to give the bookmaker a profit of 12.5 per cent?

133 What number should replace the question mark?

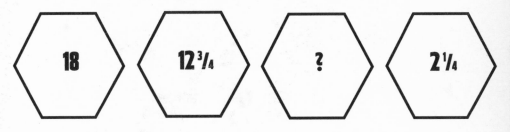

18   12³/₄   ?   2¹/₄

134 What time should appear on the 4th clock?

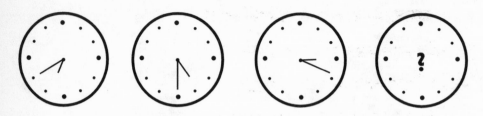

135 What number should repalce the question mark?

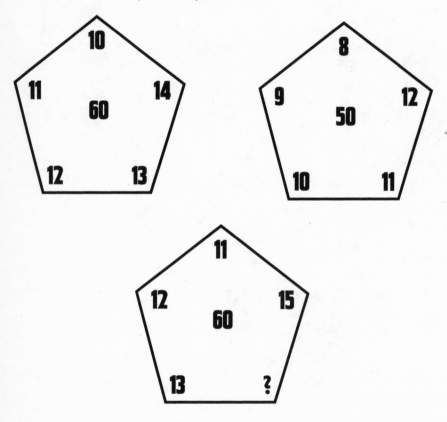

136 How many different routes are there from A to B?

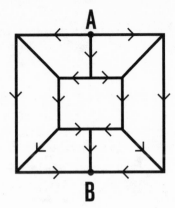

137 Which of the designs below – A, B,C or D – follows number 6?

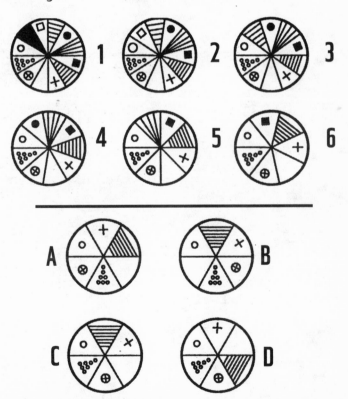

138 Using only plus or minus signs, arrange the numbers below so that they will equal 10. You must use all the numbers.

3   4   5   6   7   8   9

139 Which is the odd one out?

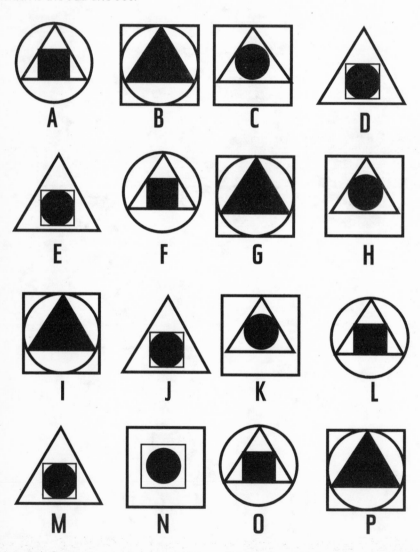

Safe Combination

140

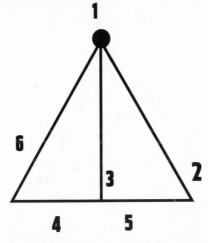

The combination of the safe is written in code below. Only people who have the above key are able to understand it, and even then not everyone finds it particularly easy to work out.

What is the combination of the safe?

The Great Book of Brainteasers

Round the Hexagons

141 Draw the contents of the bottom hexagon

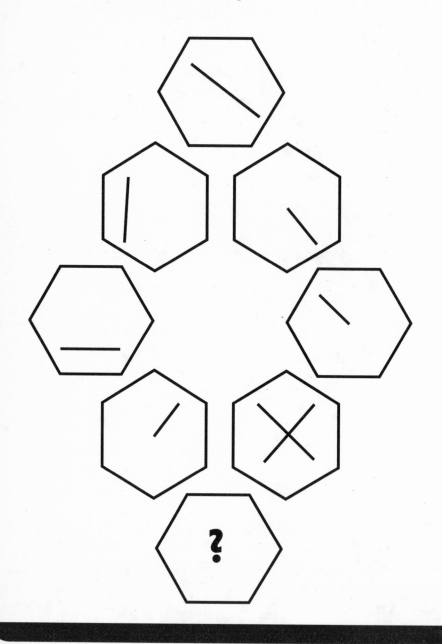

142 Choosing from the numbers on the right, what is X?

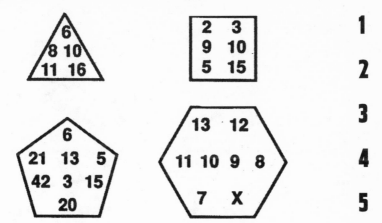

1

2

3

4

5

143 Which of the clocks at the bottom – A, B, C or D – should follow number 5?

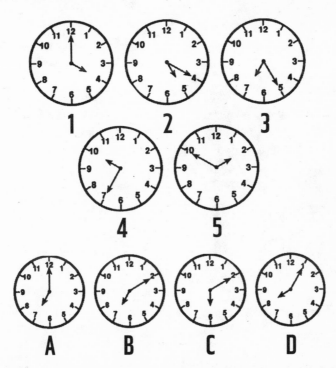

144 What is X?

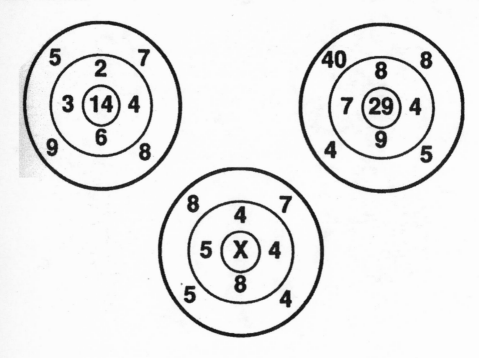

145 Multiply the number that is midway between the lowest and the highest number by the one that is midway between the number that is nearest to the lowest number and the one that is nearest to the highest number.

5	16	28	23
19	7	4	38
21	15	30	39
22	3	6	34
12	25	37	8

146 Which of the shapes below – A, B or C – follow those above?

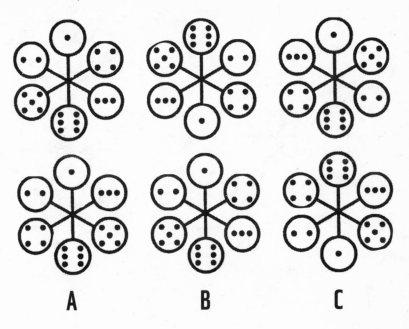

A   B   C

147 What goes into the empty brackets?

31	(1324)	
16	(6183)	42
17	(7132)	38
47	( )	23
31	(1376)	48
58	(8542)	67

148 Which is the odd one out?

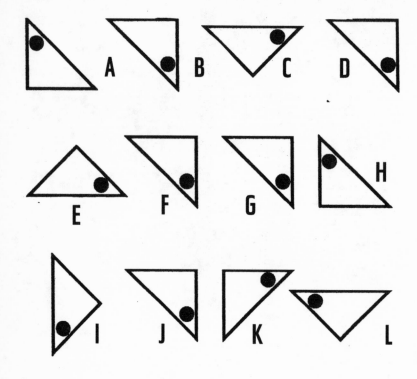

149 What goes into the bottom square?

| 41 |
| 46 |
| 56 |
| 67 |
| 80 |
| 88 |
| |

150 How many cubes can you count here?

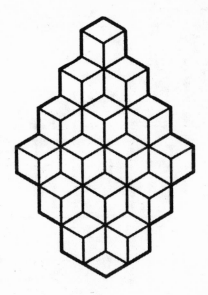

151 Which is the odd one out?

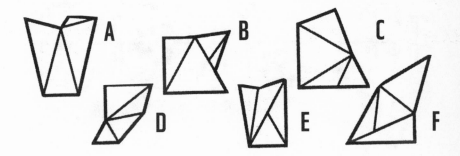

G-G-Griddle

152 What numbers should replace the question marks?

6	8	2	1	4	3	6	8	2	1
3	4	3	6	8	2	1	4	3	4
4	1	6	8	2	1	4	3	6	3
1	2	3	6	8	2	1	6	8	6
2	8	4	3	4	3	4	8	2	8
8	6	1	?	?	6	3	2	1	2
6	3	2	?	?	8	6	1	4	1
3	4	8	2	8	6	3	4	3	4
4	1	6	3	4	1	2	8	6	3
1	2	8	6	3	4	1	2	8	6

Stranger the Fiction

153 "Life's funny", said an old friend when I bumped into him the other day. "Listen to this, I was born in March, yet I celebrate my birthday in August, and last February I married my mother".

How is this possible?

154 There are five groups of teeth here, with four identical sets in each group. Match the five groups and state which teeth will not mesh with any of the other sets.

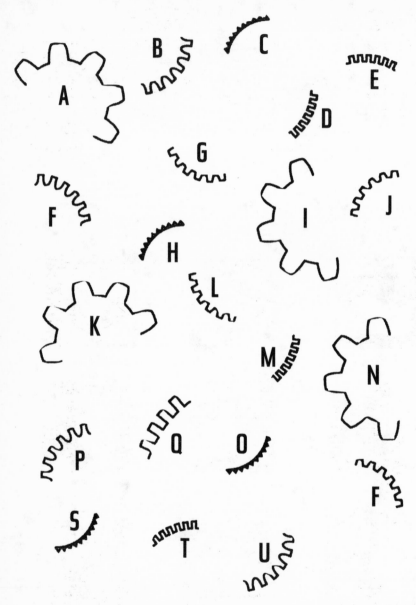

155 What are X and Y?

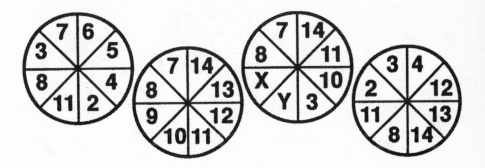

156 Which one is wrong?

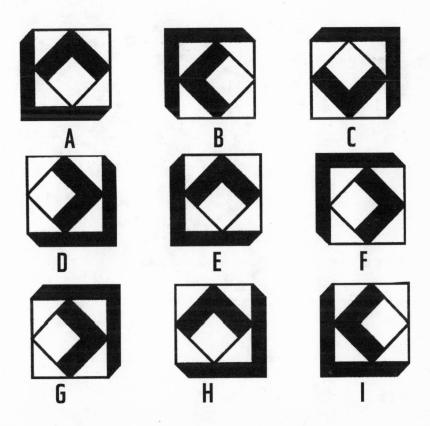

157 Which two make a pair?

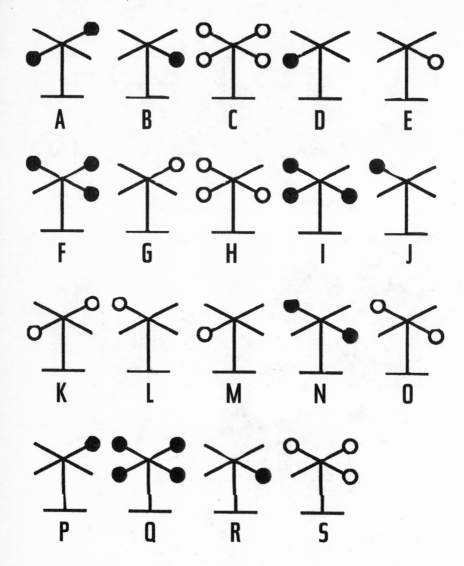

158 What are X, Y and Z?

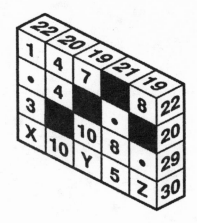

159 Which of the designs at the bottom should occupy the empty space?

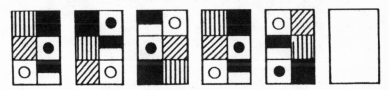

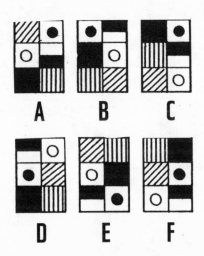

A   B   C

D   E   F

160 What comes next in the series?

625 1296 25   36   5   -

161 Study the top cards and find what city is represented by the bottom cards.

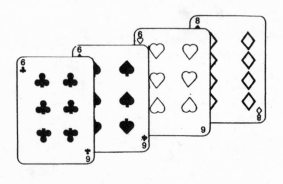

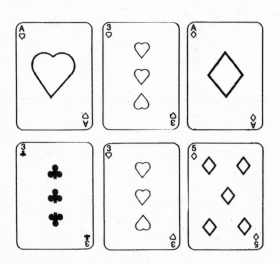

162 What goes into the brackets?

$$144 \quad (3625) \quad 125$$
$$96 \quad (1618) \quad 126$$
$$112 \quad (\quad) \quad 144$$

163 Which of those at the bottom comes next?

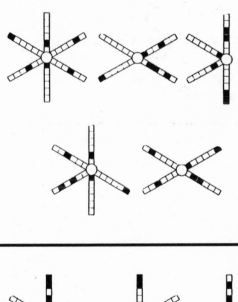

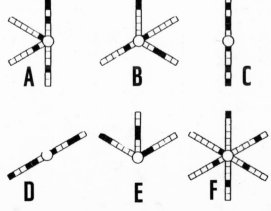

Olympic Games

164

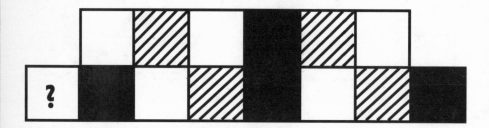

The official had just finished building the winners rostrum at the Olympic Games when someone walked off with the bottom left-hand block. Should the missing block be black, white or striped?

Number Logic

165 Where logically would you place number 1 in the grid?

	9					
				8		
		7				
5					6	
			4			3
					2	

166 What is the last term in the bottom line?

⅕	.4	⅗	.8	1
⅓	1	1⅔	2.33	3
¼	1	1¾	2.5	3¼
⅛	.625	1⅛	1.625	–

167 What is X?

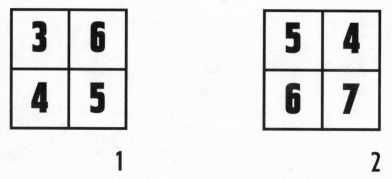

3	6
4	5

1

5	4
6	7

2

7	6
8	5

3

X	8
6	7

4

168 What should go into the empty brackets?

305	(6165)	13
280	(5670)	14
145	(2925)	5
70	(1415)	3
25	( )	1

169 Which circle should replace the question mark?

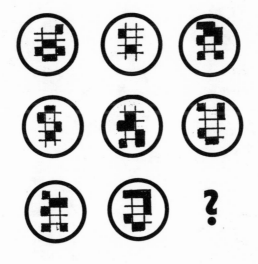

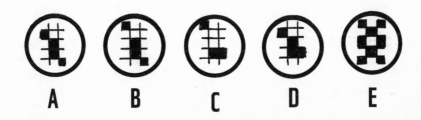

A   B   C   D   E

170 Simplify:

$$\frac{7}{11} \div \frac{28}{33} = x$$

171 Which number should replace the question mark?

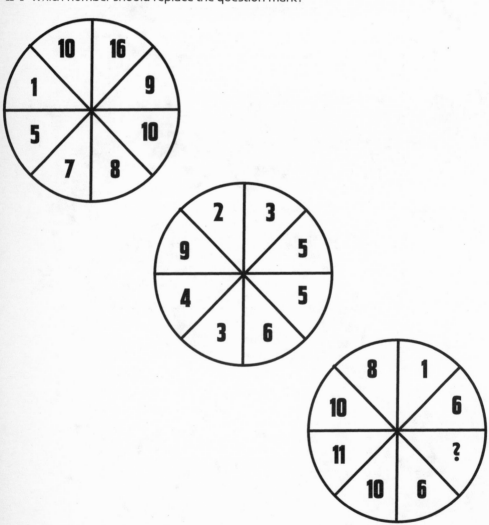

Three Circles

172 Draw three complete circles of the same size so that each circle contains one ellipse, one square and one triangle

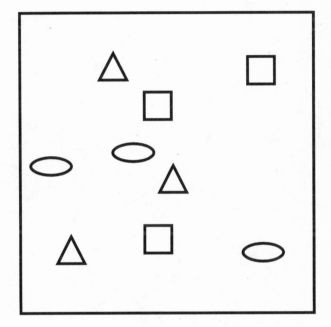

Calculation

173

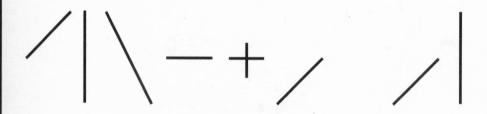

If these two numbers total 8679, what do the two numbers below total?

174 Which letter should replace the question mark?

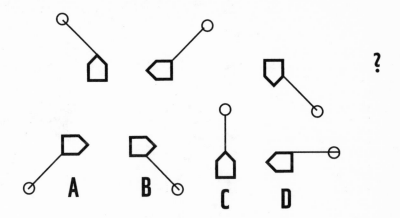

175 Divide the diamond into four equal shapes each containing one of each of the six symbols.

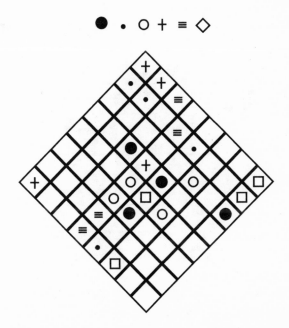

176 If you threw two dice simultaneously, what would be the odds against throwing two sixes?

177 This is an exercise in mental arithmetic, and must be solved without writing anything except the answers,

A What is the total of the odd numbers that are not prime numbers?

B What is the total of the even numbers?

C What is the total of the prime numbers?

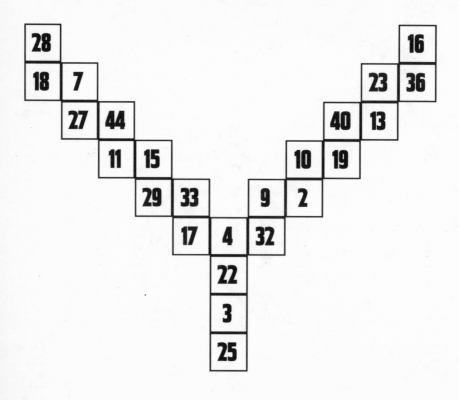

178 Which is the odd one out?

A Cassius

B Cassia

C Casca

179 What goes into the brackets?

9	(169)	4
7	(225)	8
5	(121)	6
6	( )	11

180 What is X?

4 2 3 8 4 7 1 4 0 5 6 X

181 What is the next term in this series?

3 19 7 16 8 11 14 9 12 –

The Great Book of Brainteasers

Odd One Out

182 Which is the odd one out, column A, B, C or D?

A   B   C   D

Series

183 Can you draw the next figure in this series?

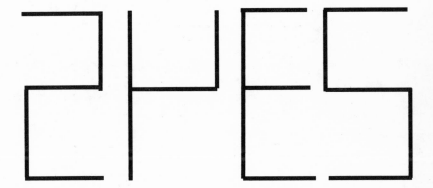

184 What is the total number of triangles in these four hexagons?

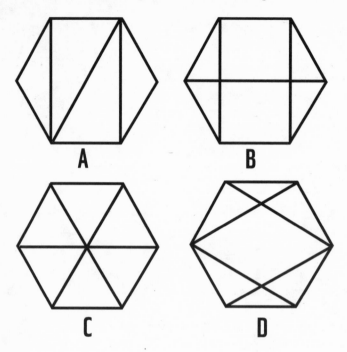

185 Which one is wrong?

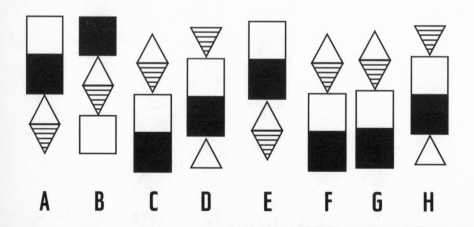

A   B   C   D   E   F   G   H

186 Take two numbers from each circle so that the total of the six numbers chosen is 100.

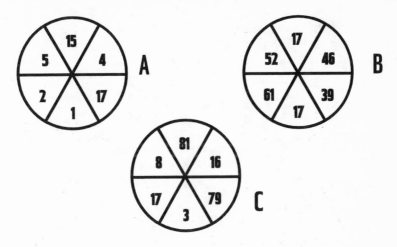

187 The three circles rotate independently of each other.

Circle A moves one number at a time clockwise;
Circle B moves two places at a time anti clockwise;
Circle C moves three places at a time anti clockwise.

In how many moves will all the eights be together again?

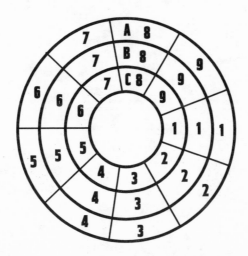

The Collectors Bequest

188 A rich collector of gold coins left detailed instructions as to how his gold coin collection of between 300 and 400 coins was to be distributed to his five sons and five daughters after his death.

First of all one gold coin was to be given to his butler, then exactly a fifth of those remaining went to his eldest son. another coin was then given to his butler, then exactly a fifth of those remaining went to his second eldest son. This procedure was repeated until all his five sons had received a share, and the butler had received 5 gold coins. Then after the fifth son had received his share, the coins still remaining were equally divided between his five daughters.

How many coins were originally in the collection?

Twins and Triplets

189 My sisters Alice and Beth each have five children, twins and triplets, although Alice had the twins first, whereas Beth had her trip[lets first.

When I saw Alice the other day she happened to remark that the sum of the ages of her children was equal to the product of their ages. I pointed out that whilst that was extremely interesting, what was even more interesting was that Beth could say exactly the same about the ages of her children.

How old are my sister's children?

Section Three

Answers

1 C

The first five patterns indicate that they arre globes, rotating anti-clockwise.

2 B

3 K

It should be like C, E and P

4 4

The top left-hand number is the result of adding the two bottom numbers. The top right-hand number is the result of dividing the bottom two numbers. If this procedure is followed throughout, X must be 4, to make the top horizontal pair 36.

5 A-K, B-P, C-M. D-J, E-O, F-L, G-I and H-N

6 35

The highest prime number is 17, and the lowest even number is 6. The remaining numbers add to 137.

7 D

8 9

9 210

The 10 highest numbers (19, 7,16, 8, 11, 14, 9, 12, 5 and 20) total 121
The 10 lowest numbers (1, 18, 4, 13, 6, 10, 15, 2, 17 and 3) total 89

10 The reason Frank replied so quickly is that he had spotted that the digits 7 - 4- 6 - 1 add up to 18, and when the sum of the digits are divisible by 9 exactly, then the number itself is also divisible by 9 exactly. Therefore, in whatever order you arrange these four digits, the number produced will divide exactly by 9.

However, on this occasion, Frank was not correct, because by screwing the 6 on upside down, it becomes a 9, and then none of the resultant four digit numbers will divide exactly by 9.

11 4/1 against.

The number of pictures on the card does not affect the odds. The only thing that does affect the odds are the number of winning pictures and the number of losing pictures.

12 E
Two of the loops are too small

13 L
The midddle heart has been changed to a spade.

14 One after another

15 So were the other half

16 E
A is the same as G, B is the same as F; C is the same as D;

17 B
The top shape stays the same, the next two change shape, size and colour

18 Susan : $25 + 1 + 1 + 1 = 28$
     Helen : $10 + 10 + 10 + 5 + 5 + 1 + 1 = 42$
     Dave : $25 + 25 + 10 + 1 + 1 + 1 = 63$

19 31425
The order of the car next to last changes each time. First it drops back to last, then at the next stage it moves into the lead.

20 $X = 6$; $Y = 36$
x is the product of the top two numbers and
y is the square of x.

21 Number 1. Each row will then contain:
(i) A scalene triangle (one with unequal sides);
(ii) A right-angle triangle – which is at present missing from the second row;
(iii) An isosceles triangle (one with two equal sides);
(iv) An equilateral triangle (one with all sides equal).

22 (i) Globe A; (ii) Globe G
The globes are rotating anti-clockwise.
In (i) there are two vertical rows of spots situated adjacent to each other. At X one of
these rows (the centre one on the first globe) will be on the blind side and only one row
will be visible.

In (ii) there are three vertical rows of spots on one side of the globe only. On the other side there are no spots. Therefore at Y there will be one row visible, while in the next position of the globe all three rows will be on the blind side.

23 22, 286
Alternate numbers starting at 7, advance by 4, 5 and 6. The alternate numbers starting at 91 are 13 times the previous number.

24 The figure rotates $1/4$ turn anti-clockwise. the difference in shading remains constant throughout. In F the small oute circle and the triangle have changed places.

25 B

26 x = 840
y = 168
z = 24
Values of the shapes as indicated are: square = 4, circle = 5, and triangle = 6. The value of the rectangle is not indicated, but is obviously 7. This is ascertained from the relationship between 4 (square) and 28, or 5 (circle) and 35. From this it can also be seen that the values of overlapping areas are obtained by multiplying the values of the individual shapes that make up those areas.
Confirmation of this is given by 140, which is the product of 4, 5 and 7.
Therefore, X is the product of the circle, square, triangle and rectangle; Y is the product of the triangle, rectangle and square; Z is the product of the triangle and square.

27 5

28 H
The faces are made up of four straight lines, five curves, two dots and one circle. In H there are only three straight lines.

29 28, 42, 41, 53
Four sequences alternate between columns:
Columns A & C
2, 5, 8, 11, 14 etc
Columns B & A
2, 4, 6, 8, 10 etc
Columns C & D
1, 5, 9, 13 ,17 etc

Columns D & B
3, 6, 9, 12, 15 etc

30 Taking alternate digits:
$9 + 7 + 5 + 4 + 3 = 28$
$8 + 6 + 2 + 1 = 17$
As the difference between the sums of these two digits is 11, the number is divisible by 11 exactly.
This would also apply if the difference between the sums of the two digits was any multiple of 11.

31 37
All the others are divisible by 7

32 5 and 5
Here the spacing may have confused you. Had the digits been placed as follow:
11   13   12   16   13   19   14   22   15   25
you would probably have recognised that there were two alternate sequences, one ascending 1 at a time (11, 12, 13, 14, 15) and the other ascending 3 at a time (13, 16, 19, 22, 25).

33 A $= 11$
B $= 26$
C $= 36$
Examination of the numbers given shows that each number is obtained by multiplying the opposite lower number by five and adding one. In the first circle 5 times $3 + 1 = 16$ and 5 times $4 + 1 = 21$. In the third circle 5 times $1 + 1 = 6$.

34 E
Acute angles have symbols at the end of the lines, as shown in the first row. Obtuse angles and right angles have different symbols.
In the second row the colours of the symbols are reversed (black becoming white and white becoming black), and in the third row they are reversed again.
Therefore, in E the circle and square are the wrong colours.

35 A, B, C and D are made up of circles and squares.
In A there is a circle inside a square inside a circle;
In B there is a square inside a circle inside a square;
In C there is a circle inside a circle inside a square;
In D there is a square inside a square inside a circle.
The third row is made up of triangles and circles, conforming in the same way.
In A the centre figure (the circle) is black; in B the midddle figure (the circle) is black; in C the outer figure (the square) is black; in D none of the figures is black.
The third row must conform in the same way.

36 X= 3
Y = 4
Z = 9
The total of each line, horizontally, vertically and diagonally will then be 15.

37 184
Double the first nu,mber and add 1;
double the second number and add 2;
double the third number and add 3.
Continuing in this manner:
double the sixth number (89) and add 6.

38 15
The lower number is the sum of the number above it and its preceding number.

39 1,024
The first number is squared to give the second number, which is then halved to give the third number. This is turn is squared to give the next answer, and so on.

40 Number 2.
In the first row there is one horizontal line (in the 7),
one vertical line (in the 1), one diagonal line (in the 7) and one circle (in the 6).
In the second line there are two of each.
In the third line there are three of each.
In the fourth line there are four of each.
There ARE four circles (in 896), but only three vertical horizontal and diagonal lines.
Number 2 is the only figure which supplies all three.

Section Three Answers

41 104

Divide the number inside the shape by the number of sides of the shape. Thus 9, divided by 3 (sides of the triangle) gives 3; 20 divided by 4 (sides of the square) gives 5, and so on. You then arrive at the progression: 3, 5, 7, 9, 11 and 13. Therefore in number 6, which is an octagon, the number inside should be 104, which divided by 8, gives 13 – the final number of the progression.

42 32

Number the sides of the first cube 0, 1, 2, 3, 5, 7
Number the sides of the second cube 1, 1, 2, 4, 5, 8
Several numbers are achieved by turning the 6 over and displaying it as a 9.

43 Put the letter T in each blank space. Now start at the bottom left hand square and read up the first column, then along the top and eventually spiralling into the centre to spell out the word prestidigitation. A very magic word presented very squarely indeed!

44 8

A vase with a broad black band round the centre has a row of circles round its neck; if there is a broad black band with a thin line below it round the centre, there is a row of rectangles round the neck; if there is a thin line near the bottom of the vase there is a row of diamonds near the neck.
When there is a broad black band round the centre with a thin line above it there should be a double line going round the neck, but in number 8 there is only a single line.

45 F

In the first row the balls are arranged as follows:
A: 1 black ball; B: 2 black balls; C: 3 black balls; D: 4 black balls.
In the second row the WHITE balls should follow the same arrangement, so that F should have two white balls instead of three.

46 3

The total of the numbers on each side of the large triangle should be the same as the total on the same side of the small triangle. The total of the numbers on the left-hand side of the small triangle is 17, made up of 8, 1, 1, 1 and 6. The numbers given on the side of the large triangle are 2, 1, 4, 1, 2 and 4, giving a total of 14. Therefore the remaining number must be 3, to bring the total up to 17.

47 X= 420

Opposite numbers are obtained by multiplying the smaller number by one less than itself. In the first circle: 3 multiplied by 2 gives 6 and 8 multiplied by 7 gives 56; in the second circle 9 multiplied by 8 gives 72 and 12 multiplied by 11 gives 132. In the third circle 14 multiplied by 13 gives 182 and 21 multiplied by 20 gives 420.

48 B

Each pattern consists of four straight lines, four curves and four dots, except B, which has five curves.

49 square root of 7 = 2.646

50 A

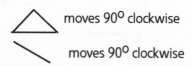

● moves 90° clockwise   △ moves 90° clockwise

● moves 90o clockwise   ╲ moves 90° clockwise

51 F

A, D, E and B, C, G are the same

52 1A There is a dot missing

53

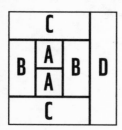

54 They are the numbers 2, 4, 6, 8 complete with mirror-image.

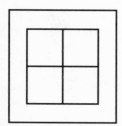

55 1 am

56 C
Diamonds change position, centre dot changes colour and side dots move and change colour.

57 G
The handle is in the wrong position, as compared with B and D.

58 29
Opposite faces of a die add up to 7. Therefore, moving horizontally from left to right and starting in the top row, opposite faces are: 6 4 1 3 5 2 1 3 4

59 8
This is an ordinary 'doubling-up' series, but wrongly spaced. When correctly spaced, the answer becomes obvious: 1 2 4 8 16 32 64 128

60 A is 24; B is 7; C is 23; D is 7
There are four series. Starting with the first term and taking every fourth term thereafter:
3 4 5 6 7(d)
Starting with the second term and continuing in the same way:
27 26 25 24(a)
Starting with the third term:
1 3 5 7(b)
Starting with the fourth term:
32 29 26 23 (c)

61 C

62 X is 15; Y is T; Z is 20
There are three series.
Starting with the first term and taking every third term thereafter: A L M O S – the only letter that will complete a word is T (ALMOST) – represented by Y. The number that follows each letter represents the position in the alphabet of that letter. Therefore, T – represented by Y – should be followed by 20 (T is the 20th letter) – the value for Z
Starting with the third term and taking every third term thereafter: 3 6 9 12 15 (the value for X).

63 X is 33; Y is 117; Z is 173

Moving down in the left-hand vertical column, the numbers increase by 4, 5, 6 and so on. 235 should be increased by 8 to give 33 – the value for X.

The middle vertical column increases by 10, 11, 12 and so on. 102 should be increased by 15 to give 117 – the value for Y.

The right-hand vertical column increases progressively – 13, 15, 17, 19 and so on. 148 should be increased by 25 to give 173 – the value for Z.

64 Tom : £52, £78, £94   = £224
Dick : £24, £46, £42 = £112
Harry : £30, £104, £130 = £264

65 1 in 24 or 23 to 1 (3 x 3 x 2 x 1)

The chances of spotting three balls correctly was exactly the same, as if three balls were spotted correctly, then four must be also.

66 A

67 55

In each quarter, add the numbers in the outer ring, then those in the next ring, and then the next.

In the top left quarter these totals descend:
40 39 38 37 (the single number in the centre).
In the top right quarter they descend:
23 22 21 20 (the single number in the centre)
In the right lower quarter they descend:
115 114 113 112 (the single number in the centre).
Therefore, in the lower left quarter they descend:
58 57 56 – and then, 55 (X).

68 E

Both lines are shorter than those in the other angles.

69 A
The figure is rotating anti-clockwise, three faces at a time. The designs on the respective faces can be discovered by examining the figures at the top, which are in this sequence.

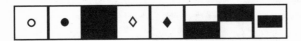

70 XXXVI
First change the Roman numerals into modern numerals:
1 3 6 10 15 21 28
It can be seen that the terms increase by:
2, 3, 4, 5, 6 and 7.
Hence the final number must increase the previous one by 8 (28 increases to 36, or XXXVI in Roman numerals).

71 G is of lesser area than the others, which are all of the same area.

72 FIR
the first letter is indicated by the position of the hour hand relative to the hours – in this case 6, that is sixth letter (F).
The next letter is shown by the position of the second hand. Here it is on the 9th second, and the ninth letter is I.
The third letter is indicated by the position of the minute hand. As it points to the 18th minute, it shows that the third letter is R – the 18th letter of the alphabet.

73 36

74 B

75 Express all ther tems as vulgar fractions:
$1^2/_3$ $2^3/_4$ $3^4/_5$ $4^5/_6$ $5^6/_7$ $6^7/_8$
Now it is obvious that the terms progress like this
123   234   345   456   567   678
and that the final term must be 789, expressed as a vulgar fraaction as in the examples:
78/9.

76 15 miles
The man walks 10 miles at 4 mph = 2.5 hours
The dog runs 2.5 hours at 6mph and covers 15 miles

77 24 minutes
As I leave according to my usual schedule, it must be before 6.30pm when I pick up my wife. Because we have saved 12 minutes, that must be the time that it takes me to drive from the point I picked her up to the station, and back to that same point. Assuming it takes me an equal 6 minutes each way, I have, therefore, picked her up 6 minutes before I would normally do so, which means 6.24pm. So my wife must have walked from 6pm to 6.24 pm. or for 24 minutes.

78 21
If x represents my present age, then X + 4 = 5 (x - 16). Therefore x + 4 = 5X - 80, from which: 84 = 4X, so X = 21

79 5

80 15
The balls move as follows:

Black ball	White ball
2	7
4	9
6	11
3	7
1	8
5	1
8	5
10	8
7	1
9	6
11	2
13	14
15	15

81 0
Spaced correctly the series becomes:
1 31 2 28 3 31 4 30 5 31 6 3 –
The series is based on the days and months of the year – the month followed by the number of days. June has 30 days, so the final term should be 30.

82 A Orange
B Red
C Indigo
D Cerise
E Magenta

83 D

84 61 (127) 71
The numbers on each side of the braackets alternately increase by 2, 3, 4, 5, 6, 7, 8 (and hence 9 and 10). To discover the number inside the brackets: double the number on the left and add 1, then 2 then 3, then 4, and finally 5 (122 + 5 = 127).

85 2' 8$^1/_2$"

86 Assume Horus is the greatest
"I am not" said Horus (LIE)
"Anubis is" said Isis (LIE)
"Isis is lying" said Anubis (TRUTH)

87 So that
1. No two consecutive numbers appear in any horizontal, vertical or diagonal line from which it follows that:
2. No two consecutive numbers appear in adjacent (horizontal, vertical, diagonal) squares.

13	10	7	3
1	4	15	11
8	12	2	6
16	14	5	9

88 38 inches

89 14 (7 + 7 + 11) - (3 + 8) (= 25 - 11 = 14)

90 Fill the hole with water, and the ball will float to the top.

91 $\underline{13} \times \underline{96} = 2$
     24   26

92 12 (outer = inner)

93 E

94 B
The very small centre suit becomes the large outer suit. The next smallest inner suit becomes the next largest outer suit. The next smallest inner suit becomes the next largest outer suit. The largest outer suit becomes the smallest centre suit

95 245   246   247
Each set of numbers starts by doubling the last number in the previous set and adding first 1, then 2, and so on. The last number in the penultimate set is 120, so the first number in the final set is 245 (240 + 5).

96 5116
Divide the number on the right outside the brackets by the number on the left outside the brackets to give the first number inside the brackets. The two digits on the right inside the brackets are the square of the right-hand digit of the number on the left outside the brackets. The remaining digit (the second inside the brackets) is the square of the digit on the left of the number on the left outside the brackets.

97 7
Male forenames are:
Leonard
William
David
Jim
Eric
Tom
(Alternate letters in the outer ring)

Female forenames are:
Iris
Mavis
Sarah
Vera

Ann
Amy
(Alternate letters in the inner ring)

98 32

99 A 3,129 units
B £106.38

100 Cousin Margaret. The statements of Aunty Mary, Uncle Jim and cousin Margaret are
true.

101 29 cats each killed 73 rats

102 271

1st throw (5) becomes	15
2nd throw (4) becomes	19
3rd throw (4) becomes	4
4th throw (2) becomes	28
5th throw (6) becomes	72
6th throw (3) becomes	93
7th throw (2) becomes	38
8th throw (2) becomes	2
	271

103 A 4
B 3
C 2
In A the cube is rotating anti-clockwise vertically
In B it is rotating anti-clockwise vertically
In C it is rotating clockwise horizontally

104 A $3^1/_4$ miles. It is equal to 26 furlongs
B 4 quarts. It is equal to approximately 4.5 litres
C 78 millimetres. 3 inches is equal to 76 millimetres approximately.
D 1 pint. It is equal to 4 gills.

105 14
F is the largest
C is the smallest

A is 56 square centimetres
B is 55.25 square centimetres
C is 54.94 square centimetres
D is 55.44 square centimetres
E is 62.72 square centimetres
F is 71.91 square centimetres

106 8 and 6
64 (the square of 8) is deducted from 100 leaves 36 (the square of 6). Conversely, the square of 6, when deducted from 100, leaves 64 (the square of 8).

107 9
Divide the top number by the sum of the two facing numbers and the series becomes 2, 3, 4, 5 and 6 (if X is 9).

108 X is 22 and Y is 13
Fairly simple deduction, especially if you realized that there were no alternatives in the third horizontal row, which led to the solution for the first vertical row.

109 42
Each number represents its position in the square relative to the other numbers. So 21 has two blank squares above it and one blank square below it.

110 1901-1954. It is not possible to read 1955 boggle style.

111 A False
B True
C False
The near-side wheels rotate anti-clockwise, but the off-side wheels rotate clockwise! In C the acute angle is slightly more than 60 degrees, because by the time the minute hand reaches 10, the hour hand will have moved slightly past the figure 4.

112 J
The upper branches should point downwards, as in D, E and N.

113 D
All the others are divisible by 17

114 E
The lines are not parallel, as they are in all the others.

115 B
The only dice that has no centre spot. Alternatively, the spots add to 10 whereas all the others add to 9.

116 A, C, B, A. A scores 99; B scores 100; C scores 107.

117 315

The number in the centre squares is the product minus the sum of the three numbers in the corner squares around it. For example, in the top left hand quarter:
The product of 2, 3 and 4 is 24 and the sum of 2, 3 and 4 is 9: 24 - 9 = 15 – as shown in the adjacent corner square.

118 CHILDREN
Present time indicated – CH, A. Forward to 5.15 – IL, B. Back to 12.50 – DR, C. Back to 11.20 – EN.

119 A scores 78
B scores 80
C scores 84

120 + + + ÷ +, + + + + + ÷

121 Nails £1.20, Grease £1.25, Blades £1.50, Hammer £3.16

122 20

Because opposite sides of a die always total 7, the bottom face of the top die must be 6 (7-1). Faces 2 plus 3 and 4 plus 5 must both total 7. The total of the five faces is, therefore, $7 + 7 + 6 = 20$.

123 JONQUIL

The moves result as follows:

	Ball A	Ball B	Ball C
1st move	G	8	J
2nd move	H	9	O
3rd move	A	4	N
4th move	E	6	Q
5th move	U	7	U
6th move	K	6	I
7th move	I	8	L

124 A, B J and K

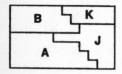

125 1 Ernie

3 Bert

5 Dave

7 Alf

9 Charles

126 C

Both circles C and A contain numbers that are squares of each other: Circle A (7-49; 12-144, 17-289, 3-9); circle C 12-144, 21-441, 15-225, 8-64)

127 $646 + 6 = 652$

128 C

Figures are produced from merging figures below, except that like portions disappear.

129 8 minutes

$$\frac{1}{9} + \frac{1}{24} - \frac{1}{36} = 0.12 \qquad \frac{1}{0.12} = 8 \text{ approx}$$

130 52642163

The numbers change from the number above in the following sequence:

ABCDEFGH   to   FDGBHEAC

131 216
   625

132 6 to 1 against

133 $7\frac{1}{2}$

134 12.10

135 9

136 10

137 C

Beginning with the segment containing O at approximately 10 o'clock in number 1, move clockwise. The segment next to it is removed in number 2 and in each subsequent figure. The number of segments in the circles decreases by one each time, so that from the initial 12 segments, the final circle contains only 6 segments.

138 Because only plus and minus signs are used there are many possible arrangements of these numbers.

Four examples are:

3+8-7+6-5+9-4

8-6-7+5+9+4-3

4-3+9+8+5-7-6

9-5+6-7+8+3-4

Any permutation of the numbers shown above (with the appropriate signs) would have satisfied the question. Of course, if division or multiplication had been required, the number of possible answers would have been very limited.

139 N

In no other figure is there a square within a square.

140 63145232152

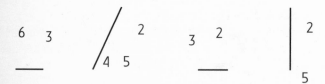

141 Starting from the top, the third hexagon in each straight row of three is the combination of lines from the previous two hexagons

142 2

The total of the numbers in the triangle (3 sides), 51, is divisible by 3; in the square (4 sides), 44 is divisible by 4; in the pentagon (5 sides), 125 is divisible by 5. Therefore, in the hexagon (6 sides), the total of the numbers must be divisible by 6. As the present numbers total 70, 2 must be added to make 72. Of the numbers offered, only 2 will bring the total to a number divisible by 6.

143 B

The minute hand moves to where the hour hand was in the previous clock; the hour hand advances first one hour, then two hours, then three, and so on. After number 5 the hour hand must advance 5 hours (to 7).

144 3

Subtract the total of the numbers in the inner ring from the total of the numbers in the outer ring. In the third circle the outer ring totals 24 and the inner ring 21.

145 441

The lowest number is 3 and the highest number is 39, so the midway number is 21. The number nearset to the lowest number is 4 and the number nearest to the highest number is 38, so the midway number is 21 again. 21 multiplied by 21 is 441.

146 C
The top and bottom circles change place each time; the other circles move clockwise throughout.

147 7848
The first two numbers inside the brackets reverse the number on the left outside the brackets. The next two numbers inside the brackets reverse the number on the right outside the brackets in the next line.

148 C
The spot is on the right of the right angle; in all the others it is on the left.

149 104
Each number is the sum of the digits in the previous number added to the previous number; 88 + 16 = 104

150 24

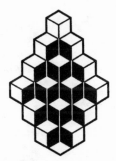

When viewed from above, there are 15 cubes; a further 9 can be seen when they are viewed from underneath. These nine can be seen more clearly if you focus your attention on the cubes with white bases and black side faces emphasizes here.

151 A
In A there are two right-angled triangles, one isosceles triangle and one scalene triangle. In all the others there are: one right-angled triangle, one equilateral triangle, one isosceles triangle and one scalene triangle.

152 4   1
   1   2

Start at the bottom left-hand corner and work up the first column, then along the top and round the perimeter, gradually spiralling into the centre and repeating the numbers 143682

153 He was born in August in a town called March, became a priest and married his widowed mother to her second husband in February

154 A-I-K-N,
B-F-P-U
C-H-O-S
D-E-M-T
G-J-L-R

155 X is 10 and Y is 9
Consider the same segments that are occupied by x and y in the other circles:

8	9	10(X)	11
11	10	9(Y)	8

156 F
The black sides of the centre square rotate anti-clockwise; the black sides of the outer square rotate clockwise. In F the black sides of the centre square have rotated clockwise.

157 B and R

158 X is 12, Y is 0 and Z is 3

159 D
The black square moves anti clockwise, first one position, then two, then three, and so on. All the other squares move in the same way.

160 6
There are two separate series here. Starting with the first term and taking alternate terms thereafter:
625   25   5
Each term is the square root of the previous term.
Starting with the second term:

1296   36   6
Again, each term is the square root of the previous number.

161 MOSCOW
This problem is based on the fact that 26 cards make half of a full deck of playing cards, and there are also 26 letters of the alphabet. These 26 letters are represented by the cards at the top:

Clubs	Ace to 6	A to F
Spades	Ace to 6	G to L
Hearts	Ace to 6	M to R
Diamonds	Ace to 6	S to Z

Thus the cards at the bottom are

Ace of hearts	13th letter	M
3 of hearts	15th letter	O
Ace of diamonds	19th letter	S
3 of clubs	3rd letter	C
3 of hearts	15th letter	O
5 of diamond	23rd letter	W

162 1416
In the first line divide the number on the left by 4 and the number on the right by 5, placing the results inside the brackets. In the second line divide the number on the left by 6 and the number on the right by 7, placing the results inside the brackets. Following this procedure, in the third line divide the number on the left by 8(14) and the number on the right by 9 (16), placing the results inside the brackets (1416).

163 A
From an examination of the black stripes on the vanes, the following facts emerge:

Rotates anti-clockwise 1 position

Rotates anti-clocwise 2 positions

Rotates clockwise 1 position

Rotates clockwise 2 positions

Rotates anti clockwise 1 position

Rotates anti-clockwise 2 positions

The Great Book of Brainteasers

164 Striped.

Whoever had built the podium had started at the left and built the bottom row, then continued along the top row from right to left in the sequence striped/black/white

165 Immediately to the left of the number 2

Start at the top right-hand corner and work along the top and back along the next row, counting 9 then 8 then 7 etc before entering each subsequent number

166 21/8 (approx 2.125)
Convert all the fractions into vulgar fractions:

1/5	2/5	3/5	4/5	5/5
1/3	3/3	5/3	7/3	9/3
1/4	4/4	7/4	10/4	13/4
1/8	5/8	9/8	13/8	$(1^7/_8)$

The final fraction could be $1^7/_8$ or $2^1/_8$
But as in the examples, vulgar fractions alternate with decimal fractions throughout. Also, as in the examples, the answer must be expressed in a unit and afracation:
$2^1/_8$
(You may have converted all the fractions into decimal fraactions. In all but the second row this would have been valid, giving a final answer of 2.125. There are however, two fallacies:
a) there are no perfect decimal fractions for 1/3 or $1^2/_3$, as they are recurring decimals, as in 2.33 recurring;
b) the already established alternating sequence of vulgar and decimal fractions should be maintained.

167 9

The numbers move one position clockwise at a time. Starting with 3 in the first square, the progression is:

3   4   5   6

Starting with 6 in the first square:

6   7   8   (9)

Starting with 5 in the first square:

5   6   7   8

Starting with 4 in the first square:

4   5   6   7

168 55

Divide the number on the left by 5 and multiply the number on the right by 5, entering the two results inside the brackets:

25   (55)   1

169 D

Sections only appear black in the final circle when they are a white in both the previous circles looking across and down.

170

$$\frac{7}{11} \times \frac{33}{28} = \frac{3}{4}$$

171 5

Each smaller segments in A, B C add up to 20

172

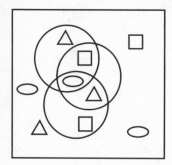

173 9825

Turn the page upside down and add up the two numbers

174 A

moves 90° clockwise   moves 90° anti-clockwise

175

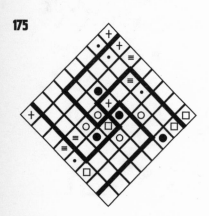

176 20 to 1 against

177 A 130
B 25
C 122

A	9	15	21	25	27	33				
B	4	10	16	18	22	28	32	36	40	44
C	3	7	11	13	17	19	23	29		

178 B Cassia is a tropical tree; Cassius and Casca were conspirators against Julius Caesar

179 289
The sum of the two numbers outside the brackets is squared to give the number inside the brackets.
289 is the square of 17 – the sum of 6 and 11

180 The middle pair of numbers (7 and 1) add to 8. The numbers from the middle to the right pair with their corresponding numbers on the left to add to 8

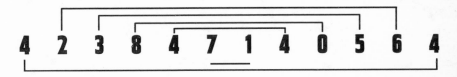

181 5
They are consecutive numbers on a dart board.

182 C
The others, cut in half vertically, all form words, i.e. elf, cell and fleece

183

So that when viewed in a mirror the numbers 1,2,3,4,5 appear in sequence

184 26
A contains 4;
B contains 6;
C contains 6;
D contains 10

185 F
The top shape moves to the bottom in each following column.
F should be:

186

A	16	17
B	17	17
C	16	17

187 9 moves

A	7	6	5	4	3	2	1	9	8
B	1	3	5	7	9	2	4	6	8
C	2	5	8	2	5	8	2	5	8

188 3121

189 Alice has twins aged 3 and triplets aged 1
Beth has triplet aged 2 and twins aged 1

Section Four

The Great Book of Brainteasers

1 The total of the three teeth meshed at point A is 6 (3, 2, and 1). The three teeth meshed at B total 28 (5, 11 and 12). When X rotates anti-clockwise to Y, what will be the total of the six teeth meshed at A and B?

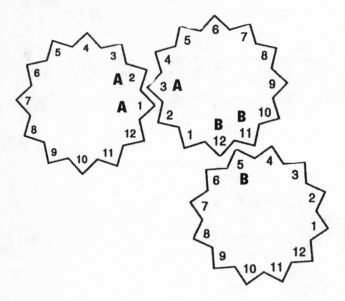

2 Which row is the odd one out?

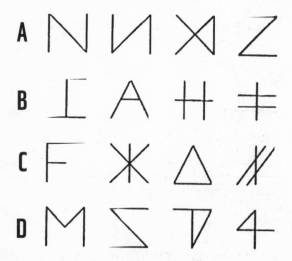

3 Which two make a matching pair?

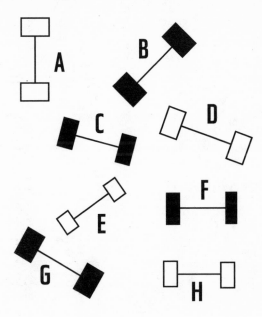

4 Taking one number from each column and using each number only once, how many groups of three that add up to 10 can you find?

1	8	1
6	5	3
9	4	1
3	1	3
5	1	2
2	0	1
4	7	0
7	4	2
0	0	2
8	9	1

5 A clock showed the exact time at midnight on 31 December 1987. If it gained two seconds every day, what time would it have shown at midnight on 31 December 1988? Give the exact time in hours, minutes and seconds.

6 Which is the odd one out?

A 9 8 6 3 1 4 7

B 6 1 5 3 2 0 3

C 4 7 9 0 1 8 2

D 1 6 7 2 1 0 4

E 3 2 4 4 2 8 6

F 4 6 7 3 1 1 2

G 7 8 8 1 1 9 4

7 What are A, B and C? (There are three clues.)

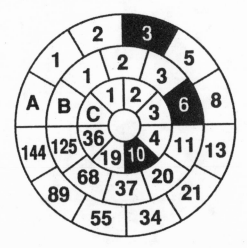

8 If 54 balls are placed into the three receptacles, so that there are twice as many in the cylinder and bucket combined as there are in the box, and twice as many in the box as there are in the bucket, how many balls are there in the cylinder?

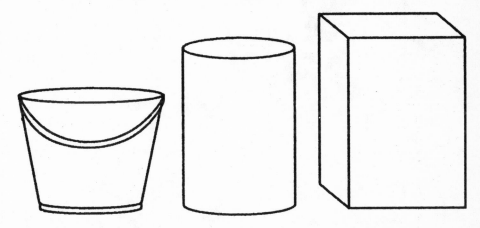

9 This problem is for mental solving only! Do not use a pencil and paper. Add the alternative numbers in A to the alternate numbers in B and divide the result by the sum of the alternate numbers in C.

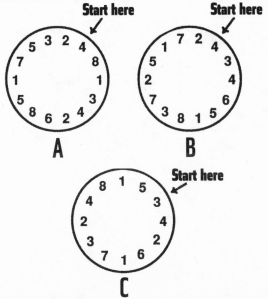

The Great Book of Brainteasers

Routes

10 How many different routes are there from A to B. Each route must not travel over the same piece of road more than once.

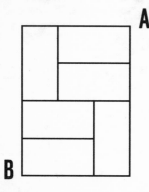

For example, one possible route is shown below

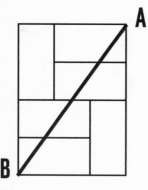

Fifteen Magic

11

4	3	8
9	5	1
2	7	6

In the above each horizontal, vertical and corner to corner line totals 15. But what if the number 8 is repositioned as below? Is it still possible to place a different number in each square so that each horizontal, vertical and corner to corner line again totals 15? You will find, that with a bit of lateral thinking, it is possible.

8		

12 In these epicyclic gears, when pinion A completes three revolutions where will the tooth marked X on pinion B be? Choose from A, B, C and D below

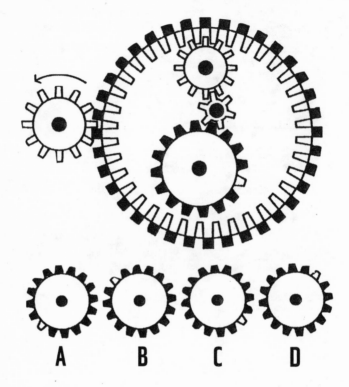

A   **B**   **C**   **D**

13 Three receptacles contain certain amounts of water as indicated below. How much water would have to be poured from A into B and C so that each receptacle contains the same?

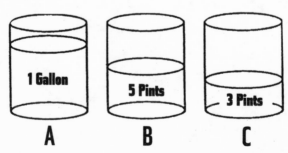

1 Gallon   5 Pints   3 Pints

A   **B**   **C**

14 Which is the odd one out?

15 What are X, Y and Z?

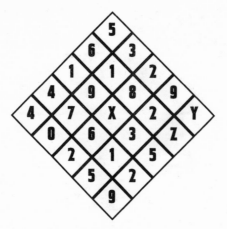

16 Here is a map of Australia. If you flew direct from Perth to the following towns in the order listed, which of the three routes shown below would you follow? Adelaide Melbourne Brisbane Sydney

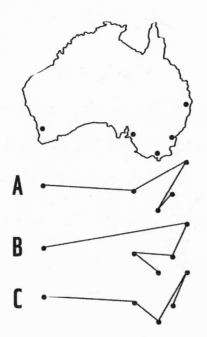

17 Consider pairs of opposite numbers on the dartboard shown below. Subtract the sum of the five lowest pairs from the sum of the five highest pairs.

18 A holiday brochure quotes as follows:

14 days £210

Long Stay £62 per week after first fortnight

Children under 10 half price

Children under 5 free

Single room supplement £1.50 per day

How much would it cost a man to take his wife and two children - one four years old and the other nine years old - and his 17-year-old nephew for six weeks? His nephew will have his own separate room.

19 What is X?

11 4 8 7 6 X 4 1
0 5 2 1 1 9

20 These two clocks are erratic time-keepers: clock A loses 15 minutes in every hour, while clock B gains 20 minutes in every hour. In how many hours will they again show an exact hour, and what time will each clock show then?

21 In each row there is one die that does not agree with the other dice in the same row. State the three dice.

Sequence

22   **3**

     13

     1113

     3113

     2123

     112213

     312213

     212223

     114213

     ?

What comes next?

Dials

23 What number is missing from the bottom dial?

257

312

327

342

?

24 What is X?

3 12 83 130 3 130 313 1303 1 X 31

25 What is X?

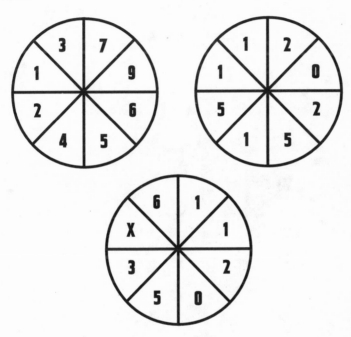

26 Multiply the number that is midway between the lowest number and the one that is nearest to the highest number by the number that is midway between the highest number and the one that is nearest to the lowest number.

39 9 26 49 5
35 51 43 14 41
8 11 7 38 30

27 Which is the odd one out?

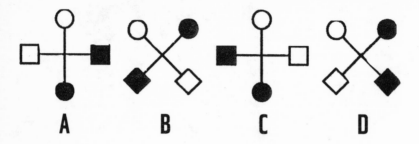

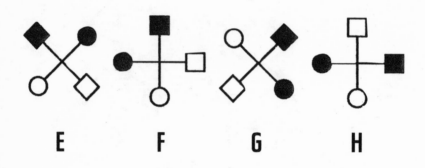

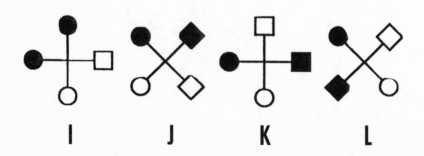

28 Which five of the pieces shown below will form the square?

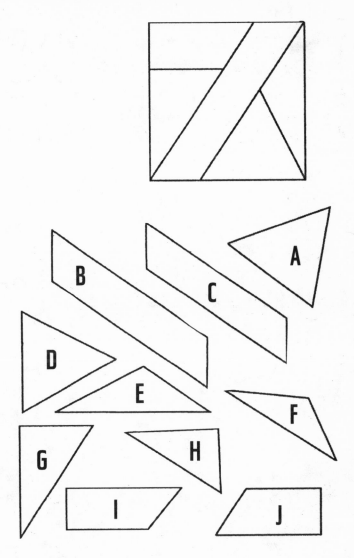

29 How would you arrange the weights on the pans of the scales so that you could weigh the following?

A. 19 kilograms B. 25 kilograms C. 31 kilograms

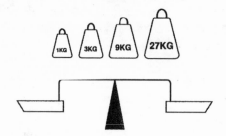

30 What goes into the empty brackets?

1 2 3 4 (4 1 6 3 5 8 7) 5 6 7 8

6 2 7 1 (1 6 3 7 8 4 5) 8 3 5 4

3 8 5 4 (4 3 2 5 1 6 7) 1 2 7 6

4 7 6 2 (   ) 3 6 5 1

31 A revolves at 40 revolutions a minute; B revolves $1^{1}/_{2}$ times as fast as A; C revolves twice as fast as B; and D revolves half as fast as all the others put together. At how many revolutions a minute does D revolve?

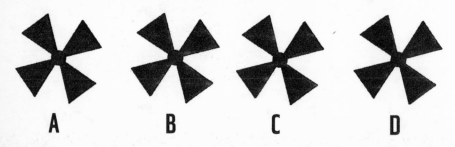

A   B   C   D

Hymn Numbers

32 "What are these numbers?", asked a new member of the congregation. "They are hymn numbers", replied his companion. "So why is there a question mark at the
bottom", replied the stranger. "Reverend Jones always does that", said his companion, "the congregation has to try and work out the number of the last hymn for themselves during the service".

What should be the number of the last hymn?

15

1

9

21

?

The Great Book of Brainteasers

The Stranger

33 Alan and his sister Sue had gone to meet their mother at the railway station. Suddenly Sue gasped out loudly in surprise and remarked to her brother, "Do you see that man in the crowd over there?" "Its Brian", said Alan, "I don't believe it, quick, we must go and introduce ourselves".

Neither Alan nor Sue had ever met Brian before, nor had they ever seen a photograph or painting of him, neither was he a famous person.

How is this possible?

34 Each of the nine squares in the grid marked 1A to 3C, should incorporate all the lines and symbols which are shown in the squares of the same letter and number immediately above and to the left. For example, 2B should incorporate all the lines and symbols that are in 2 and B. One of the squares is incorrect. Which one is it?

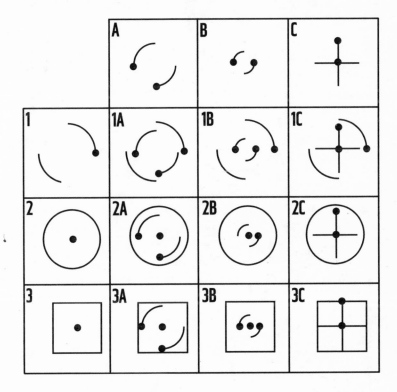

35 These 12 objects can be placed in 3 sets of 4. The sets are:
4 DOGS, 4 ANIMALS, 4 REPTILES

CLUMBER   **BONGO**   **TUMBLER**   **ROEBUCK**

POINTER   **LURCHER**   **AGUTI**   **TAIPAN**

TERRIER   **CAIMAN**   **SAURIAN**   **PADDOCK**

The Great Book of Brainteasers

36 Each line and symbol which appears in the four outer circles, above, is transferred to the centre circle according to these rules:

If a line or symbol occurs in the outer circles:
once: it is transferred
twice: it is possibly transferred
3 times: it is transferred
4 times: it is not transferred.

Which of the circles A, B, C, D, E, shown below should appear at the centre of the diagram, above?

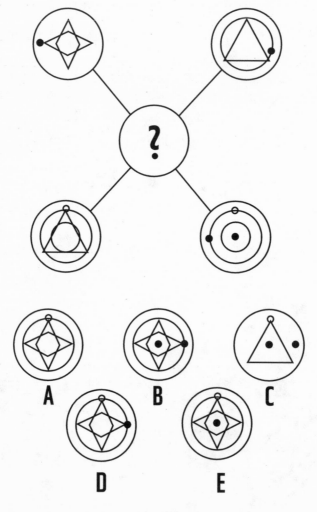

37 Each of the nine squares in the grid marked 1A to 3C, should incorporate all the lines and symbols which are shown in the squares of the same letter and number immediately above and to the left. For example, 2B should incorporate all the lines and symbols that are in 2 and B.   One of the squares is incorrect. Which one is it?

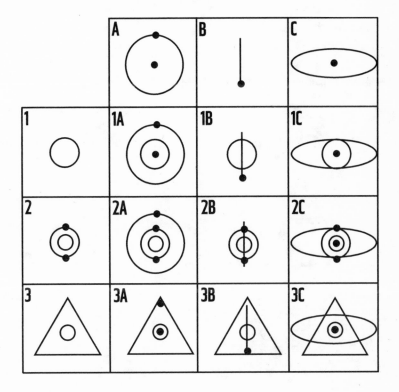

38 These objects can be placed in 3 sets of 4. The sets are:
4 VEGETABLES, 4 INSECTS, 4 REPTILES

· **MONITOR**   · **BLACK FLY**   **SKIRRET**   · **MAY BUG**

· **MILLIPEDE**   · **BASILISK**   **COCKCHAFER**   · **PIMENTO**

· **CROCODILE**   · **BROCCOLI** ˑ **ANACONDA**   **COLEWORT**

The Great Book of Brainteasers

39 Each line and symbol which appears in the four outer circles, above, is transferred to the centre circle according to these rules:

If a line or symbol occurs in the outer circles:
once: it is transferred
twice: it is possibly transferred
3 times: it is transferred
4 times: it is not transferred.

Which of the circles A, B, C, D, E, shown below should appear at the centre of the diagram, above?

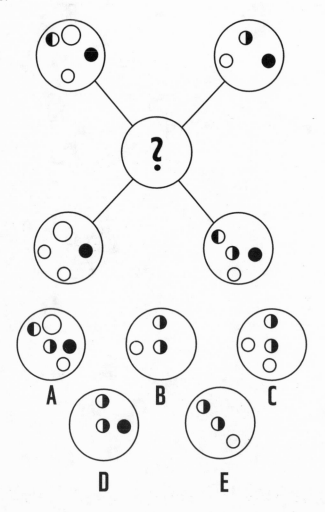

Missing Number

40 "Here's a puzzle for you", said young Tony to his classmate. "What is the missing number in this sequence?"

7, ? , 951, 620, 3

"Not sure" replied Susan, "will I need a calculator to work it out?" "A calculator might help" replied Tony.

"Aha!, I see what you mean" said Sue.

What is the missing number?

Apples

41 My neighbour returned from his orchard with an armful of apples. To my youngest son he gave half of the apples plus half an apple. To my second eldest son he gave half what he had left plus half an apple and to my eldest son he also gave half what he had left plus half an apple.

He than had no apples left.

How many apples did he have originally?

42 Which of the numbered arrows belongs to X?

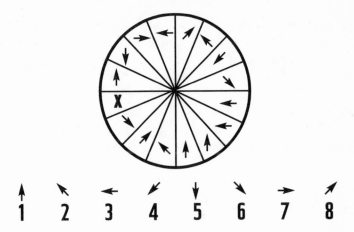

43 Pinion A is the driving pinion, while pinion B idles on its stub axle.
The black teeth of these pinions are in mesh with teeth in the outer ring.
(A) After four revolutions of A in an anti-clockwise direction, where will the black tooth of pinion B be?
(B) And where will it be when A has revolved clockwise through one revolution and then to where the tooth marked X meshes with the outer ring?

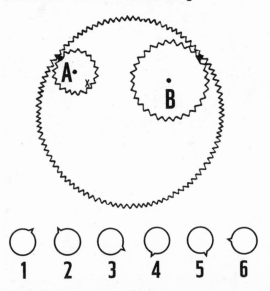

44 Which of the numbers in the bottom line should be placed under 17 in the top line?

2 3 4 5 6 7 8 9 10 11 17

7 2 17 6 13 8 3 5 4

9 15 20 33 21 25

45 What comes next in this series?

I S I T P N A A

D L I I Y N –

46 These clocks are all wrong, as indicated. If they are all correctly adjusted, which clock will show the nearest time to 12 o'clock?

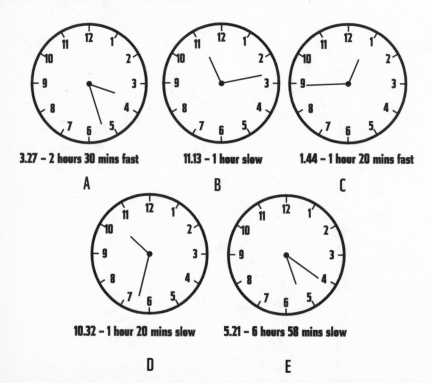

3.27 – 2 hours 30 mins fast | 11.13 – 1 hour slow | 1.44 – 1 hour 20 mins fast

A   B   C

10.32 – 1 hour 20 mins slow   5.21 – 6 hours 58 mins slow

D   E

47 Imagine that blocks X and Y are removed from the arrangement below, and that the remaining shape is turned upside-down. Which of the other shapes will be the result?

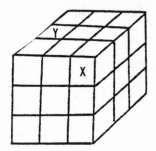

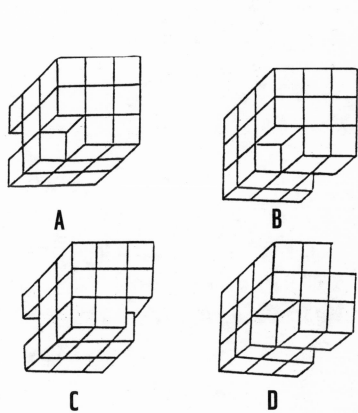

A   B

C   D

48

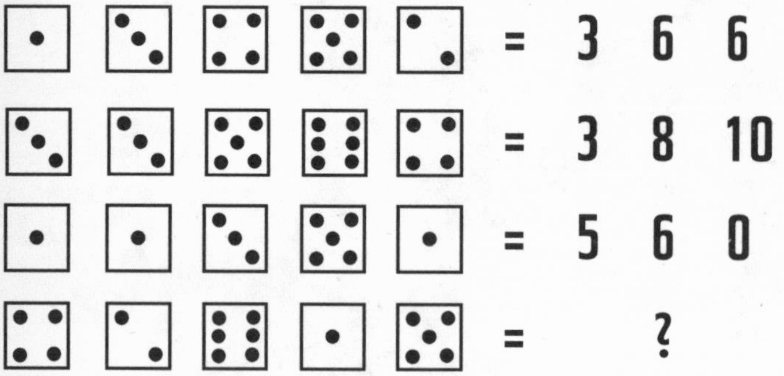

[1] [3] [4] [5] [2] = 3 6 6

[4] [3] [5] [6] [2] = 3 8 10

[1] [1] [3] [5] [1] = 5 6 0

[4] [2] [6] [1] [5] = ?

49 What comes next?

2 3 4 6 1 2 2 0

1 8 4 8 1 0 –

50 Without using a pocket calculator, which of these investments would give the greatest interest?

A £1,000 @ 5% simple interest for 4 years;

B £700 @ 8% compound interest for 3 years;

C £900 @ 7% simple interest for 3 years;

D £800 @ 6% compound interest for 4 years.

51 Discover the key from these problems and then break this NAVAL code.

				2	1
1	2			2	2
3	4	6	8	1	3
4	9	5	2	1	1
-----	-----	-----	-----	---	---
A	B	T	E	E	S

7 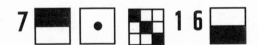 6 7

52 Give values for A, B and C:

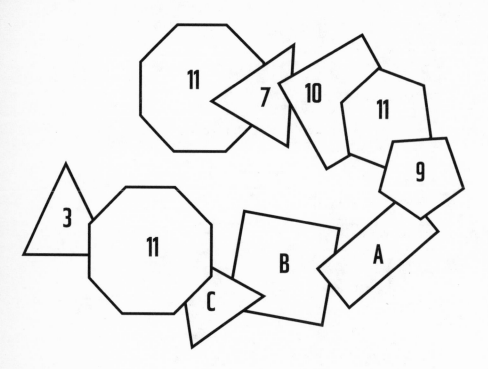

53 What is X?

15 11 19 20 X 5 3 17 2 9 6

54 What is the final term in this series?

0 8 24 48 80 –

A Missing Number

55 "What number is missing from this sequence?" asked Sally

4, 6, 2, 7, ?, 4, 8

"I think it should be 4 " replied Hilary.

"So, what comes next in this sequence?" asked Hilary

2, 4, 5, 4, 2, 4, ?

"I know it is 8 ", said Sally

"Correct" said Hilary.

"This is all beyond me", said John, "but try me with another."

"OK" said Sally, "What number comes between four and four in the sequence below?"

4, 6, 5, 7, 4 ,?, 4, 2, 3, 8, 5

Can you solve the puzzle?

The Great Book of Brainteasers

Clocks

56 The five clocks on adjoining platforms at our local train station seem to have developed a mind of their own.

The clocks on platforms 1 - 4 are shown below.

What should be the time of the clock on platform 5?

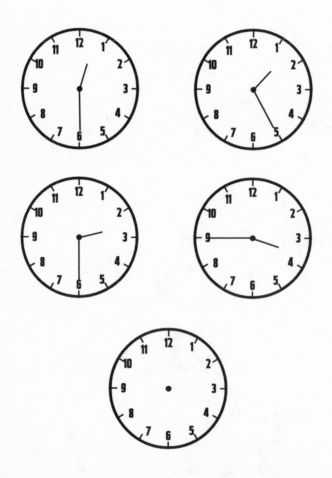

57 Which of these statements are true and which are false?
(A) 1 mile in 55 seconds shows a higher average speed that $^3/_4$ mile in 50 seconds.
(B) 2 gallons is more than 9 litres.
(C) The area of this rectangle

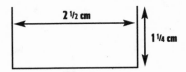

is greater than the area of this circle

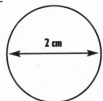

(D) Given that a jack counts as 11 and queen as 12 and a king as 13, the total number of spots on a set of dominoes is greater than that of all the picture cards.

58 What is X?

3	4	5	9	6	7	8
12	10	9	10	11	16	14
7	3	2	30	12	13	17
1	2	3	24	9	10	11
41	7	8	X	22	19	16

59 What is X?

60 What comes next in this series?

1 2 6 2 4 1 2 0 7 2 0 5 0 4 –

61 Each day the hour hand moves forward one hour, while the minute hand goes back five minutes. In how many days will the clock show eleven o'clock?

62 In the game of 'running out' at dominoes each player has to lay a domino so that the number of spots on one half matches those exposed at either end of the previously laid dominoes, as follows:

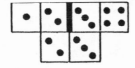

If the next player held the domino shown below it could be placed at either end, with the 1-spot matching that on the left or the 4-spot matching that in the right:

In the layout of a game shown below the order in which the dominoes were played is indicated. Can you detect the two fallacies in this? (Indicate by the numbers printed beside the dominoes.)

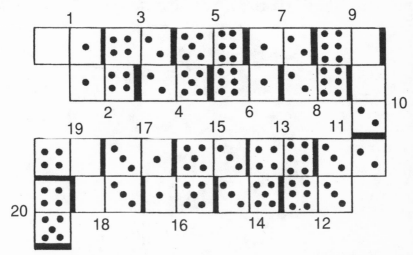

Probability

63 Two identical bags each contain eight balls, four white and four black.

One ball is drawn out of bag one and another ball out of bag two.

What are the chances that at least one of the balls will be black?

Wage Increase

64 The management offered the work-force a 2% wage increase over and above the rate of inflation providing they could increase productivity by no less than 2.7% per week.

If the company works a 6-day week and puts on a night-shift for just 2 days per week, and works one Sunday every four weeks, by how much per day over a monthly period must the work-force increase production to achieve their target?

65 A motorist drives for 200 miles. When in motion his average speed is 30mph. En route he stops for 20 minutes for refreshments and a further 5 minutes for petrol.

(A) How long does the journey take?
(B) Taking account of the delays, what is his average speed for the journey? (Answer to the nearest whole number.)

66 What should the final digit be?

2 5 26 677 45833 –

67 Which of these sums, if any, are wrong?

A	B	C	D	E
3.68	1.3	1.15	2.4	1.15
$1\,^{8}/_{25}$	$3\,^{1}/_{10}$	$1\,^{2}/_{25}$	$3\,^{1}/_{2}$	$4\,^{7}/_{20}$
2.125	2.61	1.37	1.65	2.75
$2\,^{7}/_{8}$	$2\,^{99}/_{100}$	$6\,^{1}/_{2}$	$2\,^{1}/_{20}$	$1\,^{3}/_{4}$
10	10	10	10	10

68 What is X?

2 13 7 5 6 X 15 18 24 29 36 49 51

69 What are X, Y, and Z?

1	6	3	7	2
4	9	7	5	6
53	75	Z	57	18
36	25	Y	27	8
12	X	12	18	2

70 Five towns, A, B, C, D and E, are situated consecutively so that when joined by straight roads they form the five points of an irregular pentagon.

B is 100 miles from A, its right-hand neighbour; E is 50 miles from D, its right-hand neighbour. From A to C via B is 125 miles; E is 75 miles from its neighbour, A, and 70 miles from C.

1 What is the length of the journey from A to E via B, C and D?

2 How far from B is E by the shortest route?

3 What is the distance from C to D?

71 Which of the figures below belongs to X?

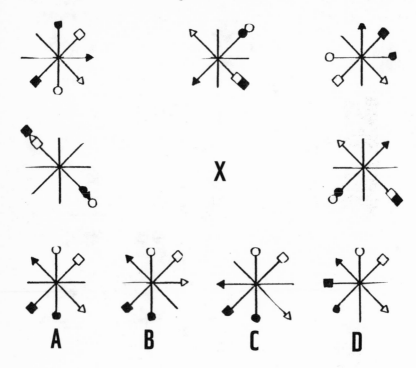

72 What is X?

2	3	12	1
4	1	5	12
9	4	17	80
6	5	24	37
3	8	32	41
5	2	11	18
7	3	X	28

73 In a cricket match, each player of one team was bowled 1st ball. Which player was 0 not out?

74

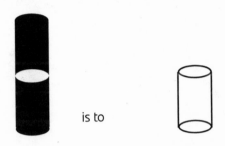

is to

as

is to

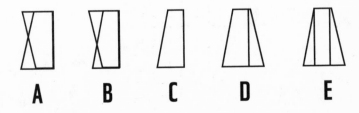

A   B   C   D   E

Time Teaser

75 Three trains start at different times on a 100-mile journey. Train A leaves 10 minutes late and stops at a station for 5 minutes. Its average speed is 40mph. Train B leaves 20 minutes late and stops at a station for 14 minutes. Its average speed is 50mph. Which train completes the journey in the shortest time?

Missing Letter

76 What is the missing letter

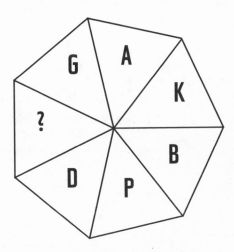

The Great Book of Brainteasers

77 Write down the tenth term of 18, 54, 162,, -------
There is a formula for finding the answer.

78 What number is missing from the grid?

16	9	7
20	15	5
8	21	?

79 We have 100 sweets in five bowls

1st and 2nd = 52

2nd and 3rd = 43

3rd and 4th = 34

4th and 5th = 30

How many sweets in each bowl?

80 These 12 creatures can be placed in 3 sets of 4. The 3 sets are:
4 ANIMALS, 4 FISH, 4 BIRDS

DOTTREL   **SQUID**   **LAMPREY**   **BUBALIS**

DASYPUS   **BITTERN**   **BANTING**   **CHAFFINCH**

MERLING   **HAMSTER**   **GROUPER**   **DOVE**

81 What number should replace the ?

| 121 | 100 | ? | 64 | 49 |

82 What time should appear on the 4th clock?

83 This clock has gone mad! Every minute the second hand goes back - first one second, then two, then three and so on; the minute hand goes forward first two minutes, then three, then four and so on; the hour hand goes back first three hours, then four, then five and so on. What exact time will it show five minutes from now?

84 What is X?

17   24   93   14   X   31   41   39   42   71

85 How many minutes before 12 noon is it if 50 minutes ago it was four times as many minutes past 10?

Palindromes

86 Was it a car or a cat I saw is an example of a palindromic sentence, in that it is the same when read forwards or backwards.

A palindromic number, therefore, is one that is the same when read backwards or forwards, as for example, the number 4521254, or the sequence; 23, 961, 42, 41, 693, 2.

Below is a series of numbers which are not palindromic, however, by applying a simple formula to each of the numbers they can be quickly transformed into a palindromic sequence.

3, 11, 12, 21, 2, 14, 1, 13

What is the formula and what are the resulting numbers?

Dotty

87

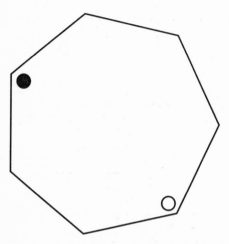

At each stage the black dot moves counter-clockwise and the white dot moves four corners clockwise.

In how many stages will both dots be in the same corner together?

88 6 3 7 4 is to G F D C

as

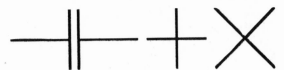

is to

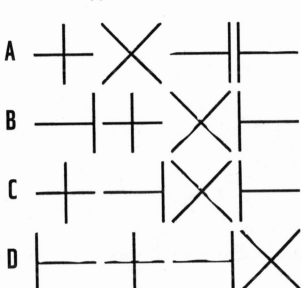

89 Which is the granny knot among the reef knots?

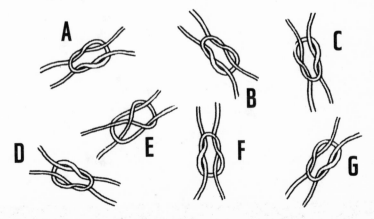

90 Add the sum of the prime numbers listed below to that of the even numbers and divide the result by 75.

4 5 6 7 8 9 10 11 12 13
14 15 16 17 18 19 20 21 22 23

91 What is X?

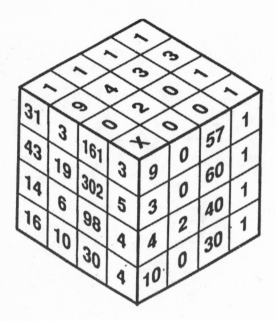

92 What is X?

31	6
4	9

7	35
8	5

7	10
4	39

3	X
43	13

93 Which of the figures below comes after number 7?

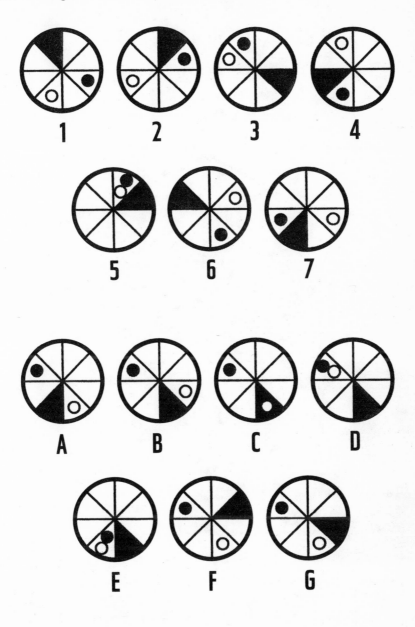

94 What are X, Y and Z?

95 Using two, three and four of these numbers, make three totals of 100:

5 9 17 19 22 36 41 42 64

96 There are 134 sweets coloured red and white in a bag. If there were two fewer red ones there would be twice as many red ones as white ones. How many of each colour are there?

97 What is X?

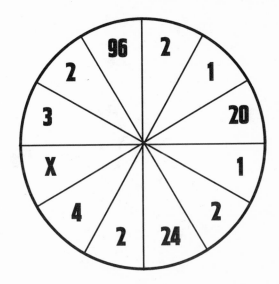

98 Multiply the lowest even number in A by the highest odd number in B; add the lowest even number in C and divide by the highest prime number in D.

7	8	9
10	6	11
1	5	3

A

B

74	66	70
65	67	72
66	69	68

7	5	6
9	8	4
3	1	10

C

D

3	8	11	14
15	7	9	21
13	19	16	18

Cards

99 Insert the remaining numbers between 1 - 9 on the cards so that the five-figure number formed by the top row is six times greater than the four-figure number formed by the bottom row.

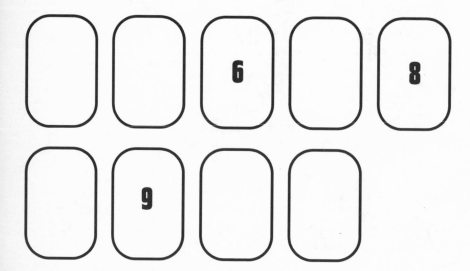

Winnings

100 Alan won £30 on the horses.

"That's lucky" said Kate, "Now you have five times as much money as you would have had if you had lost £30".

How much money had Alan after he had won £30?

101 What goes into the empty brackets?

147 (72) 312

55 (110) 218

111 (   ) 2

102 Decide which of these statements are true and which are false.

A Sydney is the capital of Australia.

B Julius Caesar invaded Britain in 55 BC.

C. Beethoven wrote only one opera.

D Gauguin was a Spanish post–impressionist painter.

103 What is the total of the numbers that are squares of whole numbers?

24   38   117   16   128   46

245   175   32   256   18   62

104 What comes next?

8 2 4 8 2 16 8 128 16 –

105 When the black pinion has made 3 ¹/₂ revolutions clockwise, where will the tooth marked X be on the white pinion?

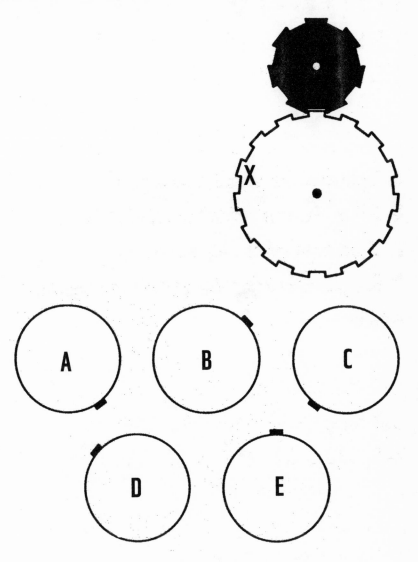

The Great Book of Brainteasers

106 The black ball moves clockwise, first to the next corner, then missing one, then two and so forth (missing an extra corner each time.) The white ball moves anti-clockwise in the same way. In how many moves will they be side by side?

107 Which two of these shapes will form a perfect square?

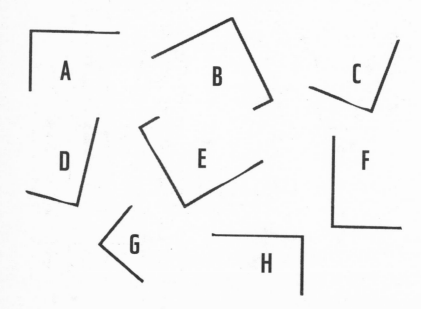

108 What is the largest total you can score in moving from A to B without moving backwards?

```
                                16
                                15
                                14  6  5
                                13     9
                                12     6
 4  2  1  18  3  2  11     3
 2         17         10     2
 4          2          9  8  2
 6          1          8     2
 1          5          7     1
 3  1  1    4          6     1
            2          5  3  1  4
            3  2  1    4        1
                       3        2
                       2  1  3  1
                       1
```

109 Eastwich is 12 miles from Westwich. Middlewich is midway between them. Northwich is 8 miles from Middlewich. How far from Northwich is Westwich?

110 The four vanes extending from four faces of the octagon move as follows: [•] one face clockwise [• •] two faces anti-clockwise; [• • •] three faces clockwise; [• • • •] four faces anti-clockwise. What will be their positions after four moves? (Choose from A, B, C, or D.)

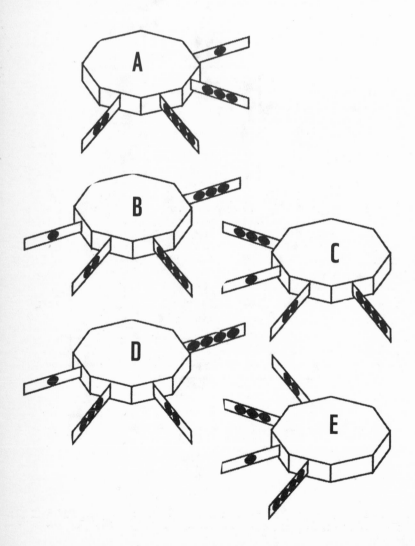

Boring party

111 By 7 pm all the party guests had arrived but by 8 pm a third of them had departed. By 9 pm a third of those remaining had also departed. By 10 pm the same happened again and a third of those remaining had also departed. Finally the party ended at 11 pm by which time a further third of those remaining had also departed, and by 11 pm only 16 guests still remained.

How many guests were originally at the party at 7 pm?

The Great Book of Brainteasers

Tennis Championship

112 A total of 421 matches were played in our local County Men's Singles Amateur Tennis Championship this year.

Apart from three contestants who scratched out of the preliminary round because they were away on holiday, and one player who scratched out of the second round due to sustaining an injury in the previous round, all matched were played.

Can you say how many people entered the Championships?

113 Which number is the odd one out?

8 9 3 6 5 4 2

114 A man entered a casino. The croupier offered £100 if he could throw a 6 with a standard die. If he failed he would have one more chance. How much should the croupier ask for a non-returnable stake?

115 A wire 1/100 inch in diameter is tightly wound around a ball of 24 ins. Diameter. What is the length of the wire?

24" diameter

116 $x + y + y = 1$

$x^2 + y^2 + y^2 = 2$

$x^3 + y^3 + y^3 = 3$

$x^4 + y^4 + y^4 = ?$

What number should replace the question mark?

117 Each of the nine squares in the grid marked 1A to 3C, should incorporate all the lines and symbols which are shown in the squares of the same letter and number immediately above and to the left. For example, 2B should incorporate all the lines and symbols that are in 2 and B. One of the squares is incorrect. Which one is it?

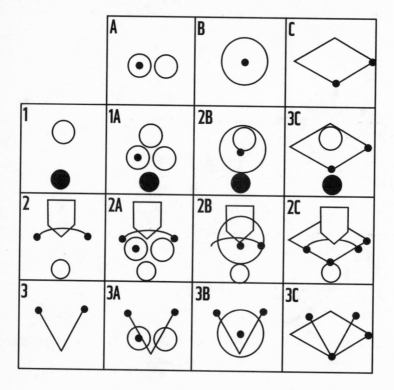

118   **124**

816

326

412

82?

What number should replace the question mark?

119 What number should replace the X?

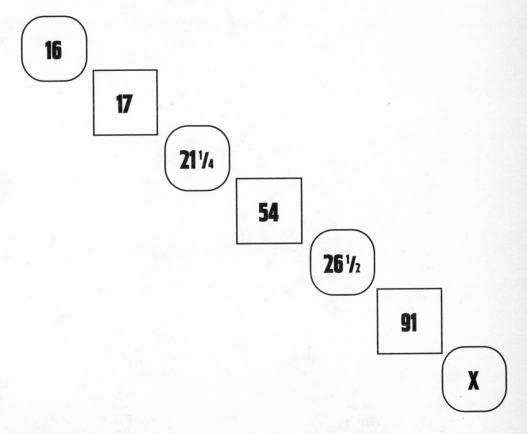

Farmyard

120 In the farmyard are a number of pigs and hens.

There are twice as many hens as pigs and if you add the total number of heads between them to the total number of legs, you get 154.

How many are there of each animal?

Walls

121 If a man and a half can build a wall and a half in a day and a half, how many walls do six men build in 6 days?

122 What is X?

5 3 4 1 2 4 2 8 6 X

123 Which of the following statements are true and which are false?

A. At 12.30 the hands of a clock form an angle of 180 degrees.

B. 15/16th is the same as 0.9375.

C. The Andes are south of the Rockies.

D. 15 capital letters of the alphabet consist entirely of straight strokes.

124 Take the number that is midway between the highest and lowest numbers that are divisible by 13. Multiply this by the lowest even number, and subtract the highest odd number.

117	8	63	43
143	12	97	39
136	27	91	3

125 Which is the odd one out?

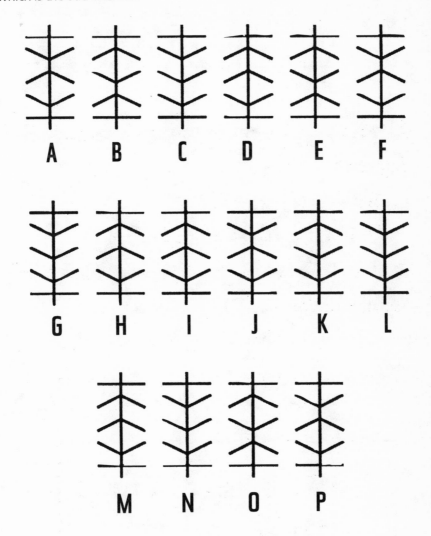

126 What is X?

1 7 8 14 X 30 20 6 14 7 8

127 On the dart-board shown below the outer ring doubles the numbers and the inner ring trebles them. Player A starts on a single 20 and moves clockwise in alternate segments. The next dart lands in a double, and the next one in a treble, and so on (a single, followed by a double, followed by a treble). Player B starts on a single 1 and moves alternately clockwise in the same manner. What are their individual scores after each player has thrown 10 darts?

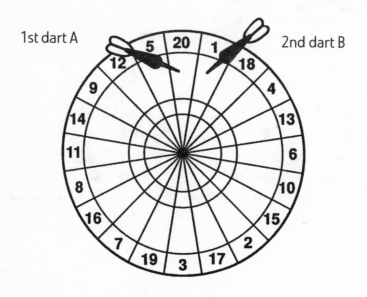

1st dart A

2nd dart B

128 Which the odd one out?

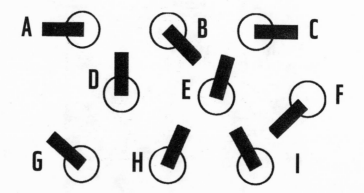

129 Which of the numbers below takes the place of X?

7 3 9 7 12 X 16 18 21 25

5 6 8 12 14 15

130 Which triangle below will not fit into the design?

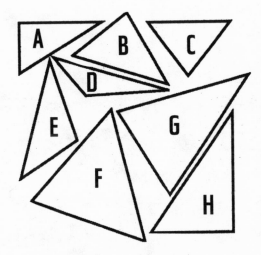

131 What is X?

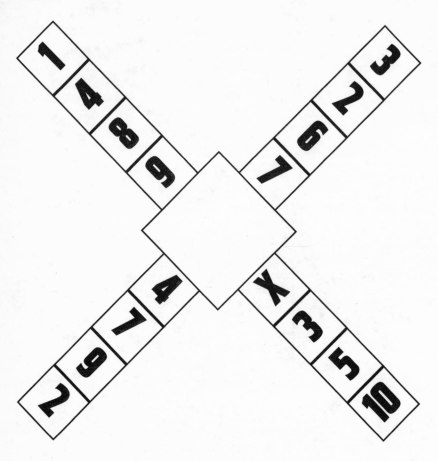

132 What is X?

6   4   18   14   X   16   30   15   32   1   28   9   8   3

Canes

133 I put two canes in my garden, one being 5 feet above the ground and the other 4 feet.
I tied a 6 foot long piece of twine 6 inches from the top of each cane. The twine hung down so that it came slightly more than 1 foot above the ground.

How far apart are the two garden canes?

Stick Stacks

134 The wind has blown a number of sticks onto the lawn in 5 distinct piles.

Four of the piles have a common feature. Which is the odd one out?

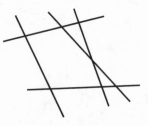

135

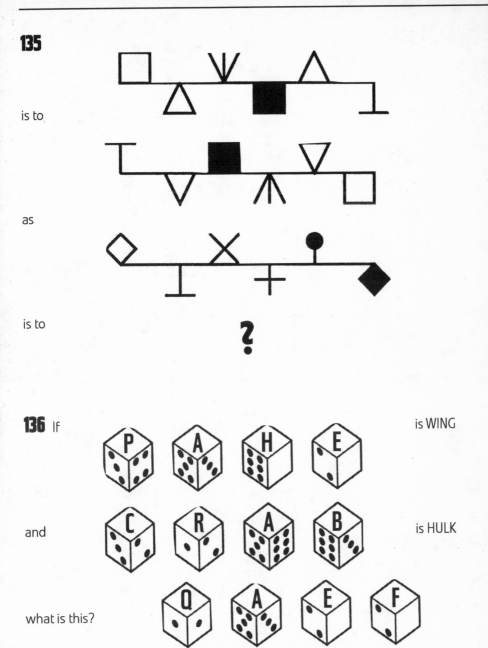

is to

as

is to

?

136 If   P A H E   is WING

and   C R A B   is HULK

what is this?   Q A E F

137 The counters are moved according to the throw of the die. The throws of the die are as follows 4, 6, 1, 2, 4. Which will be the first counter to reach 21?

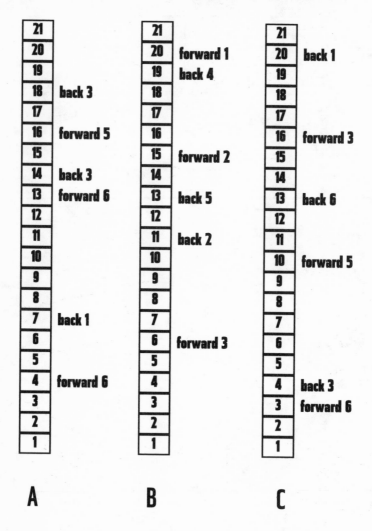

138 What is X?

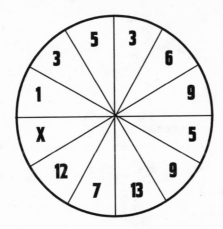

139 Arrange these into three pairs.

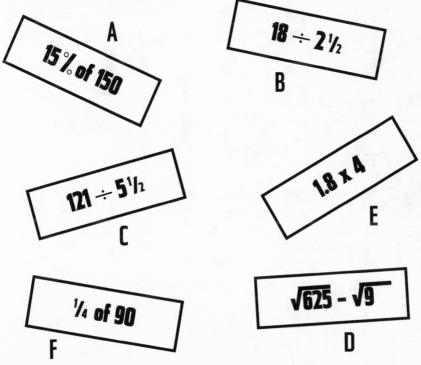

A

15% of 150

18 ÷ 2½

B

121 ÷ 5½

C

1.8 x 4

E

¼ of 90

F

√625 − √9

D

140 If **FIVE+TWENTY = TWENTY-FIVE**

TWELVE = TWENTY

NINE+TEN = FIFTEEN

What is

TWENTY-FIVE-TWELVE?

Choose one of these:

FIVE   TEN   THIRTEEN   FIFTY   NINE   ELEVEN

141 Which of these prevents a perfect fit? Is it a mortise or a tenon?

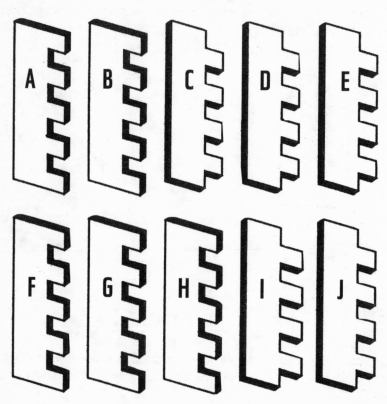

142 What should go into the empty square?

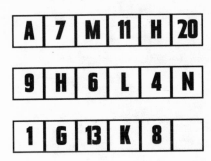

A	7	M	11	H	20

9	H	6	L	4	N

1	G	13	K	8	

143 Alf earns £110 per week and has been promised a rise of 10 per cent next year and 7 per cent the following year. Bert earns £120 per week and has been promised a rise of 5 per cent next year and 4 per cent the following year. Charlie earns £125 per week and has been promised a rise of 3 per cent next year and 2 per cent the following year. At the end of the two years who will be earning the highest weekly wage and what will be the differential between the lowest and highest paid?

144 If this card

were turned round (so that the bottom became the top and vice versa) it would look quite different:

If all the picture cards are removed from a normal pack of cards there will be 40 cards left. How many cards of that 40 would look different if they were turned round as in the example above?

POOL

145 Five pool balls are placed in a row. Which ball is immediately to the left of the ball which is two places to the right of the ball, which is one less in value than the ball which is immediately to the left of the ball two to the right of the 1 ball?

Missing Figure

146 What figure is missing from the fifth row?

1

2

3

4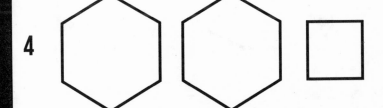

5

147 What do these dates have in common?

15 February 1984

2 July 1983

16 December 1983

148 What is X?

149 Add all the square numbers to their relative square roots and subtract the sum of the numbers remaining.

25	5	2	82	11
98	440	64	537	302
1225	35	15	225	7
19	4	9	3	8

150 Lucy, Mary, Ann, Lily, Jenny, Jim, George, Bert, Tom, and Fred sat on the two long sides of a rectangular table the ladies alternating with, and sitting opposite to, the men. Fred sat in a centre position. Lily sat opposite George. Mary sat next to Fred and three places from George. Jenny sat four places to the left of Lily. Ann sat two places from Mary. Tom sat opposite Mary. Bert sat three places from Jenny. Copy the rectangle and indicate where everyone sat.

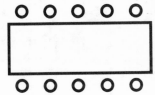

151 Which is the odd one out?

1 2 B 3 C 5 D G 8 J 9 P

152 The six faces of a cube are numbered as follows:

Which of those below is wrong?

153 Which of the dominoes below - A, B, C, D, E or F - will complete those above?

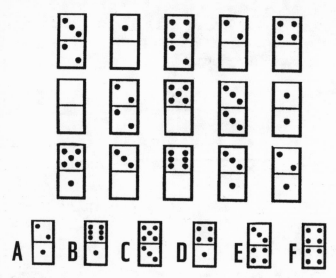

154 Which of the four hexagons at the bottom should occupy the space left by the second hexagon at the top?

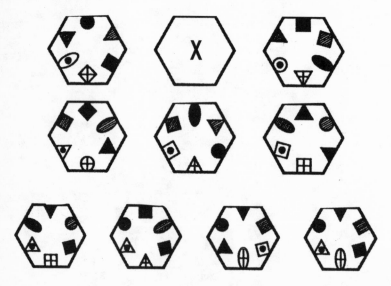

155 What is X?

1 2 4 3 4 8 5 6 12 7 8 16 9 10 20 11 X 24

156 Which of the dominoes on the right should be placed at A, B, C, and D so that the spots in each row, horizontally and vertically, total 16?

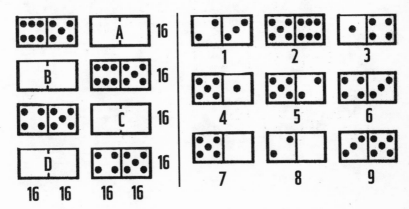

157 Which is the odd one out?

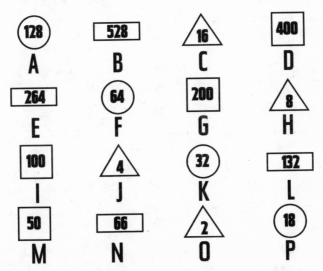

Potatoes

158 "How much does that sack of potatoes weigh", asked the farmer.

"68 lbs plus one fifth of its own weight" replied the grocer.

How much does the sack of potatoes weigh?

Foiled Again

159 What is the value of foil?

TALK   =   10

TALC   =   6

TAIL   =   8

TOIL   =   4

FAIL   =   9

FOIL   =   ?

160 What is X?

1 2 8 4 2 9 4 3 X 2 6 7 4 5 6 1 7 3

161 Four motorists drove for 50 miles. A averaged 30 mph for 25 miles and 20 mph for 25 miles; B averaged 25 mph throughout; C averaged 20 mph for 15 miles and 35 mph for 35 miles; D averaged 15 mph for 18 miles and 30 mph for 32 miles. Who did the journey in the shortest time and who took the longest time?

162 Which of the figures at the bottom - A, B, C or D - belongs to number 5?

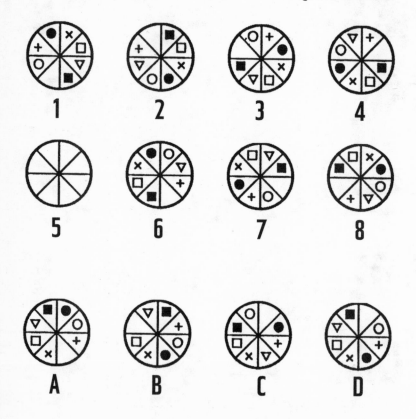

163 What is X?

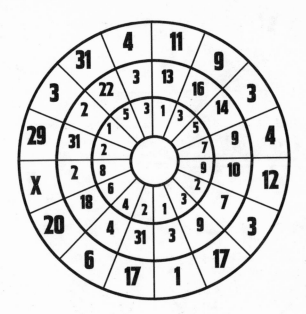

164 How many 4-card permutations can you make in a pack of 52 playing cards?

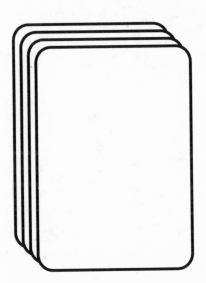

Section Four

Answers

1 40

2 3D. M has four strokes: all the others have three strokes.

3 B and G

4   10
    181   901
    253   370
    541   442
    613   802
    712   091

5 12 hours, 12 minutes, 12 seconds

6 F In all the others the middle three digits add to 10.

7 A=233, B=230 and C=69
The clues lie in the black sections, which indicate that, in the case of A, each number is the sum of the previous two numbers; in the case of B, each number is the sum of the previous three numbers; in the case of C, each number is the sum of the previous four numbers.

8 27
There are 9 balls in the bucket and 18 balls in the box

9 5
Alternate numbers in A add to 30; alternate numbers in B add to 40; alternate numbers in C add to 14. 70 divided by 14 is 5.

10 72

11

$4\frac{1}{2}$	3	$7\frac{1}{2}$
8	5	2
$2\frac{1}{2}$	7	$5\frac{1}{2}$

12 A

Pinion A has 12 teeth, so 36 teeth will rotate in three revolutions. Pinion B will rotate clockwise. Although there are intermediate pinions between A and B, which may have led you to believe they would rotate in the same direction, the inner teeth on the very large annular ring will cause pinion B to rotate in the opposite direction to A.

13 $2\frac{2}{3}$ pints

Each container will then hold $5\frac{1}{3}$ pints - that is : $\frac{1}{3}$ pint to B and $2\frac{1}{3}$ pints to C.

14 K

A-H-N, B-I-P, C-M-O, D-L-F and E-G-J.

15 X is 2, Y is 1, Z is 3

All rows should add to 20.

16 C

17 26

18 £1,666

19 5

The first term is the sum of the last three terms in the bottom row. The second term is the sum of the next last three terms. This procedure is continued throughout, so X is the sum of 0, 1 and 4.

20 12 hours

Clock A will show 12 o'clock; Clock B will show 7 o'clock.

21 D, J and L

In the top row the face shows the addition of the other two faces; the exception is D. In the middle row the front face shows the addition of the other two faces: the exception is J. In the bottom row the right-hand face shows the addition of the other two faces; the exception is L.

22 31121314

Each number describes the number above, starting with the smallest digits.
So, 114213 has 3 x 1, 1 x 2, 1 x 3, 1 x 4

23 357

They are times without the dots with 15 minutes added each time, 2:57, 3:12, 3:27, 3:42, 3:57

24 30

Correctly spaced, the series becomes, 31, 28, 31, 30, 31, 30, 31, 31, 30, 31, 30(X) and 31 - that is, the number of days in the months of the year.

25 8

The corresponding sectors in all 3 circles add to 10. Starting at 1 in the first circle, the corresponding numbers thereafter are 1 and 8 (X).

26 783

The lowest number is 5; the nearest to the highest number is 49; the midway number between them is 27. The highest number is 51; the nearest to the lowest number is 7; the midway number between them is 29. 27 multiplied by 29 is 783.

27 I

28 A, B, E, G and J

29 A. 27 and 3 kilograms on one side; 1 kilogram on the other side. B. 27 and 1 kilogram on one side; 3 kilograms on the other side. C. 27, 3 and 1 kilogram on either side.

30 2 4 6 6 3 1 5   The digits are transposed in the same order throughout, but in each case the second digit on the left outside the brackets is omitted.

31 110   A=40 rpm, B=60 rpm and C=120. A, B and C together revolve at 220rpm; therefore D revolves at 110 rpm.

32 5

The numbers coincide with the positions of the five vowels, A, E, I, O, U in the alphabet.

33 They knew that Alan was a twin but that he had been separated from his twin brother at birth. Brian was the missing identical twin who they immediately recognised in the crowd.

34 2B (dot missing)

Section Four Answers

35 DOGS
LURCHER
CLUMBER
POINTER
TERRIER

ANIMALS
BONGO
TUMBLER
AGUTI
ROEBUCK

REPTILES
CAIMAN
SAURIAN
TAIPAN
PUDDOCK

36 B. The diamond occurs once vertically and once horizontally. The dot occurs on the right and in the centre.

37 2A (dot missing)

38 VEGETABLES
PIMENTO
COLEWORT
SKIRRET
BROCCOLI

INSECTS
MINIPED
MAYBUG
COCKCHAFER
BLACKFLY

REPTILES
BASILISK
ANACONDA
MONITOR
CROCODILE

39 C. The black and white dots appears twice; the white dot appears twice.

40 84
The numbers can be read diagonally on the face of a calculator working left to right.

7	8	9
4	5	6
1	2	3
0		

41 Youngest son $3.5 + 0.5 = 4$
Second eldest son $1.5 + 0.5 = 2$
Eldest son $0.5 + 0.5 = 1$

42 4
Start with the arrow above X. In the opposite segment it is turned 90 degrees anti-clockwise. The next is turned 90 degrees clockwise. This alternating rotation is continued. Therefore, in the opposite segment to X the arrow must be turned 90 degrees clockwise (No 4).

43 A 5; B 1
There are 20 teeth on A and 30 on B. The large annular ring will rotate in the same direction as the driving pinion.

(A) After 4 revolutions of A the outer ring will rotate anti-clockwise through 80 teeth, causing the idling pinion to rotate through 2 revolutions (60 teeth) and an additional 20 teeth. (B) The driving pinion will rotate through 30 teeth - the same number as on the idling pinion, which will bring the black tooth on B to where it was originally (1).

44 20

Even numbers have prime numbers beneath them. Prime numbers have even numbers beneath them. 17 is a prime number, and must have an even number beneath it. The only even number in the third line is 20.

45 A. There are three separate series. Starting with the first letter and taking every third letter thereafter – ITALY: Starting with the second letter and taking every third letter thereafter – SPAIN: from the third letter – INDIA.

46 D

When adjusted, the clocks show the following times:
A from 3.27 to 12.57 B from 11.13 to 12.13 C from 1.44 to 12.24 D from 10.32 to 11.52 E from 5.21 to 12.19

47 B

Removing blocks X and Y leaves the following: diagram Turned upside-down, this corresponds with B.

48 2 4 12

The first number equals the number of CENTRE spots.
The second number is the total of the spots that surround the centre spots.
The third number is the total of the remaining spots.

49 0

There are three separate series, though digits representing tens are not placed adjacent to the units. For example, 12 is shown as 1 2. Starting with the first term, each third term thereafter multiplies the previous term by 3:
2 - - 6 - - - - 18 - - - - -
Starting with the second term, each third term thereafter multiplies the previous term by 4:
- 3 - -12 - - - - 48 - - -
Starting with the third term, each third term thereafter multiplies the previous term by 5:
- - 4 - - - 20 - - - - 100.
The final term (to complete 100) is 0.

50 D

(A) would show £200 interest;

(B) would show £182 interest;

(C) would show £189 interest;

(D) would show £210 interest.

51 SUBMARINES HAVE BEEN SIGHTED IN THE NORTH ATLANTIC.

From the sum on the right it is obvious that S is 7. It must be decided whether the middle one is an addition, because it would then have a three digit answer. As it must be a subtraction, E must be 6 and T must be 1. The left-hand problem must be an addition, so B must be 5 and A must be 9. Substituting these letters in the code:

```
S - B - A - - - E S
- A - E
B E E -
S - - - T E -
- -   T - E
- - - T -
A T - A - T - -
```

Certain possible words now become apparent, such as SUBMARINES and ATLANTIC. The third word (4 letters) and the sixth word (3 letters) are worth considering:

```
B E E -   T - H
```

The first must be BEER of BEEN, and the second must be THE, TIE or TOE. As it is unlikely that the seventh word ends in TI of TO, but could probably end in TH, it is reasonable to assume that the sixth word is THE. By substituting H wherever it occurs:

```
S - B - A - - N E S   H A - E   B E E N
S - - H T E -   - N   T H E   N - - T H
A T - A N T - -
```

Even if by now the other words do not become apparent, the last word should be obvious:

A T - A N T - - (remembering that this is a naval code).

This will supply L, I and C, and the rest should fall into place.

52 A is 8; B is 7; C is 11.

Starting at the octagon (11) at top left and moving clockwise, add the number of sides to the figure to the number of sides on its adjacent figure.

The figure before A is a pentagon (5 sides) and has a value of 9 (5 added to A, which is a square). Therefore, A (4 sides) is added to B (also 4 sides), giving A value of 8.

B (4 sides) is added to C (a triangle), giving B a value of 7.

C (3 sides) is added to the next figure (an octagon), giving C a value of 11.

53 8

The first term (15) is the sum of the last two terms (9 and 6); the second tern (11) is the sum of the next two last terms, and so on. Therefore, X (8) is the sum of 5 and 3.

54 120 .

The basic series is:

1 3 5 7 9 11

In each case deduct 1 from the square of the numbers in this series.

55 3

The numbers represent the numbers of letters in each word of the question.

56 The numbers indicated by the short hand followed by the long hand are successive square numbers : 16, 25, 36, 49, 64

57 3.

(A) TRUE

(B) FALSE

(C) FALSE

(D) TRUE

58 1

The middle number is the difference between the sums of the three numbers on the left and the three numbers on the right.

59 30

In the second circle the number in the segment opposite the corresponding segment in the first circle is doubled. The number opposite X in the first circle is 15, so X is 30.

60 0

Correctly spaced, the series is:

1 2 6 24 120 720 5040

that is, multiplying by 2, 3, 4, 5, 6 and finally 7.**61** 6 days

	hour hand	minute hand
1st day	6	5
2nd day	7	4
3rd day	8	3
4th day	9	2
5th day	10	1
6th day	11	12

62 14 and 15
14 is wrong because 5 has been placed beside 4; 15 is wrong because that domino has already been used (No. 14).

63 Three chances in four
The possible combinations are
        black - black
        white - white
        black - white
        white - black
There is only one of these combinations where black does not occur, therefore, the chances of drawing at least one black ball are three chances in four.

64 2.7 percent

65 (A) 7 hours and 5 minutes .
(B) 28 mph .

66 0
Each number is the square of the previous number with 1 added:
2 is 1 squared (1) plus 1
5 is 2 squared (4) plus 1
26 is 5 squared (25) plus 1
677 is 26 squared (676) plus 1
458330 is 677 squared (458329) plus 1

67 C and D

68 3

The first term is the difference between the last two terms; the next is the difference between the next two last terms, and so on. X (3) is the difference between 15 and 18.

69 X is 35

Y is 28

Z is 50

The number on the left in the top line is doubled to give the number on the right in the bottom line; the next number on the top line is multiplied by 3 to give its corresponding position in the bottom line; the next is multiplied by 4, and the next (7) is multiplied by 5 to give 25 (X) in the corresponding position in the bottom line.

The same procedure is followed in the second line from the top to establish the numbers in the second line from the bottom, so that 7 in the second line from the top becomes 28 (Y) in the second line from the bottom.

The number in the middle line is the sum of the other four numbers in the vertical column, so Z is the sum of 3, 7, 12 and 28 (Y), that is - 50.

70 (1) 195 miles; (2) 95 miles; (3) 20 miles.

71 C

▦	moves 2 places anti-clockwise
☐	moves 2 places clockwise
●	moves 1 place clockwise
○	moves 3 places anti-clockwise
▲	moves 3 places clockwise
△	moves 4 places either way

72 30

The number in the third vertical column is the difference between that in the right-hand column and the sum of the squares of the two left-hand columns.

73 1st over   1 3 4 5 6 7

2nd over   2 9 10 11   NOT OUT 8

74 B

One of the figures drops down on top of the other and the figures become transparent.

75 B

A takes 2 hours, 45 minutes

B takes 2 hours, 34 minutes
C takes 2 hours, 40 minutes

76 V
Start at A and work clockwise to alternate segments in the sequence
ABcDefGhijKlmnoPqrstuV

77 $18 \times 3 = 54$, we require $18 \times 3^7 = 354294$

78 -13
$16 - 9 = 7$, $20 - 15 = 5$, $8 - 21 = -13$

79 27,25,18,16,14

80

ANIMALS	FISH	BIRDS
DASYPUS	LAMPREY	BITTERN
BANTING	MERLING	DOTTEREL
HAMSTER	SQUID	CHAFFINCH
BUBALIS	GROUPER	DOVE

81 81
$(121 = 11^2) - (100 = 10^2) - (81 = 9^2) - (64 = 8^2) - (49 = 7^2)$

82 10.35
3.20 - 5.45 - 8.10 - 10.35
Add 2h 25m each time

83 2 hours, 15 minutes, 20 seconds .

84 13
Reverse each number from first to last or vice versa. X is the reverse of 31.

85 14 minutes

86 Multiply each number by 3 to produce the sequence: 9, 33, 24, 63, 6, 42, 3, 39

87 Never. Three corners counter-clockwise in a heptagon is the same as four corners clockwise. The dots, therefore, will always keep the same distance between them.

The Great Book of Brainteasers

88 C

Substitute numbers for letters according to their alphabetic position. Thus, the first relationship is between 6 3 7 4 and 7 6 4 3. The figures at the bottom are transposed in the same order.

89 E .

90 3

Prime numbers total 95; even numbers total 130; 225 divided by 75 is 3.

91 3

Divide the totals of the left-hand facing columns by the totals of the corresponding right-hand facing columns to give the totals of the rows on the top face.

92 6

From the first circle the numbers move one segment clockwise into the next circle. The series are:

31	35	39	43	(adding 4 each time)
6	5	4	3	(subtracting 1 each time)
9	8	7	6(X)	(subtracting 1 each time)
4	7	10	13	(adding 3 each time)

93 C

The black segment moves clockwise, first to the next segment, then missing one, then two and so forth. The black spot moves in the same way, but anti-clockwise. The white spot moves clockwise, one segment at a time.

94 X is 10, Y is 6, Z is 4.

In the first circle add numbers in opposite segments: 20, 19, 18, 17, (X being 10). In the second circle 16, 15, 14, 13, (Y being 6). In the third circle 12, 11, 10, 9 (Z being 4).

95 64 and 36; 64, 19 and 17 or 41, 42 and 17 or 42, 36 and 22; 5, 9, 22 and 64.

96 90 red sweets, 44 white sweets.
You probably solved this by elementary deduction, which, unusually, might have proved quicker than by algebra. Deduct 2 from 134, divide by 3 (to give white sweets) multiply by 2 and add 2 to give the red sweets. If you use algebra: let X be the number of red sweets and Y the number of white sweets.

$$x + y = 134$$
$$x - 2 = 2y$$

therefore $\quad 2y = 134 - y - 2$
so $\quad\quad\quad 3y = 132$
and $\quad\quad\quad y = 44$
then $\quad\quad\quad x + 44 = 134$
and $\quad\quad\quad x = 90$

97 5
Starting at 3 moving clockwise, numbers in the upper half paired with opposite numbers in the lower half equal 4, by first adding, then multiplying and then dividing. This sequence is repeated, so that 20 (opposite to X) must be divided by 5 (the value of X) to give 4.

98 22
6 multiplied by 69 is 414; 414 added to 4 is 418; 418 divided by 19 is 22.

99

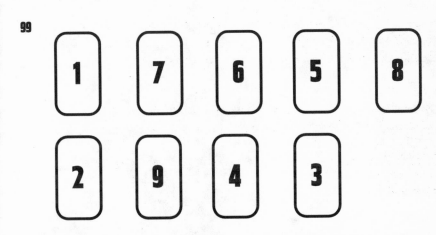

100 £45

101 6

Multiply the sums of the digits on each side of the brackets: 12 (the sum of 1, 4 and 7) multiplied by 6 (the sum of 3, 1 and 2) equals 72 (inside the first brackets); 10 (the sum of 5 and 5) multiplied by 11 (the sum of 2, 1 and 8) equals 110 (inside the second brackets); 3 (the sum of 1,1 and 1) multiplied by 2 (on the right side of the brackets) equals 6 (inside the third brackets).

102 A. FALSE, B. TRUE, C. TRUE, D. FALSE

Canberra is the capital of Australia; Gauguin was a French post-impressionist painter.

103 272

The only numbers that are squares of whole numbers are: 16 (4 squared) and 256 (16 squared).

104 2048

Divide the first two numbers to get the third. Multiply the next two to get the fourth. Then continue, dividing and multiplying alternately. The final number is 128 multiplied by 16 - that is, 2048.

105 B

106 Because it is a seven-sided figure they will never be side by side. After the first move they will always be two, four or six corners apart.

107 B and F

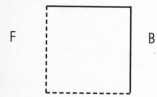

108 151

The two possible routes on the left of the straight vertical route will give a total of 151.

109 10 miles

As X is a right-angled triangle, 100 (10 squared) is equal to 36 (6 squared) plus 64 (of which 8 is the square root). This, of course, is based on Pythagoras' theorem: 'The square on the hypotenuse is equal to the sum of the squares on the other two sides.'

110 B

The vanes move as follows:

one face clockwise, finishing at '8 o'clock' approximately;

two faces anti-clockwise, finishing at '7 o'clock';

three faces clockwise, finishing at '10 0'clock';

four faces anti-clockwise, finishing at '5 o'clock' approximately.

111 81

112 425 entries

421 matches were played, so there must have been 420 losers. Add the 3 who scratched out in the preliminary round, plus the player who scratched out from the second round, then add the winner of the tournament, and you arrive at the total number of entries, 425.

113 4

The only number that consists entirely of straight lines.

114 $\dfrac{1}{6} = \dfrac{6}{36}$　　　　$\dfrac{1}{6} - \dfrac{5}{6} = \dfrac{5}{36}$

TOTAL　　$\dfrac{11}{36}$　　$\dfrac{11}{36} \times 100 = £30.60$

115 3770" Pi: 24" x $3^1/_7$ = 75.4. Take half = 37.7" x 100 = 3770

116 4 $^1/_6$

117 2B. There is a dot missing

118 5

1, 2, 4, 8, 16, 32, 64, 128, 256

119 31 $^3/_4$

There are 2 Series + 5 $^1/_4$, + 37

120 14 pigs
28 hens

121 24
One man builds 2/3 of a wall in a day. Six men will build 4 walls a day, and 24 in 6 days

122 10
The last number (represented by X) is double the first number; the penultimate number is double the second number; this pattern is continued throughout.

123 A is false (the angle is 165 degrees of 195 degrees)
B is true
C is true
D is true (AEFHIKLMNTVWXYZ)

124 585
The highest and lowest numbers divisible by 13 are 143 and 39 respectively. 91 is mid-way between them. 91 x 8 = 728
728 - 143 = 585.

125 K
It has no counterpart and should be as B, E and O.

126 10
The first number is the difference between the last two numbers, the second number is the difference between the penultimate and antepenultimate numbers, and this pattern follows throughout. X is the difference between 30 and 20.

127 A scores 195 and B scores 203
They score as follows:

A		
20 (single)	9 (treble 3)	
36 (double 18)	7 (single)	
39 (treble 13)	16 (double 8)	
10 (single)	42 (treble 14)	
4 (double 2)	12 (single)	

Total	195	

B   1 (single)   57 (treble 19)
         8 (double 4)   16 (single)
         18 (treble 6)   22 (double 11)
         15 (single)   27 (treble 9)
         34 (double 17)   5 (single)

Total   203

128 F
The black bar has been moved further out from the circle.

129 12
There are two series. Starting with the first term and taking each alternate term thereafter - 7, 9, 12, 16, 21 - the numbers increase by 2, 3, 4 and 5.
    Starting with the second term and taking each alternate term thereafter - 3, 7, (12), 18, 25 - the numbers increase by 4, 5, 6 and 7.

130 B

131 8
Start at 1 and move clockwise. Then consider the second section in the next vane, followed by the third section in the next vane and finally the fourth section in the next vane: 1, 2, 3, 4. Now start at 3 in the second vane (at the top) and move downwards through successive vanes: 3, 5, 7, 9. Next start at 10 in the third vane (at the top) and move in the same way: 10, 9, 8, 7. Finally, start at 2 in the remaining vane (at the top) and move in the same way: 2, 4, 6, (8).

132 2
The first term doubles the last term; the second term halves the penultimate term; the third term doubles the next to last; and so on. Therefore, X must double 1.

133 They are practically touching.
Deduct 6 inches from the top of each, then deduct 1 foot off the bottom of each. So there is just enough twine to go down one cane 3.5 feet and back up the other 2.5 feet.

134 C
The sticks form three triangles, in the others they only form two.

135

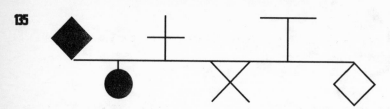

Transpose the symbols in the same way as in the example. (This is in fact only a matter of reversing the order of the symbols and placing them on the opposite side of the central line.)

136 Sigh
Add the number of spots on each die to the letter shown. For example, Q plus 2 is S.

137 A. They move as follows:

	Counter A	Counter B	Counter C
1st move	10	4	1
2nd move	12	9	9
3rd move	15	17	15
4th move	21	18	19
5th move	-	21	21

138 17
Starting at 1, moving clockwise and missing two segments each time gives 1, 3, 5, 7. Starting at the next number, 3, and moving in the same way gives 3, 6, 9, 12. Starting at the next number, 5, and moving in the same way gives 5, 9, 13, (17).

139 A-F (each is 22.5), B-E (each is 7.2), C-D (each is 22)

140 FIVE
Add the number of straight strokes that make up the words:
FIVE (10) plus TWENTY (18) = 28
TWENTY-FIVE = 28
TWELVE = 18
TWENTY = 18
The only word at the bottom that contains 10 strokes (the difference between 28 and 18) is FIVE.

141 I; it is a tenon
A, B, F, G and H are all mortises (cavities to receive tenons); C, D, E, I and J are all tenons. The projections on I are too long.

142 T
In the bottom row numbers are substituted for letters (or letters for numbers) compared with the top row. T (the 20th letter) corresponds with 20 in the top row. (The middle row has no bearing on this comparison and is merely a 'red herring'.)

143 Charlie and £1.85
Alf's weekly wage will be £129.47; Bert's weekly wage will be £131.04; Charlie's weekly wage will be £131.32. The difference between Alf's and Charlie's wage is £1.85.

144 22
The cards that would look different are

heart	club	diamond	spade
Ace	Ace		Ace
3	3		3
5	5		5
6	6		6
7	7	7	7
8	8		8
9	9		9

145 The 5 ball

146 A square
Add the number of sides of the figures in each row. The result is successive square numbers: 1, 4, 9, 16, 25

147 They all fall in the middle
15 February was the middle of February (1984 being a leap year); 2 July was the middle day of the year 1983; and 16 December was the middle of December.

148 7
The numbers in the lower half are the sum of the two numbers in the opposite upper half (2+7=9; 7+9=16; 9+5=14; 5+4=9. Hence 4+3=7 (X).)

The Great Book of Brainteasers

149 124

The sum of the square number and their relative roots - 25, 5, 64, 8, 1225, 35, 15, 225, 4, 2, 9 and 3 - is 1620. The sum of 82, 11, 98, 440, 537, 302, 7 and 19 is 1496. 1620 less 1496 equals 124.

150

Jim   Mary   Fred   Ann   George

Jenny   Tom   Lucie   Bert   Lily

151 1

It is the only straight stroke; all the others have curves.

152 F

Compare with right-hand cube above.

153 D

All combinations of dominoes that represent numbers from 0 to 6 are included, with the exception of 4/1 (5).

154 D

This can be seen by following the sequence of shapes from the third hexagon at the top. All the interior shapes move one place anti-clockwise, but the shading (as established in the first of the top hexagons) remains in the same position throughout.

155 12

There are three series. Starting with the first term and taking every third one thereafter: 1, 3, 5, 7, 9, 11. Starting with the second term and proceeding in the same way: 2, 4, 6, 8, 10, (12) X. Starting with the third term and proceeding in the same way: 4, 8, 12, 16, 20, 24.

156 A-1, B-3, C-6, D-5

The result is as follows:

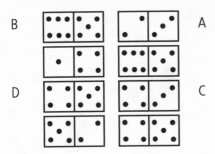

B · · · A

D · · · C

157 P
The numbers are progressively halved according to the shapes that surround them, so P should be 16 to fit into the sequence 128, 64, 32, 16.

158 85 lbs

159 5
Count the number of straight lines in each word. Deduct curved lines from the total if any appear in the word

160 8
The first two numbers equal the last one; the third number is the sum of the two before the last; the sum of the next two (4 and 2) is the fourth from last (6). This pattern is followed throughout.

161 C took the shortest time, D took the longest time.
The times taken were: A-2 hours and 5 minutes, B-2 hours, C-1 hour and 45 minutes, D-2 hours and 16 minutes.

162 D
Each segment moves clockwise in alternate circles, missing one segment each time.

163 0
The totals of the three numbers in opposite segments are halved and doubled alternately. The three numbers opposite X total 20 (7, 9 and 4); therefore, the total of the three numbers in the segment occupied by X must be 10. As the present total is already 10, X must be zero.

164 6,497,400 (52 x 51 x 50 x 49)

Section Five

The Great Book of Brainteasers

1 What are A, B, C and D?

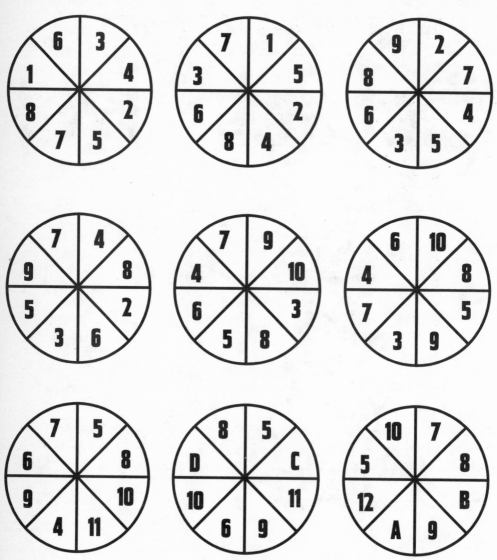

2 What is X?

90 180 12 50 100 200 X 3 50 4 25 2 6 30 3

3 Write down the numbers 1, 3, 9, and 27, leaving the appropriate spaces, and insert arithmetical signs (+, x, - or ÷) to give these results.

A 40

B 30

C 16

D 22

E 39

F 9

G 63

4 In a cricket match five batsmen, A, B, C, D and E, scored an average of 36 runs. D scored 5 more than E; E scored 8 fewer than A; B scored as many as D and E combined; and B and C scored 107 between them. How many runs did each man score?

5 In the diagram below you must first eliminate: A. three alternate numbers that add to 72 B. three alternate numbers that add to 114 C. three alternate numbers that add to 12 D. four alternate numbers that add to 16 E. four alternate numbers that add to 64 F. five adjacent numbers that add to 50 G. five adjacent numbers that add to 140 H. five adjacent numbers that add to 190. Some of the numbers may be used twice. What is the total of the numbers that you have not used?

1	2	3	4	5	6	7

						8

15	14	13	12	11	10	9

16

17	18	19	20	21	22	23

						24

31	30	29	28	27	26	25

32

33	34	35	36	37	38	39

						40

6 If you join all the dots divisible by 3 in ascending order, and then those divisible by 7, also in ascending order, what pattern will result? Use you eye only, and do not use a pointer.

●	●	●	●	●
6	4	18	5	7

●	●	●	●	●
1	22	2	20	8

●	●	●	●	●
28	10	21	11	14

●	●	●	●	●
16	23	13	25	29

●	●	●	●	●
35	17	33	19	39

7 From the three examples above, decide what goes into the empty brackets below.

635 (53) 714

294 (18) 832

153 (21) 264

742 ( ) 498

8 What are A, B, C and D in the bottom two circles?

9 What is X?

737	**382**
461	**955**
392	**745**
183	**297**
468	**246**
732	**58X**

10 The exact position of the hands on these clocks point to whole numbers or fractions of numbers. Thus, the first clock shows a total of 12 $^1/_2$ (the minute hand points to 6 and the hour hand to 6 $^1/_2$). Give the total represented by all three clocks. What will the total be in 2 $^1/_2$ hours time?

11 What are X and Y

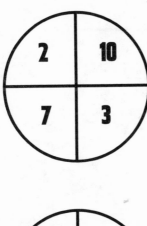 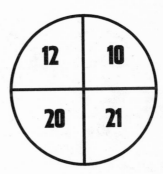

'37'

12 If the digits 1-9 are placed in the grid as follows

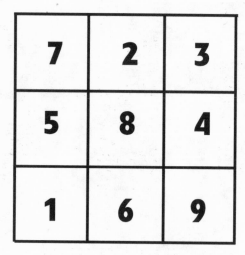

a total of 16 different numbers will be formed if each horizontal, vertical and corner to corner line is read both forward and backward.

Rearrange the digits 1-9 in the grid in such a way that if each of the 16 three-figure numbers are extended to form a palindromic six figure number, for example 723 would become 723327, and 413 would become 413314) then each of those 16 six-figure numbers will divide exactly by 37.

Trominoes

13 Consider the three trominoes below:

Now chose one of the following to accompany the above

    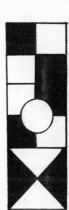

A **B** **C** **D** **E**

14 Will pinion Y rotate: A. Faster than X and in the same direction? B. Slower than X and in the same direction? C. At the same speed as X and in the same direction? D. Faster than X and in the opposite direction? E. Slower than X and in the opposite direction? F. At the same speed as X and in the opposite direction?

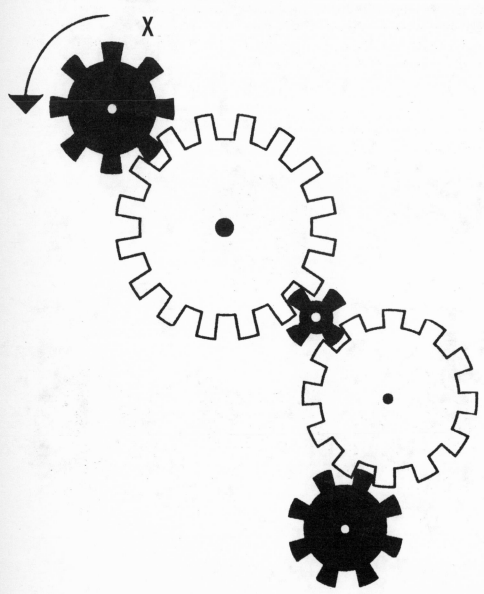

15 How many mistakes can you find here?

In the town their were shops of every description, but the biggest shop was stocked with such things as lawn mower's and garden tools. Two shops were managed by Stan and Bert, the son-in-laws of the town counsillor. Stan sold objects d'art, while Bert's shop was stocked with electrical goods. In the High Street their was a seathing mass of people and vehacles. At the end of the street there was a monument comemmoration the the local boys who were killed in the last war.

16 If this die were held in front of a mirror, which of those below - A, B, C or D - would be reflected?

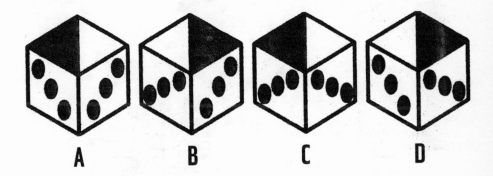

A   **B**   **C**   **D**

17 State the combined total of both these series when you have substituted numbers for X and Y.

2 5 8 11 X 17

1 4 7 4 7 10 7 Y 13 10 13 16 13 16

18 Take a two-digit number and multiply it by its square root. The result is the same as the square of half the original number. What is the original number? Then, multiply the answer by four and add the result to double the original number.

19 What are X, Y and Z?

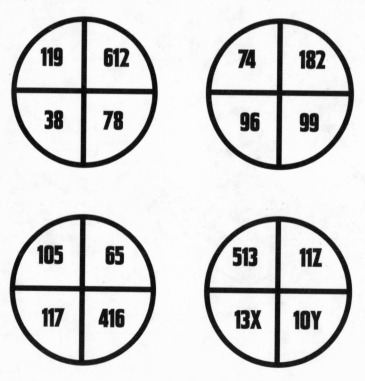

20 When the minute hand points to 9 minutes and the second hand points to 18 seconds the acute angle between them is between:

A 30 and 40 degrees

B 40 and 50 degrees

C 50 and 60 degrees

If clock A shows 8.30 and clock B shows 5.40, is the acute angle between the hands:

A Greater in A?

B Greater in B?

C The same in each?

Which of these times shows the largest acute angle between the hands?

A 2.20

B 7.25

C 8.50

21 A runner, a cyclist and a motorist compete over a 10-mile course. The runner, who averaged 10 mph, started at 1.10 pm. The cyclist, who averaged 12 mph, started at 1.20 pm. The motorist, who could only average 20 mph because of heavy traffic, started at 1.40 pm.

In what order did they finish?

Missing Numbers

22 Fill in the four missing numbers

4	7	8	3	8	5
6	5			7	4
8	1	8	6	2	
3	6	5	8	7	6
	7	2	6	3	7
8	4	7	4	7	5

The Rope Bridge

23 Four explorers in the jungle have to cross a rope bridge at midnight. Unfortunately the bridge is only strong enough to support two people at a time. Also, because deep in the jungle at midnight it is pitch black dark the explorers require a torch to guide then, otherwise there is a distinct possibility they would lose their footing and plunge to their death in the deep ravine below. However, between them they have only one torch. Young Maurice can cross the ravine in two minutes, his sister Kathleen can cross in four minutes, their father Thomas can cross in 10 minutes, however, old Colonel Tompkins can only hobble across in 20 minutes.

How quickly is it possible for all four to reach the other side?

24 Here are three bingo cards. The numbers are called out in the order shown below. Without writing or marketing the numbers, which card is the first to get a full line across, and in how many numbers called was the winning line claimed?

A

3			36	41		64	70	
	13	24			53	66	75	
	19		37		58		77	90

B

1		25		42		61		88
		29		44	56	68	71	
4	12		30	48		69		

C

	17		35		51	60		87
2		22	38		55		73	
6	18			40	59		74	

87	16	41	3	59	71	33	50	68	701
89	21	56	74	5	14	64	44	18	43
65	40	29	36	6	8	9	11	88	90

25 If you wanted pinion 2 to rotate twice as fast as pinion 1, which of the pinions below – A, B, C or D – would you mesh between them?

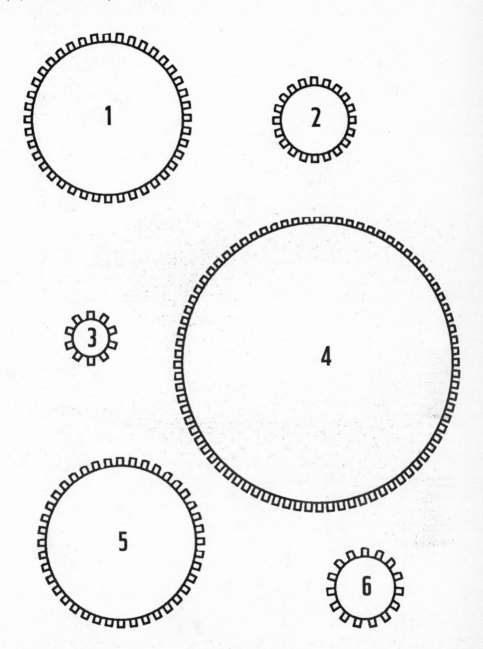

26 This hour hand moves 25 degrees backwards and then it moves 35 degrees forwards. Then it moves to the position diametrically opposite, from which it moves 100 degrees backwards. Finally it moves 60 degrees forwards. On what hour does it finish?

27 Which is the odd one out?

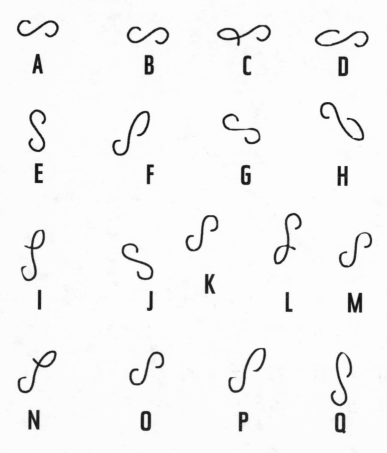

28 In this problem you must not use measuring instruments, but you may draw a freehand sketch, endeavouring to keep to fairly correct proportions. From point X, a person walks 50 metres southwest, then 100 metres east, then 120 metres north, then 50 metres west, followed by 70 metres southeast, 50 metres west, and finally 35 metres north-west. In the diagram be;low, decide which spot will be the nearest to the finishing point. Base your proportions on the first leg of the journey, which is already indicated.

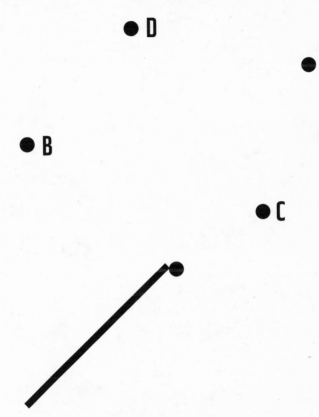

29 What is X?

6	7	12	11	5		9	13	8	X
2	4	3	9	2		3	6	7	1	2

The Great Book of Brainteasers

30 In a normal pack of playing cards some cards look different when they are turned round so that the top appears at the bottom and vice versa, as in this example of a simple letter.

If all the aces and picture cards are removed, there is only one suit that has only one card that looks different when it is turned round. What is the suit? What is the card?

31 A total of 27 loose blocks are placed in the form of a cube. Two of these blocks, indicated by X, are then removed. Which of the blocks A, B, of C will remain?

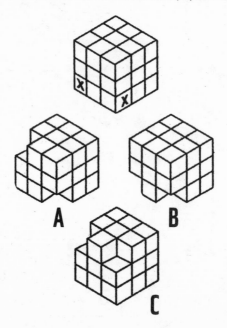

32 Which three of these numbers will add to 1000?

264   136   547   192

756   631   249   233

33 The receptacle at the top is filled with water. If its contents were poured into the six receptacles below, which of them, if any, would overflow?

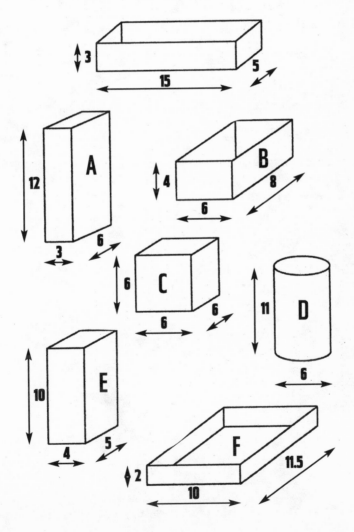

The Great Book of Brainteasers

Three Strokes of the Pen

34 "Here's a good one", said Peter, "in fact, three for the price of one actually. Have a look at these numbers below".

101010

"Some sort of binary code?", enquired Sue. "Well no, not really", said Peter, "but see how many of the following you can figure out. Write down the numbers below three times thus:

101010

101010

101010

now add just one straight line to each so that you make:

1. the first line one thousand

2. the second line one hundred one

3. the third line nine fifty"

"The first two seem easy enough", said Sue, "but I will have to put my thinking cap on for the third".

How did Sue solve the puzzle?

Two in a Bed

35 A man was working on a night shift when he suddenly received a telephone call giving him some information causing him to dash home at breakneck speed.

On bursting into his bedroom quite breathless he found his informant was quite correct and his wife was in bed with someone he had never even clapped eyes on before.

However, far from being angry he greeted them both with a friendly smile and a few hours later was bringing them both breakfast in bed.

What is the reason for this?

36 Which is the correct route from A to B?

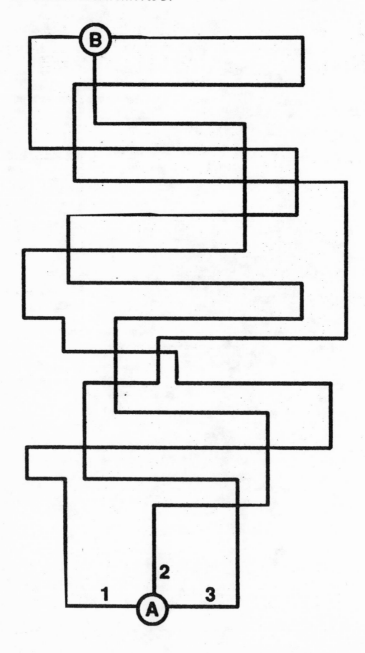

37 Which number at the bottom belongs to X? (clue: watch the spacing!)

63   14   431   74   52   6   X   915

716 654 7   14   812   449 11   600

38 What number should replace the ?

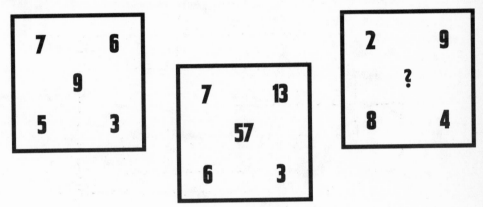

39 Which of the following is the odd one out?

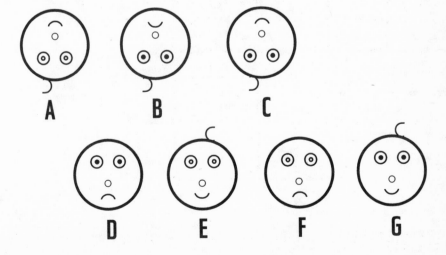

A   B   C

D   E   F   G

40 What numbers should go into the box?

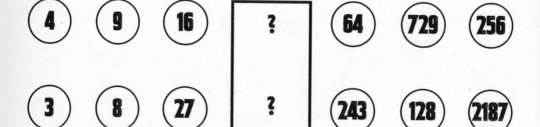

41 What numbers should replace the ?

42 Which box completes the sequence?

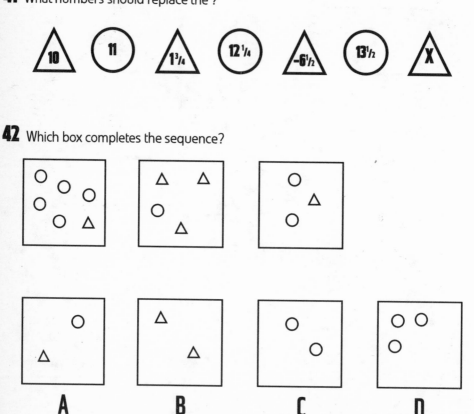

A   B   C   D

43 What number should replace X?

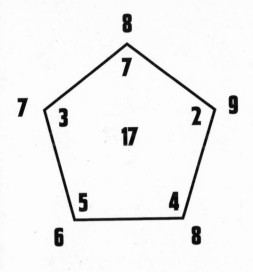

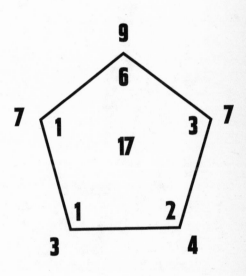

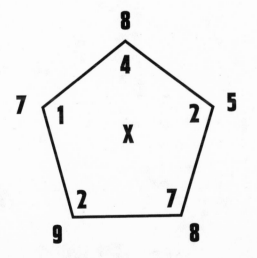

The Great Book of Brainteasers

What's their ages

44 My neighbour remarked to me that he and his wife have three children and the sum of their ages equalled the age of his wife, and if he multiplied the children's ages together it came to 1200.

How old are the children of my neighbour's wife if she had her first child when she was 17 and the third child when she was 32?

Connections

45 Insert the numbers 1-10 in the circles so that for any particular circle, the sum of the numbers in the circles directly connected to it equals the value corresponding to the number in that circle, as given in the list below.

1=15
2=10
3=9
4= 16
5 =14
6 = 5
7 =19
8 = 14
9 = 17
10 = 27

For example:
1= 7
2= 4
3=5
4=6

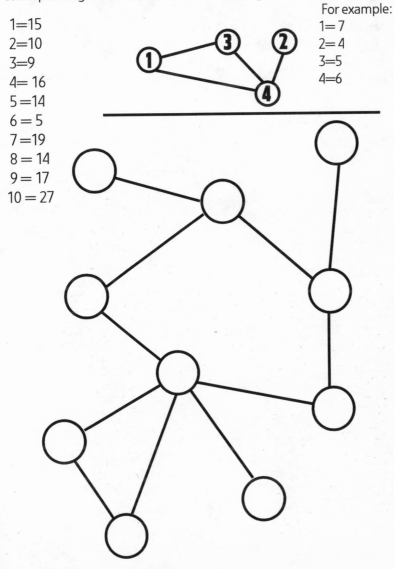

46 To continue this sequence, which figure should be repeated after H?

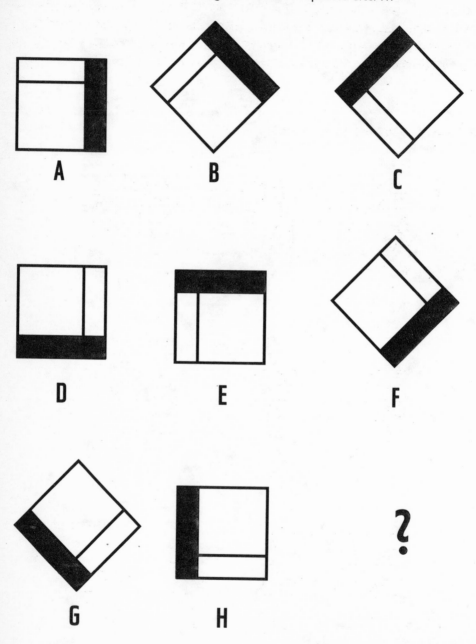

47 A shopkeeper had very little space in his crowded shop and the scales on his counter took up a lot of room which he could ill afford. Realising that everything he sold was weighed in pounds, and that the heaviest article weighed 40lbs., he decided to economise on space by using four weights only. With these four weights he was able to weigh anything from 1 lb. to 40 lbs. Inclusive. What were the weights?

48 Which of the bottom figures will complete F?

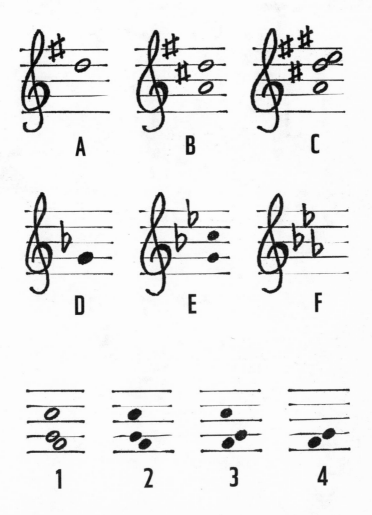

49 Complete this sequence:

$$9 \quad 3 \quad 16 \quad 4 \quad 25 \quad 5 \quad - \quad -$$

50 What are the values of A and B?

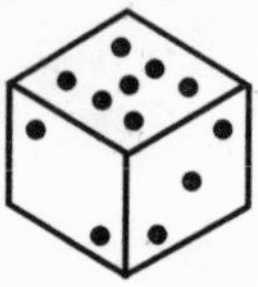

= 17

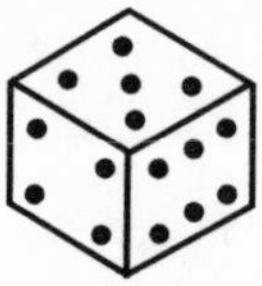

= 10

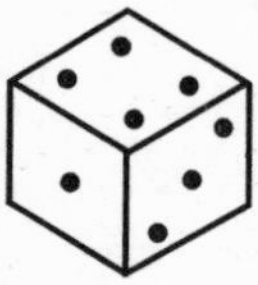

= 12

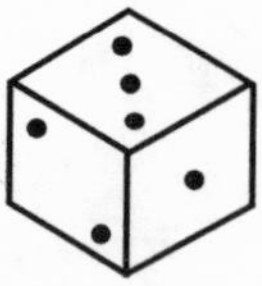

= 3

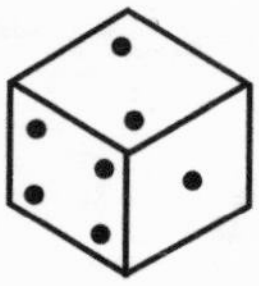

= 9

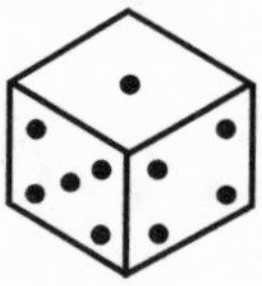

= 9

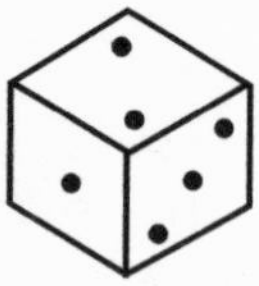

= A ?

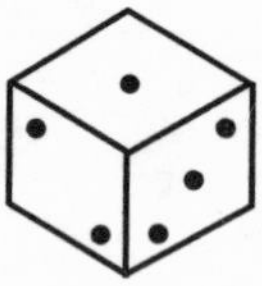

= B ?

51 Which of these fractions is out of place?

$$\frac{2}{8} \qquad \frac{5}{25} \qquad \frac{4}{64} \qquad \frac{6}{216} \qquad \frac{7}{343} \qquad \frac{3}{27}$$

52 Which of the numbered figures at the bottom should take the place of X?

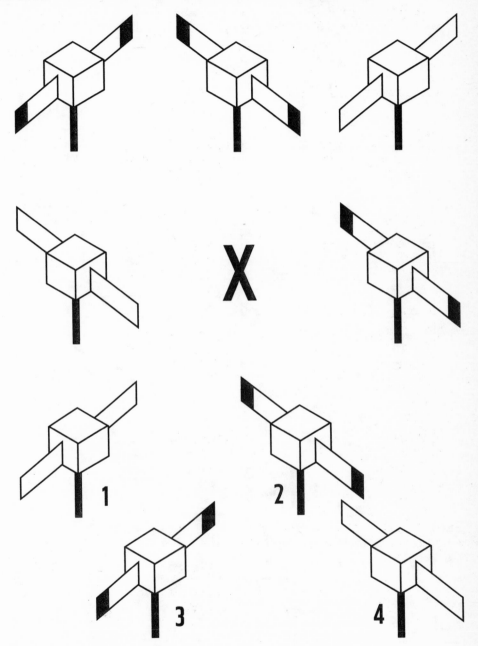

53 Give values for X, Y and Z.

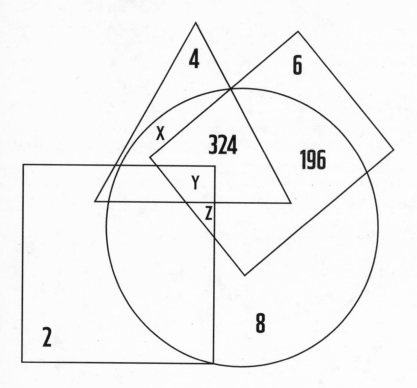

54 What is the missing number?

3	4	6	5
5	15	105	4
7	480		8
8	9	6	7

Fatal Attraction

55 Lucretia Borgia invited a prospective victim to lunch. They ate a hearty meal of roast venison, with a selection of fresh vegetables, all washed down with the finest wine imported from Bordeaux in France.

After the meal they finished off with figs and grapes freshly picked.

"Just one apple left", said Lucretia, "I insist you have that. "No", said the guest, "I couldn't". "Tell you what", said Lucretia, "we will share it", and promptly sliced it neatly in two with her sharpest knife. The guest and Lucretia started to eat their respective halves when suddenly the guest's eyes rolled towards the ceiling and he keeled over backwards stone dead.

"Another victim successfully despatched", thought Lucretia.

How did she do it?

The Great Book of Brainteasers

Archery Contest

56 During an archery contest Tom, Dick and Harry between them hit the target eleven times and had scored in total, 50. All their scoring shots are shown on the target below.

Tom said to Harry, "If I had scored half as many more I would have scored exactly the same as you would if you had scored 5 less. Also if Dick had scored 5 more he would have scored one more than I have scored now".

"Run that by me again, very slowly" said Harry.

How many did each man score, and what were their individual scoring shots?

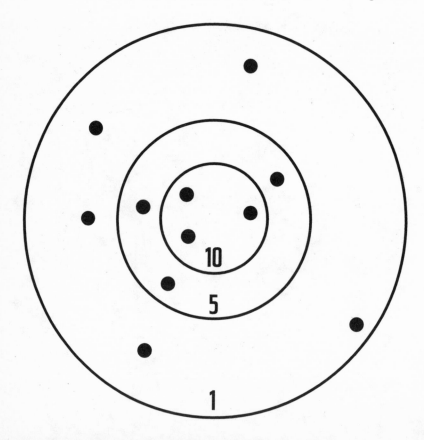

57 Continue this sequence:

2 2 2 4 5 3 16 8 4 - - -

58 Complete this series:

LI CLIII – – – MCCCLXXVII

59 Which figure is wrong?

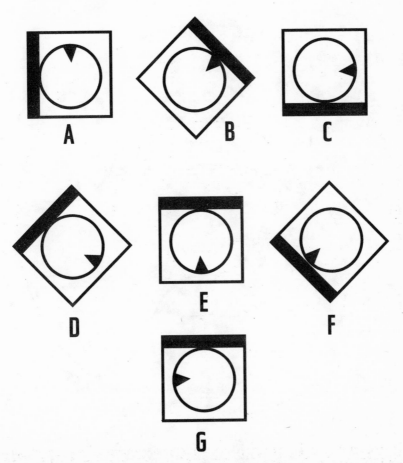

60 These were the scores as the wickets fell in a cricket match.

54	74	89	108	121	142	153	176	185
1	2	3	4	5	6	7	8	9

What was the final score?

61 Complete this sequence:

1 7 3 2 6 5 3 – 7 4 4

62 Where do the hands point at E?

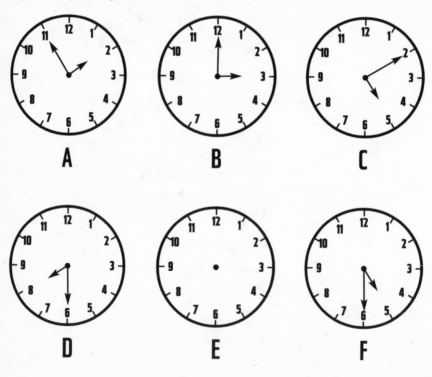

63 What is X?

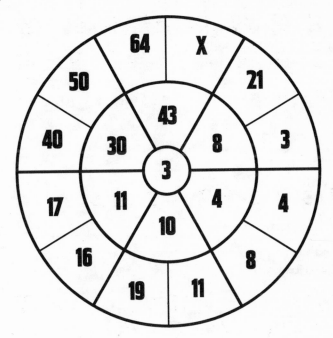

64 Which one does not conform?

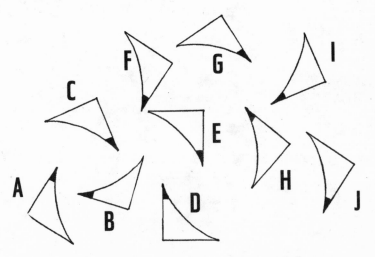

The Great Book of Brainteasers

Spring Bulbs

65 My wife sent me to the Garden Centre with exactly £100 and told me to buy bulbs to brighten up the front garden in Spring.

"I want a mixture of crocus, tulips and hyacinths", she said, "and I want you to buy some of each but spend exactly the £100, not a penny less, not a penny more, and I want exactly 100 bulbs, not one more, not one less".

When I reached the Garden Centre the bulbs were priced as follows:

£0.05 each crocus
£1.00 each daffodils
£5.00 each hyacinths.

When I got back home my wife was not impressed with my selection and mix, but at least said I had followed her instructions correctly.

How many of each did I buy?

The Happy Wanderer

66 A hiker sets off one morning at 6 am and begins to walk up the only track from the pub at the base of a small mountain to a pub at the top. He arrives at the top at 6 pm and after spending the night at the pub at the top starts down the same track at exactly 6 am the following morning, eventually arriving at the pub at the bottom at 6 pm that same night.

From these facts, is it possible to determine if there exists along the track a point that the hiker passes at exactly the same time of the day coming down the track as he did going up the track?

67 Complete this series:

1 2 3   7 8 9   28 29 30

- - -

68 How many revolutions of A will take place before the black teeth (1 and 2) on pinion B are again in mesh with black tooth (3) on pinion A *and at the same time* the black teeth (4 and 5) on pinion B are again in mesh with black tooth (6) on pinion C?

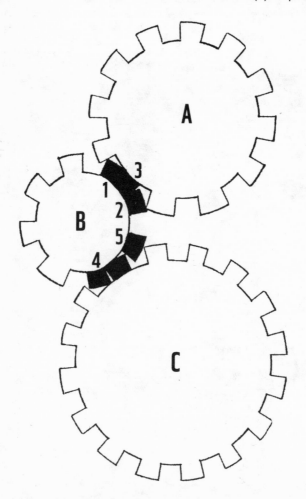

69 Which of the four figures at the bottom should follow No. 6?

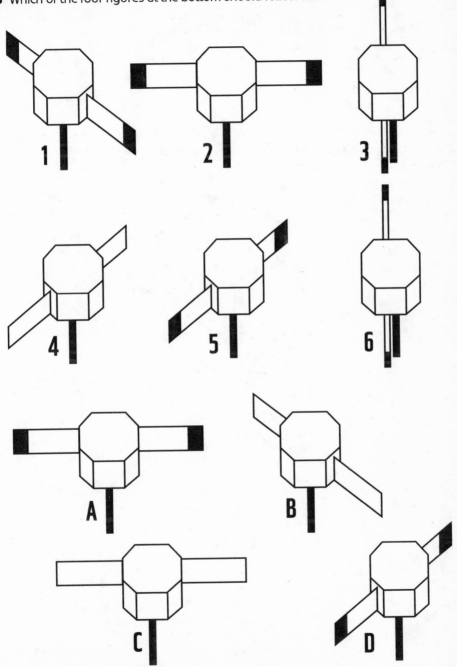

70 Which of the figures at the bottom belongs to No. 5?

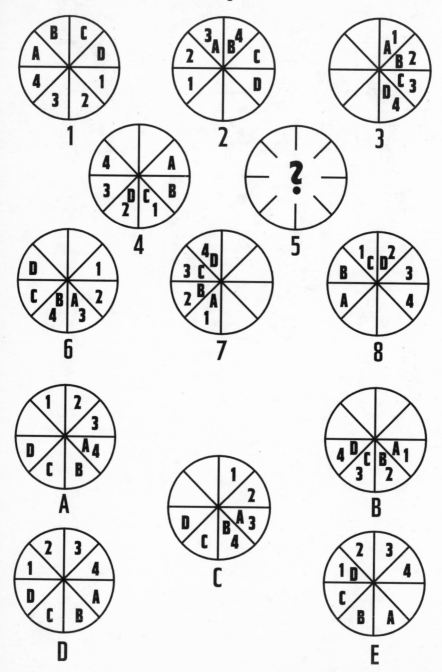

71 What completes the third circle?

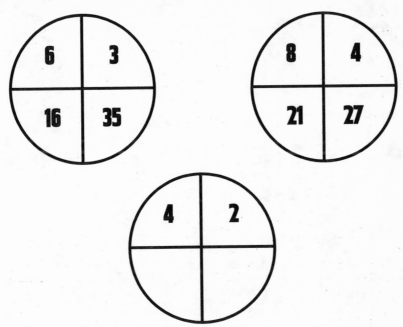

72 Supply the missing number:

35	36	40
21	18	20
14	9	10
7	14	–

73 Which of the numbered cubes at the bottom belong to A, B, C and D?

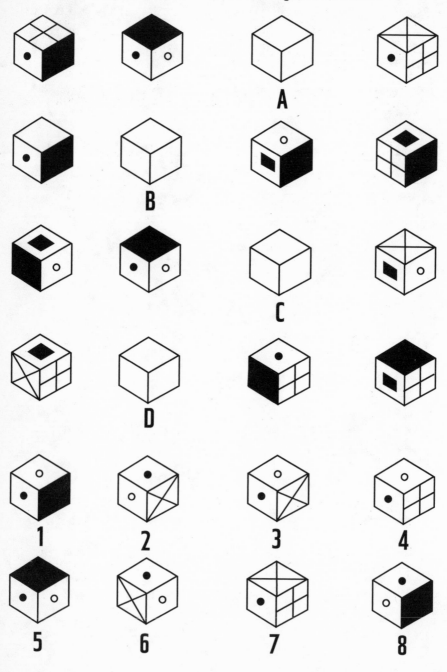

74 Which of the dice in the bottom row is SIX?

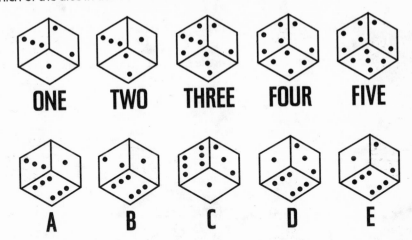

ONE   TWO   THREE   FOUR   FIVE

A   B   C   D   E

75 What is the value of x?

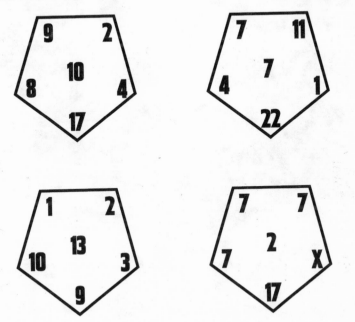

The Gramophone Record

76 A gramophone record is 12 inches in diameter. It has a 4.75 inch middle and a 0.25 inch border. The remaining 7 inches of playing surface has an average of 100 grooves to the inch. How far does the needle travel during the playing time of one side?

The Dinner Party

77 "I want to hold a dinner party", said my wife, "but I think we should invite as few guests as possible."

"OK", I said, "then as well as the two of us I suggest you invite your sister Andrea, her brother-in-law and his wife, my son Alan, my lawyer Ali and her husband and son, and Mrs Bower, the widow from next door, and her nephew who I happen to know is visiting her tomorrow."

"How many is that ?", asked my wife. "The fewest possible, as you requested", was my reply.

How many were at the dinner party?

The Great Book of Brainteasers

78 Which circle A - B - C - D or E should be placed in the blank circle in order to continue the sequence?

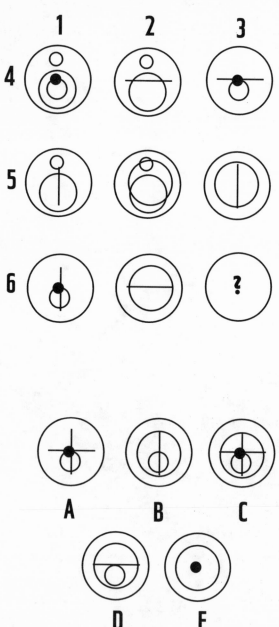

79 What number replaces the ?

18   4   10¾   11¼   3½   18½   ?

80 What number should replace the question mark?

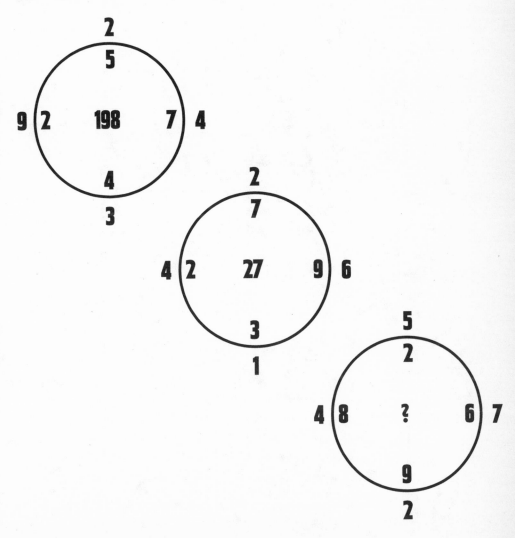

81

 is to 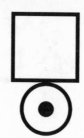 as 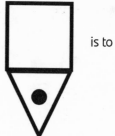 is to

A

B

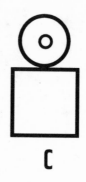

C

D

E

82 Which circle is nearest in content to A?

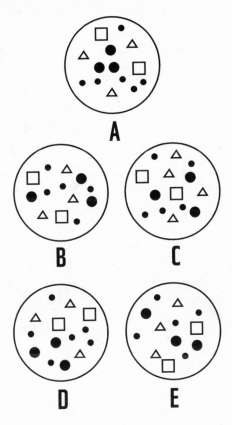

83 What degree is the same in Celsius + Fahrenheit

A 0°

B 40°

C 100°

D -10°

E -40°

The Great Book of Brainteasers

84 Take a word from each columnand find eight reptiles, each of which has a name of three words:

A	B	C
Green	Nosed	Toad
Long	Tree	Snake
Spade	Eating	Boa
Rat	Lined	Snake
Snake	Tree	Skink
Egg	Foot	Frog
Four	Tailed	Snake
Green	Eyed	Viper

85 Divide the diamomd into four equal shapes each containing one of each of the 6 symbols.

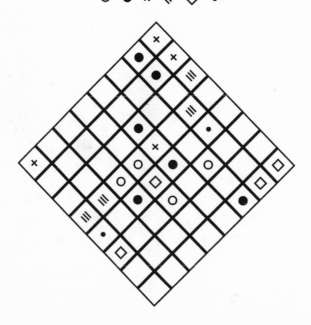

86 Which of A, B, C, D or E, fits into the blank circle to carry on a logical sequence?

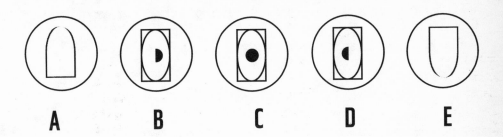

A   B   C   D   E

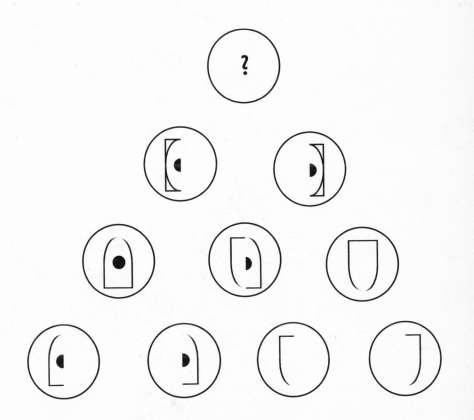

Divide a Circle

87 Draw three lines to divide the circle into three parts of identical size and shape.

The numbers in each part must add up to the same total.

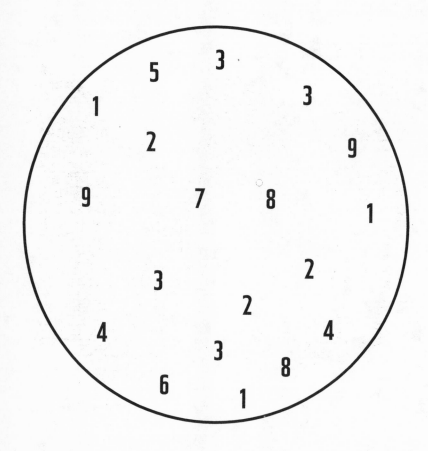

Production Line

88 A car manufacturer produces only black and white models, which come out of the final testing area completely at random.

What are the odds that four consecutive cars of the same colour will come through the test area at any one time?

The Great Book of Brainteasers

89 Which of the lower circles should take the place of No 5?

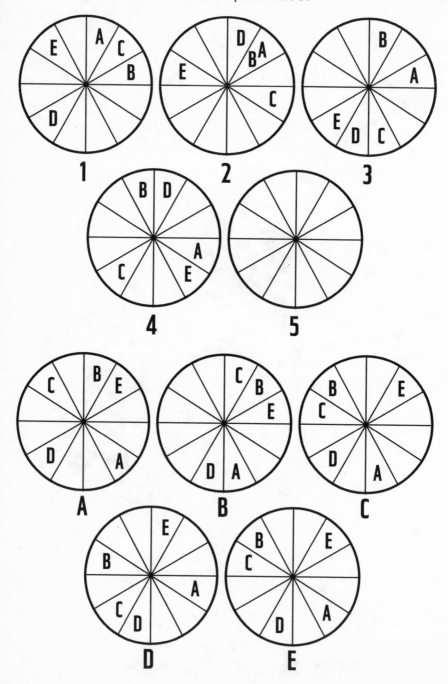

90 When a dart lands in an even number the next throw lands it in the second odd number clockwise. When a dart lands in an odd number the next throw lands it in the third even number clockwise from the previous throw. As can be seen, the first dart has already been thrown. Four more darts are to be thrown. What will be the total score of the five darts?

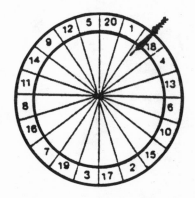

91 What famous author is this?

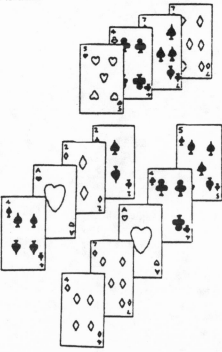

92 A clock shows 9.25. If it were held upside-down in front of a mirror, which of those below would be reflected?

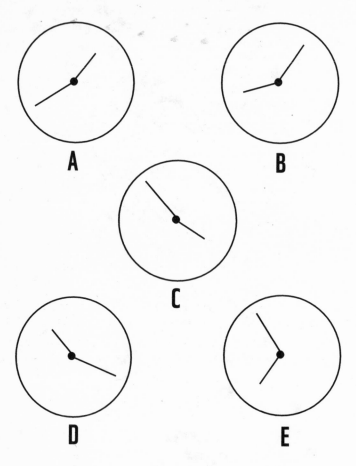

A

B

C

D

E

93 Which number in the bottom line should come next in the top line?

15 16 21 20   9 88 18 28 –

7 34 19 17 22 66

94 Find words for A, B, C, D, E, F, G and H

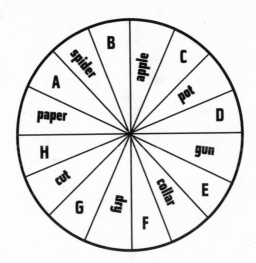

95 The top band rotates anti-clockwise. The middle band rotates clockwise. The bottom band rotates anti-clockwise. Each movement brings the next number into position, and there are eight numbers on each band, continuing in the same order on the blind sides. After 7 moves what will be the sum of the three numbers in the vertical column above A, and also the sum of the three numbers above B?

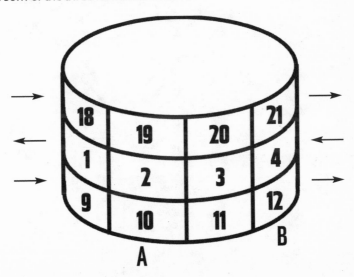

96 What is X?

97 Which of the numbered figures at the bottom should take the places of A, B and C?

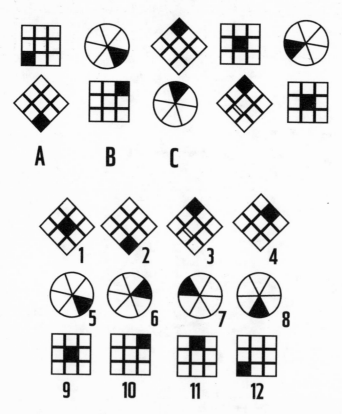

98 A advances 1 place, then 2, then 3, etc., increasing its jump by one each time.

B advances 2 places, then 3, then 4, etc., increasing its jump by one each time.

C advances 3 places, then 4, then 5, etc., increasing its jump by one each time.

Which will be the first to reach 25 EXACTLY?

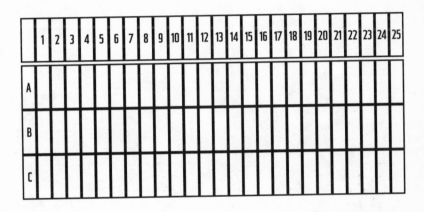

	1	2	3	4	5	6	7	8	9	10	11	12	13	14	15	16	17	18	19	20	21	22	23	24	25
A																									
B																									
C																									

99 What is X?

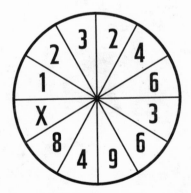

The Great Book of Brainteasers

Unique Features

100 Apart from coming between three and seven, what feature do the numbers 4, 5 and 6 have in common that they share with no other numbers?

5

4

6

Prime Number

101 A prime number is a number which is only divisible by itself and 1 without leaving any remainder. The first few prime numbers being, 2, 3, 5, 7, 11, 13.

Eight balls numbered 1-8 are placed in a bag and then drawn out at random one by one and the digits written down to form an eight-digit number. What are the chances that the number so formed will be a prime number.

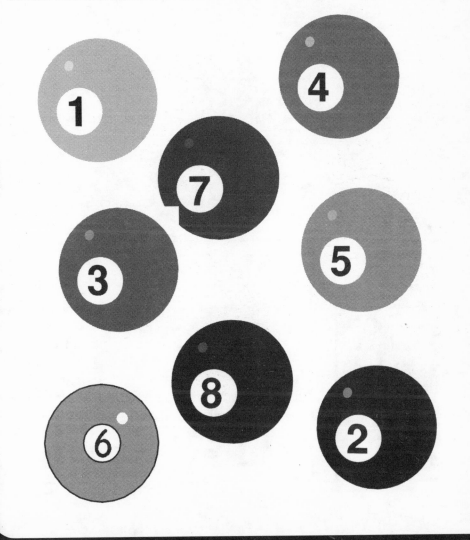

102 What is X?

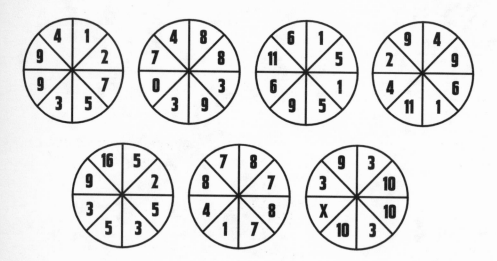

103 Add the numbers divisible by 7 to those divisible by 9 and subtract those divisible by 11.

169	**117**	**112**
135	**104**	**147**
153	**133**	**110**

104 What is X?

105 If the top house is correct, which, if any, of those below have been constructed wrongly?

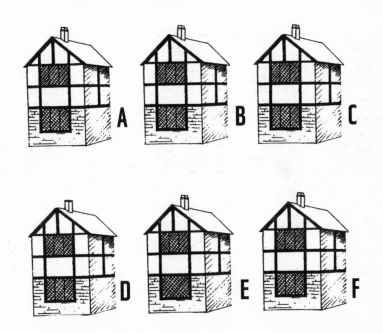

106 Alf, Bert and Charlie played a round of golf. Their combined score was 257. Alf took two more strokes than Charlie; Bert took seven more strokes than Alf; Charlie took two strokes fewer than Alf. What did each man score?

107 The black ball moves one place at a time clockwise; the white ball moves one place at a time anti-clockwise; the cross moves two places at a time anti-clockwise. In how many moves will they all be together?

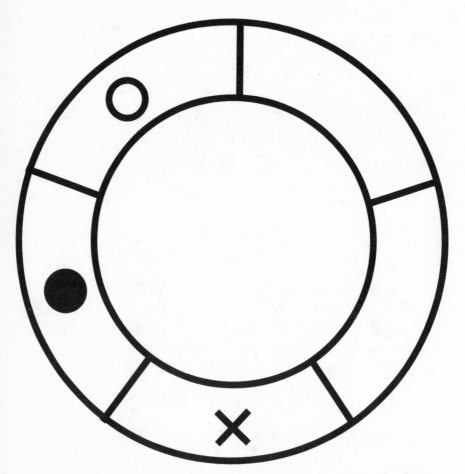

108 What is X?

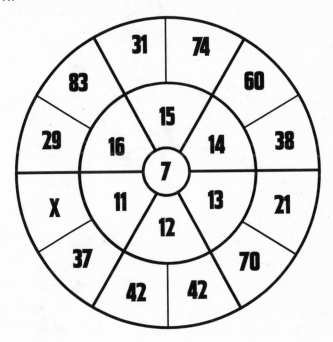

109 What is X?

21 8 46 X 2 92 16 42

110 What goes into the brackets?

1 5 8 (9 3 12) 2 7 1

3 1 6 (9 8 4) 7 3 1

1 2 3 (   ) 4 5 6

Ages

111 The ages of five family members total 100 between them.

Jean and Carol total 34 between them

Carol and Tom total 41 between them

Tom and Frank total 54 between them

Frank and Sally total 30 between them

How old is each family member?

Cheeses

112 The host brought out five bowls of cheeses and placed them before the guests.

"Just one bowl short", said the host, "I'll get it in just one minute, but first, can anyone tell me how many pieces of cheese it will contain?"

The guests scratched their heads and looked blank.

Can you say how many pieces the missing container should contain?

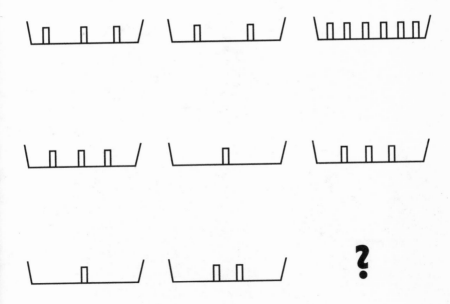

113 What is X?

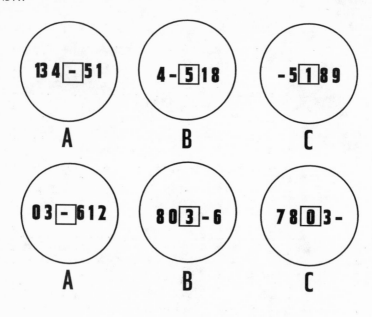

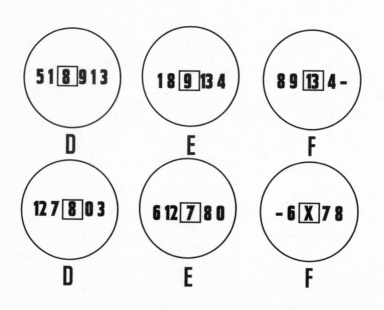

114 What is X?

3	7	5	2	1
1	2	8	9	3
4	1	6	7	12
5	5	X	5	5
7	7	7	1	1
4	4	4	4	2

115 What are X and Y?

X 19 13 8 4 1 3 6 10 15 Y

The Great Book of Brainteasers

116 The diameter of the outer circle is twice that of the inner circle. The other circle is midway between them. How many revolutions of the inner circle will there be before the three balls are again in line with each other?

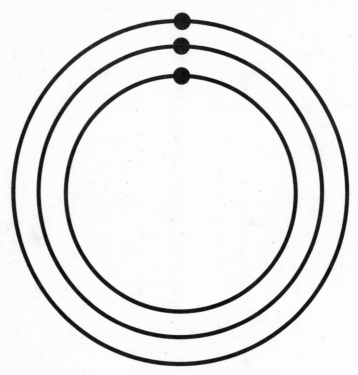

117 A boy is doing a jigsaw with 275 pieces. Each day that he fits pieces together there are fewer pieces left, and it is reasonable to assume that he fits more pieces each day because of the number left to sort out diminishes progressively. Hence he is able to fit an extra piece as each day goes by. On the first day he fits 20 pieces. How many days does it take him to complete the puzzle?

118 How far is SOUTHBURY?

The Great Book of Brainteasers

119 Which two pieces will complete the chequered square?

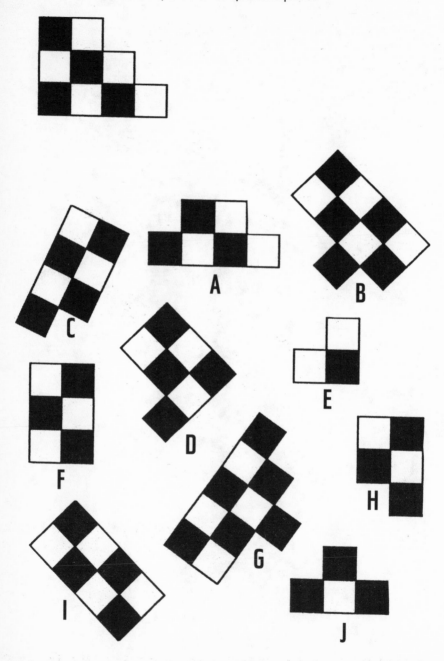

Orchard

120 A man has an orchard with fourteen trees. In order to detract thieves he wishes to build three circular fences so that each two trees are completely surrounded by fencing and is isolated from all the remaining twelve trees.

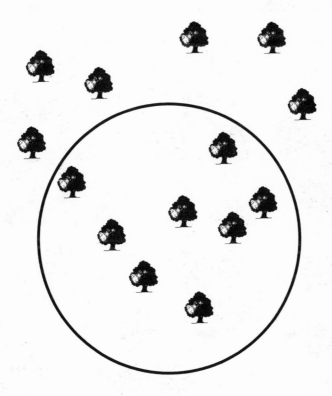

He has already built one of the fences. How should he construct the remaining two fences?

The Great Book of Brainteasers

Ceremonial Swords

121 Two Japanese tourists visit a country that forbids taking ceremonial swords on trains. Between them they have two suitcases and two ceremonial swords. Both swords are 5 feet long and the suitcases are 3.5 x 4.5 feet and 1.5 x 2 feet respectively.

How do they get both swords aboard the train without the guard noticing them?

122 What number should replace the ?

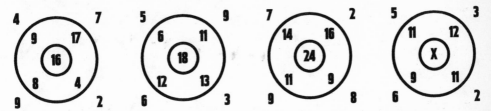

123 Which is the odd one out?

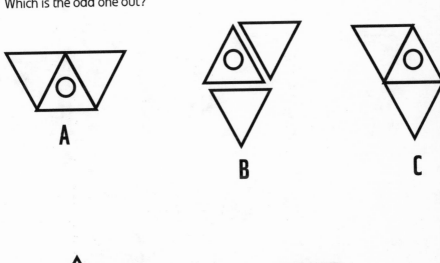

124 What number should replace the question mark?

125

 is to as

is to

A　　　　B　　　　C　　　　D　　　　E

126 What number should replace the ?

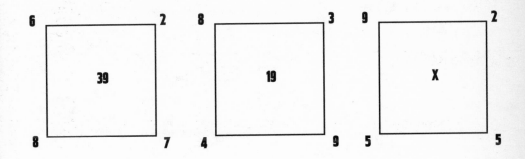

127 Which box has most in common with the box on the right?

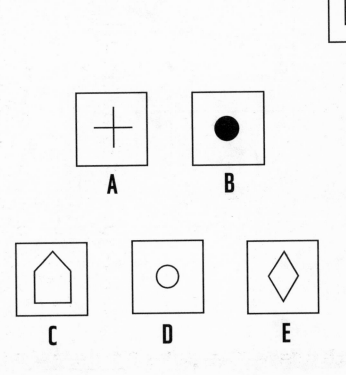

A

B

C

D

E

The Great Book of Brainteasers

128 Each of the nine squares in the grid marked 1A to 3C, should incorporate all the lines and symbols which are shown in the squares of the same letter and number immediately above and to the left. For example, 2B should incorporate all the lines and symbols that are in 2 and B. One of the squares is incorrect. Which one is it?

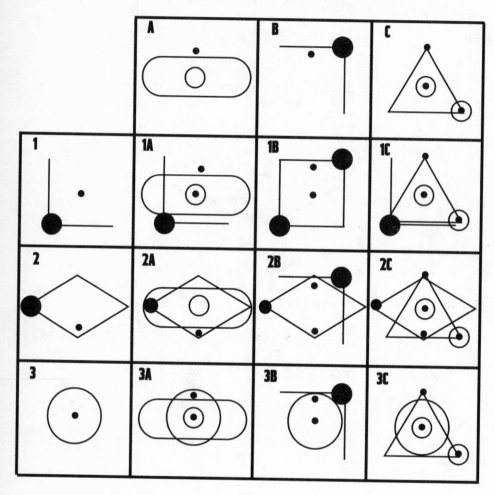

129 What is X?

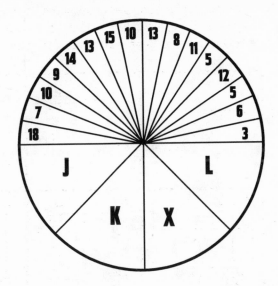

130 Which of these statements are true and which are false?

A. When the time is either 5.50 or 10.30 the hands of a clock form an angle of 120 degrees.

B. London is further south than Newfoundland.

C. Greenland is the largest island in the world.

Strange Addition

131 If + =

and + =

and + =

and + =

what does

 + | = **?**

Dear Old Uncle

132 "My dear old Uncle Jim died today", said one of my work colleagues. "Sorry to hear that", I replied, "how old was he?"

"Eighty-eight" replied my colleague. "He was born in 1933 and died in 2001".

"That doesn't add up", I remarked. "Its true enough though", said my colleague, "see if you can work it out".

What is the explanation?

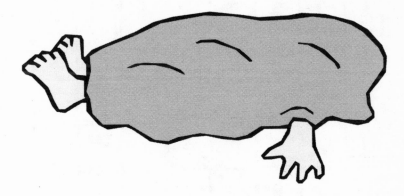

The Great Book of Brainteasers

133 What numbers do the letters represent? The first calculation is an addition; the second is a subtraction.

```
  A B C          A B C
  D E F          D E F
 ‾‾‾‾‾          ‾‾‾‾‾
 1216            254
```

134 What is the total of the numbers in the cross?

1	5	9	0	8	6	7	1
4	2	8	7	5	6	2	0
1	6	3	8	9	3	5	6
1	2	8		4	7	6	5
0	7				1	9	8
5	8	6		0	6	7	5
6	7	0	1	5	9	7	8
8	6	9	5	7	6	0	8

135 In a cross country race George was not first; John came in after Harry, Ian was not ahead of Ken: George was not in front of John; Ian was not fourth or fifth; Ken was not first.

In what order did they finish?

136 Which of the numbered cubes on the right belong in the spaces A, B, C and D?

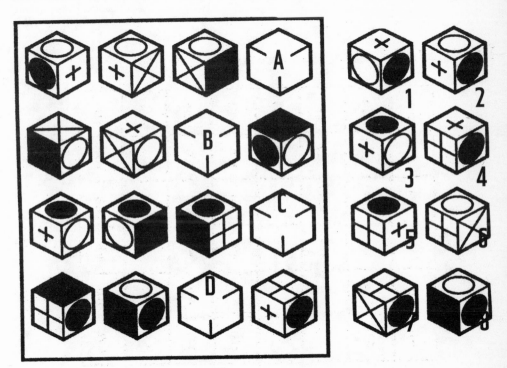

137 How many combinations of three of these numbers will add to 100?

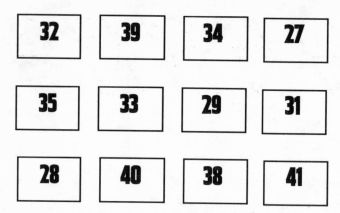

32	39	34	27
35	33	29	31
28	40	38	41

138 Two couples played each other at darts: A and B played together and C and D were partners. They used the dart-board shown below, on which the bull scores 50. Player A scored all numbers divisible by 4, plus the bull; player B scored all numbers divisible by 3, plus the bull; player C scored all numbers divisible by 7, plus the bull; and player D scored all even numbers, excluding the bull. Which team won, and what were the individual scores?

139 Which is the odd one out?

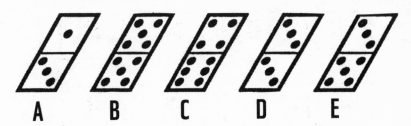

A   B   C   D   E

140 What goes into the empty brackets?

441 (14736) 144

625 (12516) 96

756 (10832) 256

108 (   ) 90

141 How can the number 18 be represented by a fraction using the digits 1 to 9 once each only?

1 2 3 4 5 6 7 8 9 = 18

The Circle

142 Draw the largest circle possible. It must be completely within the square, must not touch the side of the square and must not touch any other circle.

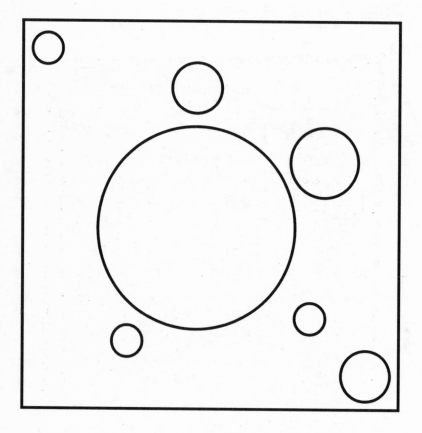

Newsagent

143 The newsagent was having a terribly slack day.

Between 10 am and 11 am he sold two copies of a magazine and five copies of a newspaper for a total of 35.90. Between 11 am and 12 noon he sold five copies of the same magazine and two copies of the same newspaper for a total of £7.40.

What is the cost of one magazine and one newspaper?

The Great Book of Brainteasers

144 These are words taht contain synonyms. If you remove some of the letters from the original word, you are left with a synonym of that word. take, for example, the word CALUMNIEs. If you delete the 1st, 2nd, 4th, 5th and 6th letter you are left with LIES – a synonym of the original word. Here are a few more examples for you to try:

CATACOMB
CHARIOT
CHOCOLATE
DELIBERATE
DESTRUCTION
ENCOURAGE
EVACUATE
EXHILARATION

FACETIOUSNESS
FATIGUE
HURRIES
ILLUMINATED
INSTRUCTOR
LATEST
MASCULINE
PASTEURIZED

145 How many different teams of 11 can be made out of 8 men and 7 women if each team must consist of 6 men and 5 women?

146

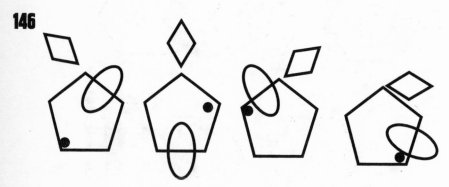

Which option below continues the above sequence?

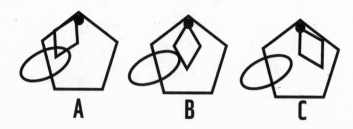

A   B   C

147 Which hexagon fits the missing space?

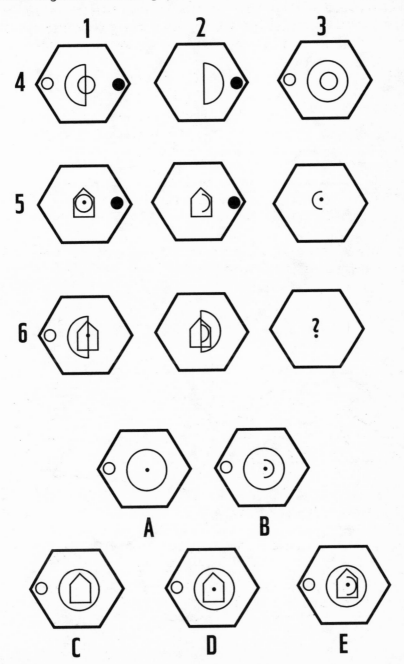

148 Give values for A, B, C and D.

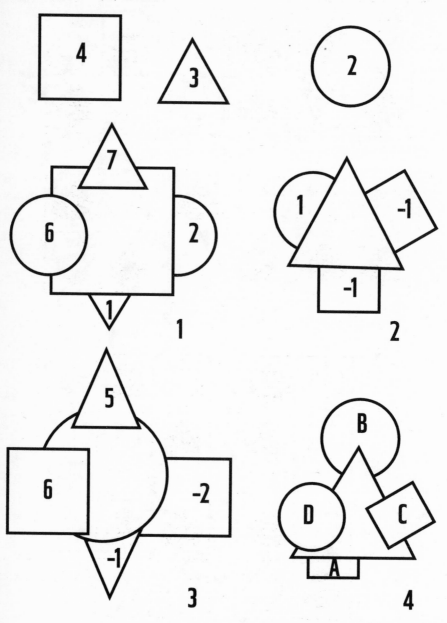

149 Which one follows F?

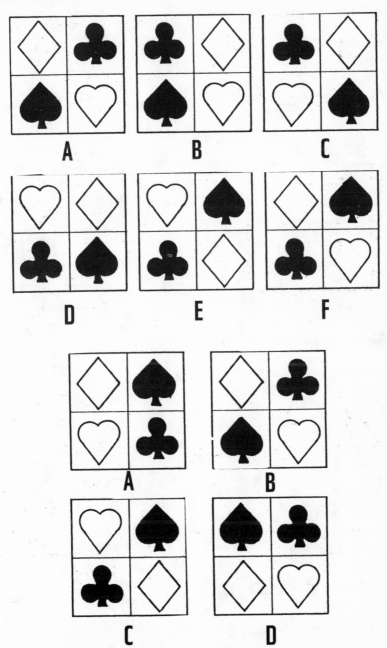

150 Which triangle is wrong?

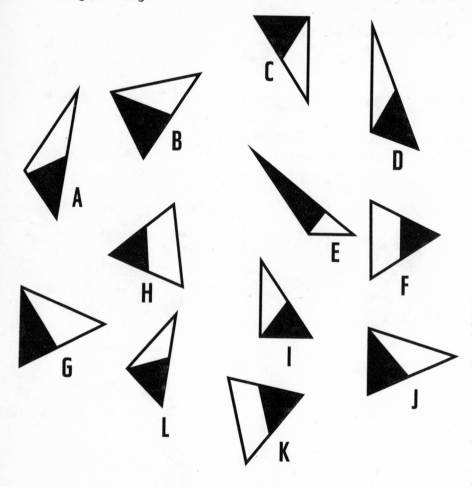

151 Subtract the sum of the prime numbers from the sum of the odd numbers (which are not prime) and add the sum of the even numbers:

3 6 7 9 11 12 14 15
16 18 19 21 27 31 33

Eleven

152 Add three matches to make eleven.

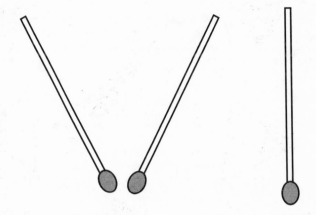

Two Halves

153 Draw just one line to divide the square into two equal halves so that the numbers in each half add up to the same total.

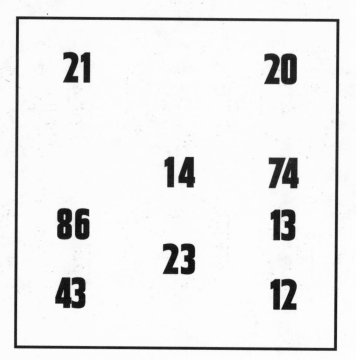

154

If

is FOG

and

is GEM

and

 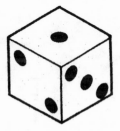 

is HIM

what is this

155 Which is the odd one out?

A. 119

B. 21

C. 91

D. 77

E. 95

F. 105

156 If

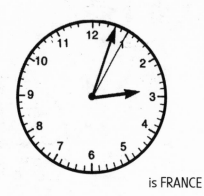

is FRANCE

where is this?

157 What are the next two terms in this series?

36 91 21 51 82

12 42 7   -   -

158 What are A, B and C?

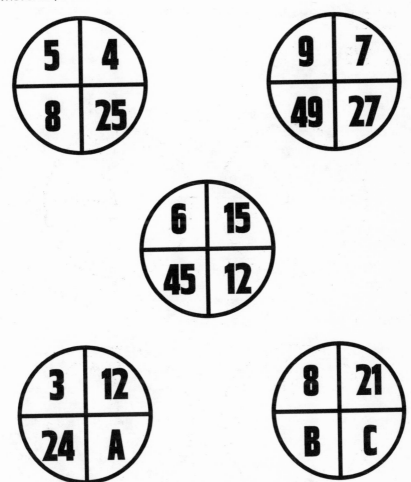

159 Which of the fractions in the bottom line should complete the series in the top line?

3.8 **²⁹/₆** **5⁶/₇** **6.875**

7¼ **8.1** **⁷⁷/₉** **⁷/₉** **8.375**

160 The black ball moves one corner at a time clockwise. The white ball moves anti-clockwise. First it goes to the next corner. Then it misses one and goes to the next corner. Then it misses two, then three and so on. A.
In how many moves will the two balls be in the same corner?
B. In which corner will they first be together?

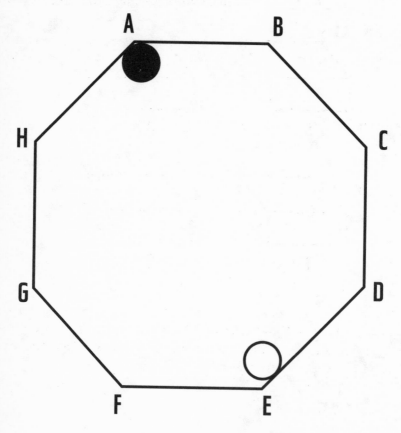

161 What should go inside the empty brackets?

9164 (8231) 4187

6194 (5573) 8174

4398 (   ) 7654

162 A is the bottom block of a column of six which measures 18.6 cms high   B is the bottom block of a column which measures 40.3 cms high   C is the bottom block of a column which measures 58.9 cms high   D is the bottom block of a column which measures 34.1 cms high. All the blocks are the same size. How many blocks are there altogether?

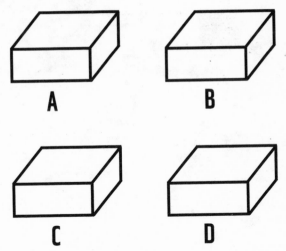

A　　**B**

C　　**D**

163 In the previous problem, if the blocks are coloured black and white alternately with a black block at the bottom and all the black blocks removed, what would then be the combined height of the remaining blocks?

Conifers

164 In my back garden are six conifers and each is a different height. The tallest is twice as high as the shortest and there is one foot difference in height exactly between each of the different sizes from smallest to tallest.

How high is the tallest conifer and how high is the smallest?

Missing Number

165 What is the missing number?

1	2	4	8
2	8	3	6
7	2	5	?
9	6	2	4

166 The four drawers look identical, but in fact each will only fit into its own compartment, as there is a very slight difference in the runners. If the drawers are removed and mixed up, what is the maximum number of combinations possible before sliding them into their correct positions?

167 This is a test of mental arithmetic (and memory). Without writing (except for your answer) how many groups of three consecutive numbers add to ten?

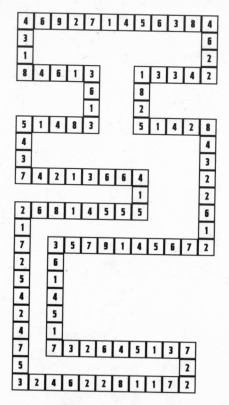

168 If pinion A rotates four revolutions anti-clockwise how many times will F rotate and in which direction? The number of teeth is indicated on each pinion.

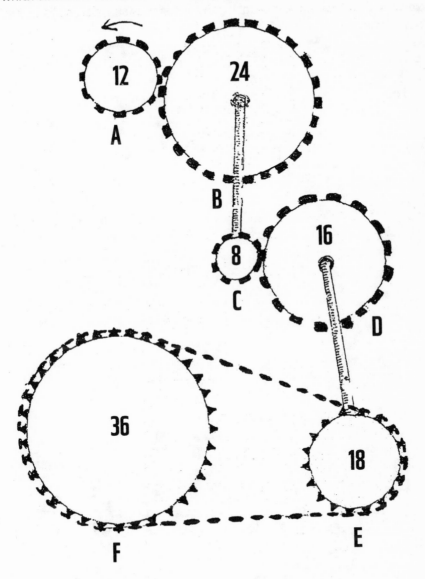

169 (A) A man travels by bus from A to D, leaving A at noon, and having to change buses at B and C. The distances involved are shown on the diagram, as well as the average speeds of the buses. All buses run on time and at each stop he catches the first available bus (as shown on the time-tables). After the first leg of the journey he takes 2 $1/2$ minutes to walk to the next bus stop and after the second leg he takes 6 minutes to reach the next bus stop. At what time does he arrive at D?

(B) If he could have caught a non-stop bus at A and if the bus averaged 20mph throughout, at what time would he have arrived at D?

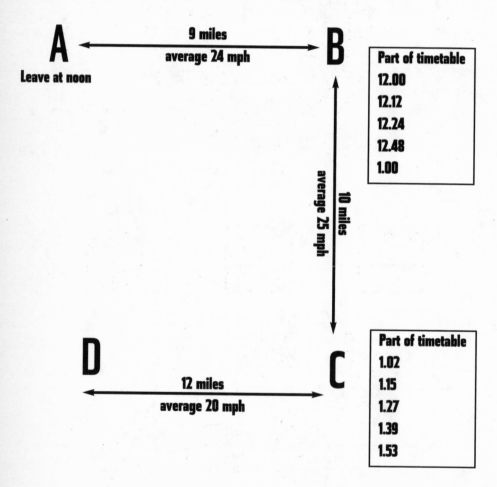

A **9 miles** average 24 mph B

Leave at noon

Part of timetable
12.00
12.12
12.24
12.48
1.00

average 25 mph **10 miles**

D **12 miles** average 20 mph C

Part of timetable
1.02
1.15
1.27
1.39
1.53

170 The ring marked A moves 3 spaces clockwise at a time. The ring marked B moves 3 spaces anti-clockwise at a time. The ring marked C moves 2 places clockwise at a time. In how many moves will all the black spaces be together for the first time?

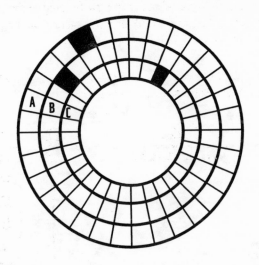

171

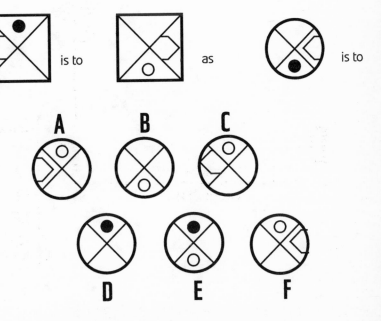

172 Which hexagon below continues the sequence?

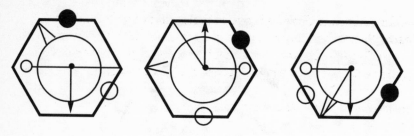

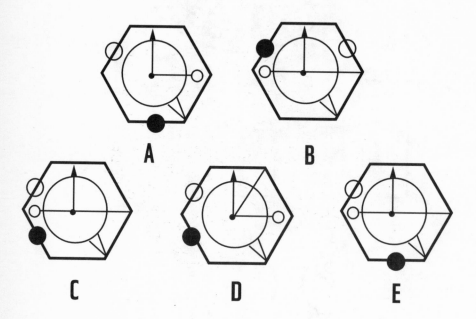

173 In 15 years time the combined ages of 2 brothers and 2 sisters will be 110. What will it be in 7 years time?

Dates Coincidence

174 My elderly Aunt and Uncle both died in the late 20th-century within a few days of each other. Remarkably they were also born within the same number of days as each other, but even more remarkable was that all the numbers of the date, month and years of their births and deaths all began with the same letter.

What were the dates of their births and deaths?

Fruit

175 How much are pomegranates?

oranges	**34 pence each**
apples	**24 pence each**
pears	**23 pence each**
pomegranates	**?**

176 What number should replace the ? To a definite rule?

177 What is the mathematical sign for greater than?

A >

B _

C <

D ⋖

E ⋗

The Great Book of Brainteasers

178 Which of A, B, C, D or E, fits into the blank circle to carry on a logical sequence?

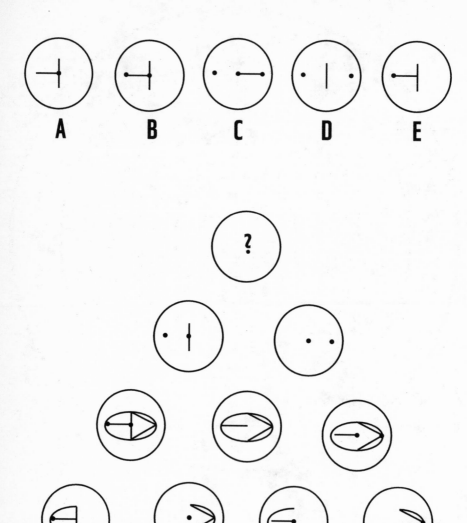

A   B   C   D   E

179 What is X?

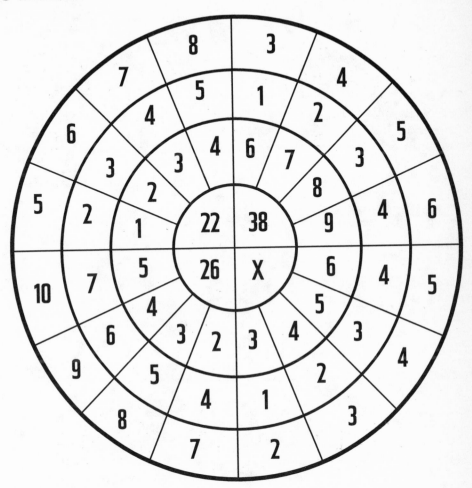

Section Five

Answers

The Great Book of Brainteasers

1 A is 11, B is 6, C is 7 and D is 4.
Take alternate sectors in alternate circles, moving always in a clockwise direction.
Starting at the first circle:

1	2	3	4	5
6	7	8	9	10
3	4	5	6	7
4	5	6	7	8
2	3	4	5	6 (B)
5	6	7	8	9
7	8	9	10	11 (A)
8	9	10	11	12

Starting at the second circle, and again going clockwise:

3	4	5	6
7	8	9	10
1	2	3	4 (D)
5	6	7	8
2	3	4	5
4	5	6	7 (C)
8	9	10	11
6	7	8	9

2 150.
The first term (90) is the product of the last two terms (30 and 3). This procedure is followed throughout, so X is the product of 3 and 50.

3 A. 1+3+9+27; B. 1÷3x9+27; C. 1-3-9+27; D. 1+3-9+27; E. 1x3+9+27; F. 1+3x9-27; G. 1+3x9+27.

4 A scored 28 runs; B scored 45 runs; C scored 62 runs; D scored 25 runs; and E scored 20 runs. If B and C scored 107, A, D and D must have scored a total of 73 runs. If A scored x runs, x+x-8+5+x-8=73, therefore, 3x=84 so x=28 From knowing that A scored 28 runs it is easy to discover how many the other players scored.

5 302.
A.22-24-26; B. 36-38-40; C. 2-4-6; D. 1-3-5-7; E. 13-15-17-19; F. 8-9-10-11-12; G. 26-27-28-29-30; H. 36-37-38-39-40. The numbers not used are 14-16-18-20-21-23-25-31-32-33-34-35.

6 A swastika

7 10
Add the sum of the digits on either side of the brackets to the sum of the digits in the brackets above. Hence: 7+4+2=13, which, by adding the digits, is 4; 4+9+8=21, which, by adding the digits, is 3; the sum of the digits in the brackets above - 21 - is 3; 4+3+3=10.

8 A is 2, B is 5, C is 8 and D is 4.
In alternate circles, starting with the first circle, the numbers advance one sector clockwise; starting with the second circle the numbers go back one sector anti-clockwise.

9 5.
The numbers in the horizontal lines add to 30. In the last line the numbers add up to 25, so X must be 5 to bring the total to 30.

10 $46 \frac{1}{4}$, $47 \frac{3}{4}$
The total now is: $12 \frac{1}{2} + 18 \frac{3}{4} + 15 = 46 \frac{1}{4}$
The total in $2 \frac{1}{2}$ hours will be $21 + 15 \frac{1}{4} + 11 \frac{1}{2} = 47 \frac{3}{4}$

11 X is 902, Y is 50400
In each circle the number in the top left quarter is the sum of the top two quarters in the previous circle; the number in the top right is the sum of the bottom two quarters in the previous circle; the number in the bottom left quarter is the product of the two numbers in the previous circle; the number in the bottom right quarter is the product of the two numbers in the bottom two quarters in the previous circle. Therefore, X is the product of 22 and 41; and Y is the product of 120 and 420.

12

7	8	9
4	5	6
1	2	3

13 D

This completes every possible grouping in threes of the four different symbols

14 C

A pinion interposed between two other pinions does not change the ratio between the others, but it does change the direction of rotation. Nor does it matter how many pinions are interposed, but because, in this case, there are three intermediate pinions, the direction of rotation will remain as in the original.

15 12

The mistakes are: there; description; mowers; sons-in-law; councillor; objets d'art; electrical; there; seething; vehicles; commemorating; the (repeated).

16 A

17 188 X is 14 and Y is 10 to complete the series.

The top series advances each number by 3, so X is 14; the bottom series advances every fourth row by 3, so Y advances 7 (the 5th term) by 3 to become 10.

18 16 and 96

16 multiplied by 4 (its square root) is 64, which is the same as the square of 8 (half of 16). 32 (double 16) added to 64 gives 96.

19 X is 7, Y is 1 and Z is 4

Add the digits in each number and the result is the same in each successive quarter moving clockwise: 119 (11), 182 (11), 416 (11), 137(X) (11), 612 (9), 99 (18 - that is, 9), 513 (9), 78 (15 - that is, 15,6), 96 (15 - that is, 6), 105 (6), 114(Z) (6); 38 (11 - that is,2), 74(11 that is, 2), 65 (11 - that is, 2), 101 (Y) (2).

20 C, A, B

21 They all finished at the same time (2.10pm)

22 The grid should contain 1 x 1, 2 x 2, 3 x 3, 4 x 4 etc.
The missing numbers are, therefore, 5, 6, 8, 8 and all numbers are placed in the grid so that the same number is never horizontally or vertically adjacent

4	7	8	3	8	5
6	5	(6)	(8)	7	4
8	1	8	6	2	(8)
3	6	5	8	7	6
(5)	7	2	6	3	7
8	4	7	4	7	5

23 34 minutes.
First Maurice and Kathleen cross - 4 minutes
Then Maurice returns - 2 minutes
Then Thomas and Colonel Tompkins cross - 20 minutes
Then Kathleen returns - 4 minutes
Finally Maurice and Kathleen recross - 4 minutes

24 CardB. 23 numbers were called.

25 Any of them

26 5 o'clock

27 H

28 D

29 3
The first number in the top line is the sum of the first two numbers in the bottom line; the next number in the top line is the sum of the second and third numbers in the bottom line. This procedure is followed throughout, so X is the sum of 1 and 2.

30 Diamonds, Seven

31 C

32 136, 631 and 233

33 A, B, C, D and E
They would all overflow except F. The cubic capacity of the top receptacle is 225 cubic units. The other containers will hold: A. 216, B. 192, C. 216, D. 207 (approximately), and E. 200, cubic units.

34 1. 1010 - 10
   2. 1010/10
   3. 10 TO 10 (9:50)

35 His wife had just given birth to a baby.

36 1

37 716
When it is spaced correctly the top line reads: 631, 443, 174, 526, 716(X), 915. Adding the digits that make up each number: 10, 11, 12, 13, 14, 15.

38 64=(8x9) - (2x4)

39 F   A=E, B=D, C=G

40

81		4 16		9
–		\ /		/ \
32		8 plus	3	27

41 14 $^3/_4$
There are two sequences: the first is –8 $^1/_4$; the second is +1 $^1/_4$

42 A
(In each box 2.0 = 1△ and 2△ = 1.0
to make next box) therefore 2C + 1△ = 2△

43 21 (7+8+5+9+8) - (4+1+2+2+7)

44 5, 12 and 20

45

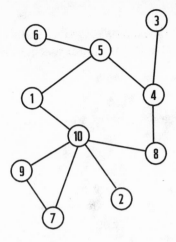

46 No. 8
The figure is rotated anti-clockwise throughout. Taking a unit as being a move of 45 degrees, in the first move (No. 2) it is turned one unit; then it is turned two units (No. 3). It is then successively turned 3, 4, 5, 6 and 7 units, bringing it to position No. 8. Therefore the next move will be eight units, in other words bringing it back to the same position as in position 8.

47 1 lb., 3 lbs., 9lbs., 27lbs.
The weights multiply by three progressively and the combined weight of all of them is 40 lbs.
If you worked it out by trial and error, it is obvious that there must be a weight of 1 lb. in order to weigh the smallest article. It would not be necessary to have a 2 lb. weight, since this could be achieved by putting a 3 lb. weight on one side of the scales and a 1 lb. weight on the other.

Individual weighings are made as follows:

2 lbs. ...3 on one side and 1 on the other.
4 lbs. ... 3 and 1 on the same side.
5 lbs. ... 9 on one side and 3 and 1 on the other.
6 lbs. ... 9 on one side and 3 on the other.
7 lbs. ... 9 and 1 on one side and 3 on the other.
8 lbs. ... 9 on one side and 1 on the other,

and so on, eventually reaching 40 lbs., when all the weights are placed on one side only.

48 No. 2.

The upper figures (in sharp keys) have open notes; the lower figures (in flat keys) have black notes. The spacing between the notes is the same as the spacing between the sharps or flats.

49 36, 6.

Each alternate number is the square root of the one before it. The square root progress in units - 3, 4, 5 and 6.

50 A=8 B=5

If an even number is at the top, add the three faces and then add the top number. If an odd number is at the top, add the three faces and then subtract the top number. Thus, in A, as there is an even number at the top, add the three faces: 3, 2 and 1, and add the top number (2), making a total of 8. In B, as there is an odd number at the top, add the three faces: 3, 2 and 1, making a total of 6, from which subtract the top number (1), giving 5 as the result.

51 $^5/_{25}$ in which the upper figure is the square root of the lower figure. In all the other fractions it is the cube root.

52 No. 2.

The figure is rotating clockwise, a quarter-turn at a time. Therefore, the fourth move at X will bring the black ends of the vanes into view again.

53 X=144
Y=400
Z=256

The values of the shapes are as follows: Square = 2 Triangle = 4   Rectangle = 6 Circle = 8. Where shapes overlap, add together the values of the individual shapes and square the result. Thus, in the examples given, where the circle and rectangle overlap the value is 196 (6+8) = 14. 14 squared = 196. Where the triangle, rectangle and circle overlap the value is 324 (4+6+8) = 18. 18 squared = 324.

54 315

The number in each of the centre squares is the product minus the sum of the three numbers in the three corner squares surrounding it. Therefore, 8 x 7 x 6, 336, minus 8 +7 +6, 21 = 315.

55 She used a knife coated just on one edge with cyanide. When she sliced the apple in two, the victim's half only was poisoned.

56 Tom 14 (2 x 5, 4 x 1)
Dick 10 (1 x 10)
Harry 26 (2 x 10, 1 x 5, 1 x 1)

57 256 11 5.
There are three series here, starting respectively with the first three numbers. The first sequence is 2, 4, 16 and 256 (each number is the square of the one before it); the second sequence is 2, 5, 8 and 11 (the numbers increase by three each time); the third sequence is 2, 3, 4 and 5 (numbers rising by one at a time).

58 CDLIX
The progression is 51, 153, 459 and 1,377 (multiplying by three each time) expressed in Roman numerals.

59 E.
The figure is turned 45 degrees clockwise each time (the pointer in the circle indicates this), and the thick side is advanced one side on each move. E is wrong, therefore. Although the figure has turned 45 degrees clockwise the thick side has not been advanced at all. It should appear as follows:

60 210
After the first wicket had fallen 17 runs were added before the next wicket fell. Thereafter the additional runs scored were 15 (2 less), 19 (2 more), 13 (4 less), 21 (4 more), 11 (6 less), 23 (6 more), 9 (8 less) and finally 25 (8 more), making a grand total of 210 - thanks to the fine last wicket stand!

61 5
There are three combined sequences here. Starting with the first number, the first sequence is : 1, 2, 3 and 4; the second number starts the next sequence of 7, 6, 5 and 4; the third number starts the third sequence of 3, 5 and 7.

62 The hour hand should point to 12 and the minutes hand should point to 2. The hour hand advances progressively by 1 hour, 2 hours, 3 hours, 4 hours and 5 hours. The minute hand advances by 5 minutes, 10 minutes, 20 minutes, 40 minutes and 80 minutes.

63 65

In each segment of the circle the two numbers in the outer ring are added and then divided by three (the common divisor indicated in the centre of the circle). The result is entered in the inner ring.

64 H.

In all the others the black point is to the right of the right-angle. In H the black point is to the left of the right-angle.

65 80 crocus
1 daffodil
19 hyacinths

66 Yes

Suppose the hiker had an identical twin who also starts from the pub at the top at 6 am and reaches the pub at the bottom at 6 pm, in other words duplicating the twins ascent. there has then got to be a point on the track where they meet each other.

67 121 122 123.

Each group of three consecutive numbers starts by first doubling the last number of the previous group and adding one (1 2 3 = 3 doubled + 1 = 7); then trebling the last number of the previous group and adding one (7 8 9 = 9 trebled + 1 = 28); finally quadrupling the last number of the previous group and adding one (28 29 30 = 30 multiplied by 4 + 1 = 121).

68 4 REVOLUTIONS

69 C

The model is rotated anti-clockwise. The first move is one face of the octagonal-shaped hub; the second two faces; the third three faces, and so on. Therefore, after position 6 the vanes are rotated six faces, bringing them to the position shown in C.

70 D.

Imagine that the circle consists of two semi-circles, each having independent movement from the other. The entire figure is rotated clockwise. In each movement the semi-circle containing the letters - A, B, C and D moves forward by one segment. The semi-circle containing the numbers 1, 2, 3 and 4, moves forward three segments each time.

71 Multiply the number in the top left-hand quarter by 6 and subtract 1. (4 multiplied by 6 = 24, less 1 = 23.) Multiply the number in the top right-hand quarter by 5 and add 1. (2 multiplied by 5 = 10, plus 1 = 11.)

72 7 - so that each column adds up to 77.

73 A = 3
B = 8
C = 6
D = 7

In the top row across the cube is turned one face at a time, with the facing black spot remaining in the same position. It can be deduced that after the black face at the top (second cube) the next face visible at the top will have a white spot.
In the second row across the black side remains in position and the face with the black spot goes to the top. In each case the remaining face can be deduced by examining the other faces in the same row. The third and fourth rows are changed in a similar way.

74 A

The bottom face indicates the actual number (six). The left-hand face shows the number of letters in the word (one = 3, two = 3, three = 5, four = 4, five = 4, six = 3). The right-hand face shows the number of vowels in the word (OnE = 2, twO = 1, thrEE = 2, fOUr = 2, fIvE = 2, sIx = 1).

75 8 (7+17)-(7+7+8)=2

76 .3.5 inches
It travels in a straight line across the disc.

The Great Book of Brainteasers

77 Four
Me and my wife
Alan my son
Andrea my sister-in-law

Andrea's brother-in-law and his wife are my and my wife
My lawyer Ali is my wife
Mrs Bower is my sister-in-law Andrea
Andrea's nephew is my son Alan

78 C

79 3 j702

There are two sequences. The first is $-7\,^{1}/_{4}$; the second is $+7\,^{1}/_{4}$

80 255 (4x5x7x2) - (2+8+6+9)

81 C

82 D. A and D have six small dots.

83 (d)- 40°

84 Spade-foot toad   Green tree frog
   Snake-eyed skink   Four-lined snake
   Rat-tailed snake   Egg-eating snake
   Long-nosed viper   Green tree boa

85

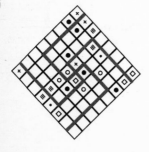

86 C

87

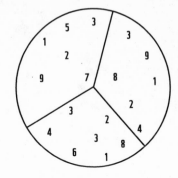

88 1 in 8 or 7 to 1

Each car to come through the final test area has an even chance of being either black or white. To repeat four times is 1 to the power 4 or 16. However, as the first car will always be black or white, only another three cars are required to complete a sequence of four white or four black cars. The chances, therefore, are two to the power of three, or 7 to 1.

89 E

a moves one place at a time clockwise;

b moves one place at a time anti-clockwise;

c moves two places at a time clockwise;

d moves to and from opposite segments;

e moves anti-clockwise, first one place, then two, then three, and so on.

90 68

1st throw...18

2nd throw...15

3rd throw...8

4th throw...9

5th throw...18 (again)

Total 68

91 MARK TWAIN

The four cards at the top indicate the first 23 letters of the alphabet:

Ace of hearts up to the 5... 1-5, or A to E

Ace of clubs up to the 7 ... 6-9, or F to I

Ace of spades up to the 7 ... 10-16, or J to P

Ace of diamonds up to the 7 ... 17-23, or Q to W

92 B

93 66
The numbers at the top are divisible by 3 and 4 alternately. The only number in the bottom line that is divisible by 3 is 66.

94 The disposition of the letters from A to H indicates that the words are considered in a clockwise direction. Starting with PAPER, and reading clockwise:
paper
(A) MONEY
spider
(B) CRAB
apple
(C) JACK
pot
(D) SHOT
gun
(E) DOG
collar
(F) BONE
dry
(G) CLEAN
cut
(H) GLASS
paper

95 A 32; B 38

	A	B
1st move	18	20
	3	5
	9	11
2nd move	25	19
	4	6
	16	10
3rd move	24	18
	5	7
	15	9

4th move	23	25
	6	8
	14	16
5th move	22	24
	7	1
	13	15
6th move	21	23
	8	2
	12	14
7th move	20	22
	1	3
	11	13
Total	32	38

96 6

Correcting the spacing, the series becomes: 1 8 27 64 125 21- That is: the cubes of: 1, 2, 3, 4, 5, 6. The cube of 6 is 216, which means that 6 must follow 21.

97 A 5; B 2; C 12.

Consider the movements of the black section in each figure. It goes diagonally across the square from bottom left to top right and then back again:

A

In the circle it moves two segments at a time in a clockwise direction:

B

In the diamond it moves alternately from top to bottom:

C

98 C.

The relative positions are shown below:

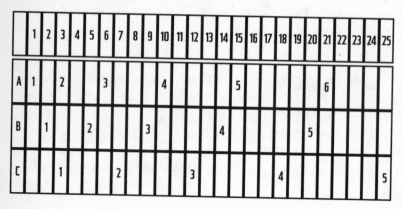

	1	2	3	4	5	6	7	8	9	10	11	12	13	14	15	16	17	18	19	20	21	22	23	24	25
A	1	2		3					4					5					6						
B	1			2			3					4					5								
C		1			2				3					4											5

99 12

Move clockwise from 1 and miss two segments each time. The series are: 1 - 2 - 3 - 4, 2 - 4 - 6 - 8, 3 - 6 - 9 - 12(X).

100 They all use the same number of segments when displayed on a calculator as the number itself, i.e.

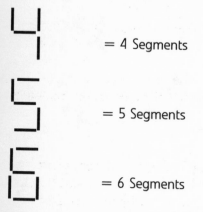

= 4 Segments

= 5 Segments

= 6 Segments

101 Nil

The sum of the digits 1-8 is 36. When the sum of the digits of any number is divisible by nine, then the number will always divide by nine and three exactly. Whichever order the balls are drawn out the sum of their digits will be 36 and the number will be divisible by at least the numbers 3 and 9.

102 4

Add alternate segments throughout: first circle = 20, second circle = 21, third circle = 22, fourth circle = 23, fifth circle = 24, sixth circle = 25. Therefore, alternate segments in the seventh circle should add to 26.

103 687

Those divisible by 7 are 112, 147 and 133 (total 392). Those divisible by 9 are 117, 135 and 153 (total 405). The only number divisible by 11 is 110, and 110 subtracted from 797 gives 687.

104 F

The letters are the initials of the numbers in the opposite segments. X is opposite to 4.

105 D and E

In D the chimney is different;
in E the bottom window is not divided.

106 Alf took 84 strokes, Bert took 91 strokes and Charlie took 82 strokes

107 3 moves

108 40

In each segment add the two numbers in the outer circle and divide by the number in the inner circle. In each case the answer is 7, as in the centre.

109 1

The first number is half the last one. The second number is half the penultimate one, and so on. Therefore X(1) is half of 2.

110 4 10 7

Add the first and last digits of the number on the left and place the result on the left inside the brackets. Add the first and last digits of the number on the right and place the answer next inside the brackets. Then add the middle numbers of those outside the brackets and place the answer on the right inside the brackets. Thus, in the last line: add 1 to 3 (4), 4 to 6 (10) and 2 to 5 (7).

111 Jean 29, Carol 5, Tom 36, Frank 18, Sally 12.

112 2 pieces

Looking across multiply the pieces of the first two bowls together to obtain the quantity in the third bowl. Looking down, divide.

113 12

Although the numbers on the globes indicate the direction of rotation, they are immaterial and are in the nature of being 'red herrings'. The important numbers are the middle ones (enclosed in square).

The second line has the same letters as the first, and this indicates that the two lines must be regarded as a pair and the two centre numbers added together. This gives (after the first globes, which add to zero:) 8, 1, 16, 16, 13 plus the value of X. Substituting letters of the alphabet according to the numbers gives: H, A, P, P, Y. As Y is the 25th letter of the alphabet and 13 is in the centre of the top globe, the bottom globe must show 12 to bring the total to 25.

114 10

The top row gives the same total (18) as the bottom row. The second row from the top gives the same total (23) as the second row from the bottom. Therefore the third row from the top must give the same total as the third row from the bottom, so X must be 10 to bring the total to 30.

115 X is 26, Y is 21

Starting at the middle, at 1, the right-hand side progresses: 1, 3, 6, 10, 15, (21) the value of Y (the difference increasing by 1 each time).

The left-hand side progresses: 1, 4, 8, 13, 19, (26) the value of X (the difference increasing by 1 each time)

116 Six revolutions

If x is the circumference of the inner circle, the others are $3x/2$ and $2/x$ respectively.

117 11 days

	Pieces fitted	Pieces left to fit
1st day	20	255
2nd day	21	234
3rd day	22	212
4th day	23	189
5th day	24	165
6th day	25	140

7th day	26	114
8th day	27	87
9th day	28	59
10th day	29	30
11th day	30	-

118 86 kilometres
Give consonants a number according to their position in the alphabet, omitting vowels.
Give vowels these values: A - 1, E - 2, I - 3, O - 4 and U - 5.

119 A and G

120

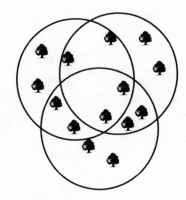

121 They put them both corner to corner in the large suitcase

122 27 (11+12+9+11) - (5+3+6+2)

123 E Circle is at end

124 58 (10 x 10) - (6 x 7)

125 C

126 9 (7 x 3) - (5 + 7)

127 E (Made up of 4 lines)

128 2A (Dot missing)

129 F

Consider the four numbers in the four opposite segments. Subtract the sum of the two lowest numbers from that of the two highest numbers. The letter derives from the alphabetical position of the result.

130 A. False B. False, C. True

In A note that the hour hand will not be exactly on the hour.

131 3 + 4 = 7

2 + 3 = 5

6 + 3 = 9

4 + 5 = 9

4 + 1 = 9 (□)

132 He was born in hospital room 1933 and died in room 2001.

133 A is 7, B is 3, C is 5, D is 4, E is 8 and F is 1

```
 735
 481
1216
```

```
735
481
254
```

134 21
Follow arithmetical progressions diagonally. Start at the top left-hand corner: 1, 2, 3, 4, 5, 6, 7, 8. Start at the top right-hand corner: 1, 2, 3, 4, 5, 6, 7, 8. Start at the third number down on the left-hand side: 1, 2, 3, 4, 5, 6. The cross is filled thus

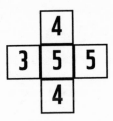

135 1st Harry
2nd Ken
3rd Ian
4th John
5th George

136 A is 8, B is 3, C is 5, D is 1
In each row the position of either the black spot or the white spot remains the same, and this gives a clear indication of the direction in which the cube is rotating.

137 13 The combinations are:
27 32 41
27 34 39
27 35 38
27 33 40
28 31 41
28 32 40
28 33 39
28 34 38
29 32 39
29 33 38
29 31 40
31 34 35
32 33 35

The Great Book of Brainteasers

138 A and B won
The individual scores were: A - 110 (4-16-8-12-20-50); B - 113 (18-6-15-3-9-12-50); C - 71 (7-14-50); and D - 110 (18-4-6-10-2-16-8-14-12-20).

139 C
It is the only domino that does not have a centre spot.

140 129
Divide the numbers outside the brackets by 3, 4, 5, 6, 7 and 8. For example, 441 divided by 3 is 147 and 144 divided by 4 is 36. In the last line divide 108 by 9 (12) and 90 by 10 (9).

141 18 = 9 + $\frac{5742}{638}$

$\phantom{18 = 9 + {}}$ 1

142

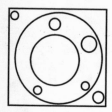

143 Newspaper £0.70
Magazine £1.20

144 190

145 588   8x7x6x5x4x3   (over) 1x2x3x4x5x6   x   7x6x5x4x3 (over) 1x2x3x4x5

146 C

147 B

148 A is -1; B is 1; C is 7; D is 5.
We know that a square is worth 4 points, a triangle 3 points and a circle 2.
A figure lying ABOVE another adds its value to that of the one below. A figure lying BENEATH another deducts its value from that of the one above. So, in the first diagram:
The top triangle (3) adds its value to the square beneath it (4) and is worth 7; the circle on the left (2) adds its value to the square beneath it (4) and is worth 6; the bottom

triangle subtracts its value (3) from that of the square (4) and is worth 1; the circle on the right subtracts its value (2) from that of the square (4) and is worth 2.

Thus in the last diagram:

square A is worth -1 (3-4);
circle B is worth 1 (3-2)
square C is worth 7 (4+3)
circle D is worth 5 (3+2)

149 D.

In square 2 the top two suits in square 1 are transposed. In square 3 the bottom two suits in square 2 are transposed. In square 4 the left vertical column in square 3 is transposed. In square 5 the right vertical column in square 4 is transposed. In square 6 the top left has been transposed with the bottom right in square 5. Therefore, in the next square the top right will be transposed with the bottom left in square 6.

150 E.

There are four different types of triangle here: equilateral (all sides equal) isosceles (two sides equal) right-angled (one right angle) scalene (all sides unequal) Each is shaded according to its type, the scalene triangle being shaded like this:

In E, however, it is shaded like this:

151 100

152

153 Both halves total 151

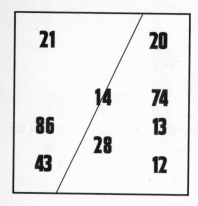

154 ICE
In the first row the spots on each cube are added and given letters equal to their position in the alphabet: 6(F) 15(O) 7(G) In the second row 1 is deducted from the total of the spots on each cube. In the third row 2 is deducted from each total. In the last row 3 is deducted from each total: 12 - 3 = 9 (I) 6 - 3 = 3 (C) 8 - 3 = 5 (E)

155 E.
All the other numbers are divisible by 7.

156 CANADA.
The hour hand of the first click is at 6; the sixth letter of the alphabet is F. The minute hand is at 18:R. The second hand is at 1:A. On the second clock, the hour hand is at 14:N. The minute hand is at 3:C. The second hand is at 5:E. Follow the same principle for the other two clocks and you get CANADA.

157 3 and 0 .
The series must be spaced correctly: 3 6 9 12 15 18 21 24 27 The terms increase by 3 throughout, so 30 is next.

158 A is 9; B is 63; C is 16 .
Prime numbers are squared in the opposite quarter; even numbers are doubled in the opposite quarter; odd numbers are trebled in the opposite quarter.

159 71/9.
Convert all the fractions in the top line into vulgar fractions: 3 4/5 4 5/6 5 6/7 6 7/8

160 A Five moves
B   F
They move as follows;

                 1 2 3 4 5
Black ball   B C D E F
White ball   D B G C F

161 1111
Consider the digits outside the brackets. The second is deducted from the first, and the fourth is deducted from the third, to give the digits inside the brackets.

162 49
Each block is 3.1cm high, as established in A
B contains 13 blocks (13 times 3.1)
C contains 19 blocks (17 times 3.1)
D contains 11 blocks (11 times 3.1)

163 71.3cm
3 blocks remain on
A   6 blocks remain on
B   9 blocks remain on
C   5 blocks remain on
D   Total height is 23 blocks – 23 x 3.1 = 71.3

164 Smallest 5 foot
Highest 10 foot

165 6
All the two figures numbers reading horizontally down the left side are doubled on the right side.

166 23
If the drawers are numbered from 1 to 4, the possible combinations are

1234	2134	3124	4321
1243	2143	3142	4312
1324	2314	3214	4213
1342	2341	3241	4231
1423	2413	3412	4123
1432	2431	3421	4132

167 28

Of all the problems throughout this book, in pre-testing there were more discrepancies in the answers to this one than any other one. Answers offered were 28, 29 or 30 in almost equal proportions. The reproduction below will clarify the answer:

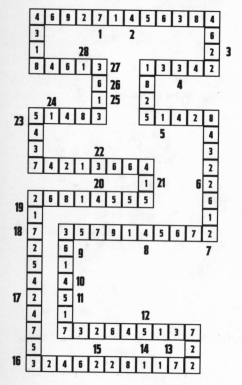

168 1/2 revolution anti-clockwise
B rotates 2 revolutions, as does C.
D rotates 1 revolution, as does E,
so F rotates 1/2 revolution.

169 (A) 2.03
(B) 1.33
(A) The first leg (9 miles @ 24 mph) takes 22 1/2 minutes. He reaches B (after walking for 2 1/2 minutes) at 12.25 and catches the first bus at 12.48. The second leg (10 miles @ 25 mph) takes 24 minutes. He reaches C (after walking for 6 minutes) at 1.18 and catches the first bus at 1.27. The third leg (12 miles @ 20 mph) takes 36 minutes, so he arrives at D at 2.03.

(B) The entire journey is 31 miles. At an average speed of 20 mph it would have taken 1 hr 33 mins, and he would have arrived at D at 1.33.

170 5 moves (see below)

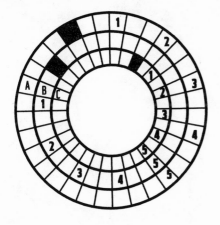

171 A

172 A

173 110-(4x15)=50 50+(4x7)=78

174 Born: Ninth November Nineteen Nineteen and Nineteenth November Nineteen Nineteen
Died: Ninth November Nineteen Ninety Nine and Nineteenth November Nineteen Ninety Nine

175 57 pence.
In the spelling of pomegranates there are 5 vowels and 7 consonants

176 85
(7x7)+(9x4)

177 (a) >

178 D

The Great Book of Brainteasers

179 22. In each quarter of the circle add the numbers in the outer ring; subtract the sum of the numbers in the next ring; add the sum of th enumbers in the next ring to give the number that goes into the inner section. Thus: the sum of 2, 3, 4, and 5 14
Subtract the sum of 1, 2, 3, 4 10
                                                      4
Add the sum of 3, 4, 5, and 6........ 18
                                                    22